Managing People at Work
A manager's guide to behaviour in organizations

Managing People at Work

A manager's guide to behaviour in organizations

Second Edition

John W. Hunt

McGRAW-HILL BOOK COMPANY

London · New York · St Louis · San Francisco · Auckland · Bogotá
Guatemala · Hamburg · Lisbon · Madrid · Mexico · Montreal
New Delhi · Panama · Paris · San Juan · São Paulo
Singapore · Sydney · Tokyo · Toronto

Published by
McGRAW-HILL Book Company (UK) Limited
MAIDENHEAD · BERKSHIRE · ENGLAND

British Library Cataloguing in Publication Data

Hunt, John W.
Managing people at work: a manager's
guide to behaviour in organizations.—2nd ed.
1. Personnel management
I. Title
658.3 HF5549

ISBN 0-07-084927-7

Library of Congress Cataloging-in-Publication Data

Hunt, John W. (John Wallace)
Managing people at work.

Includes index.
1. Personnel management. I. Title.
HF5549.H878 1986 658.3 86-10484

ISBN 0-07-084927-7

2345 WL 8987

Typeset by Eta Services (Typesetters) Ltd, Beccles, Suffolk, and
printed in Great Britain by Whitstable Litho Printers Ltd,
Whitstable, Kent

Contents

Preface

TO THE SECOND EDITION

My prime objective in writing the first edition of this book was to provide a summary of my ideas on the major areas of organizational behaviour—motivation, perception, groups, power, organizations, structures, leaders, managers and change. My objective has not changed, although some of my ideas have shifted. My second objective was to distil from a vast literature those insights which might help managers. I did not want a theoretical or academic summary of other people's work; I wanted to clarify not confuse. Moreover I had already presented a theoretical summary of many of my ideas in *The Restless Organization*.

My third objective was to present the material in a form which made it easy to read, especially for managers. For this reason, as before, I have left out precise references in the text and tried to minimize the use of academic jargon. References are given at the end of chapters, but only as guides to further reading.

The original objectives for this book remain. It was, and in this revised edition is still, intended for managers, not for academics. It is one alternative to numerous papers or academic pieces. It is a summary of my ideas, my research findings and the ideas of others who have provided me with insights into the world and work of managers.

In some cases my arguments are based on extensive research data, in others on the experiences I have had as a manager, as an academic and as a consultant.

The success of the first edition, both in hardback and paperback, led to this extensive revision. Much of the earlier material has been dropped in favour of what is now more relevant material. For example, I have reduced the material on participation in favour of more on change. I have extended the coverage of the development of an organization to include a discussion of an organization's culture. Indeed, every chapter has had revisions; nine have undergone major alteration, the other two only marginal. I hope the result is helpful to the reader.

This sort of writing does not come easily to me, as I learned when preparing the original edition. I am therefore indebted to a number of people who helped me to produce the kind of text which intelligent managers would find interesting. Among those who read all or some of the revisions were John Harter, Rob Goffee, Denis Pym, Roger Collins and Sebastian Green. I am deeply indebted to them for the time they gave me. Rosemary Gooder typed my constantly changing versions with enthusiasm, despite her very heavy workload.

To all these people I am very grateful. But to the thousands of managers with whom I have worked and with whom I continue to work on four continents, I want to express my appreciation for their willingness to debate and discuss their world, often when they knew that I had it 'all wrong'. If this book clarifies the world of work for them then I will be delighted.

John W. Hunt
London 1986

1. Individuals at work

Introduction

This chapter discusses individuals at work. It concentrates, as far as it is possible to isolate them, on influences originating within the individual. Subsequent chapters concentrate on the influence of markets, other people, strategies, structures, leaders and technologies.

Why do people behave the way they do in organizations? Why do some work so hard while others appear to do the minimum required? Why do two people have such different rates of productivity? Why do some like highly structured jobs while others want freedom and autonomy? What makes some satisfied and happy while others seem unhappy? Why do some work alone and others spend all their time in groups? Why are some people money-hungry while others are almost unaffected by monetary rewards? It is questions like these that managers want answered.

It is not very helpful to managers to be told simply that people are different. They know that already. What managers find useful are reference points against which they can map data about the individuals they have to manage. People drop clues all the time about their experiences, goals and expectations. One function of a manager is to collect those clues and use them to discover the abilities, goals, events, etc., that are important to that individual. Once they know what is important to the individual employee, managers then have the key to motivating that person for better performance. They have to link the individual's goals to those of the organization.

One of our objectives, as managers, is to attempt to predict future performances. To help elucidate this extremely complex process I will look at five major influences on how an individual behaves at work:

- Abilities
- Experience
- Goals and values
- Energy
- Expected rewards

If individuals have the necessary abilities and experience and their goals are the same as those of the organization, then, provided they find the rewards attractive and have the energy, they will work hard to achieve those goals.

Let us examine each of these factors.

Abilities

From a very early age we learn (despite parental reassurances) that some people are much better at, say, drawing or running or language than we are. For this reason abilities have attracted a great deal of attention as we attempt to devise ways of assessing their levels in individuals. Schools, colleges and universities and business organizations measure abilities religiously and, on the basis of test results, attempt to predict an individual's future performance.

Unfortunately the relationship between performance and both formal and informal assessments of abilities is a disappointing one. Ability clearly does influence performance: some people undeniably have the ability to be better at some jobs than the majority of the population. However, knowing the abilities of a person only tells us that there is potential; it is another piece of data to add to our file. Ability is not a good predictor of performance in work organizations; knowing someone has the ability will not permit a manager to predict performance.

ABILITIES AND APTITUDES

There have been numerous attempts to separate abilities (believed to be inherited) and aptitudes (the capacity to learn and develop abilities). A major issue has been whether aptitudes or abilities are unitary or complex. Can we even talk about *an* ability and measure it separately?

The most frequently cited ability groups are:

- Reasoning
- Spatio-visual ability
- Perceptual speed and accuracy
- Manual ability

From these general groups a variety of additional categories have been identified:

- Reasoning
  - Verbal
  - Numerical
  - Abstract

- Spatio-visual
  - Practical intelligence
  - Non-verbal ability
  - Creative ability
- Perceptual
  - Clerical ability
- Manual
  - Mechanical ability
  - Manual ability
  - Musical ability
  - Athletic ability

However, most of these sub-categories are mixtures of ability, interest and goals. For example, mechanical ability (or aptitude) is a complex of other aptitudes and characteristics. It consists of spatial visualization, reasoning and experience. However, despite its complexity, it can be treated as a unit and measured reliably. Other complex aptitudes that can be measured in tests are:

- Musical aptitude
- Manual aptitude

Where one or more of these ability or aptitude categories is required in a job, it is useful to test for them, provided the test results are seen for what they are—a glimpse of possible performance and not a measure of actual performance.

ABILITIES AND MANAGEMENT

Are these abilities related to 'good management'? Most top managers are above average in intelligence, but are not in the genius class. Similarly, most middle managers are average or above average in intelligence. However, no study has shown that more intelligent managers are 'better'. On the contrary, there have been some studies which show that some of the 'super' intelligent are distinctly untalented managers.

Nor have any of the other commonly assessed abilities been found to be related to managerial performance. The one glimmer of recognition of a distinct ability comes from a common-sense observation of business-school academics and senior executives that there is a perceptual-analytic aptitude which is important to managers at the top. This aptitude is often referred to as 'seeing the big picture', 'seeing the forest not the trees', or the 'helicopter ability'. This spatio-visual ability involves seeing situations in their totality, identifying their important components and their relationships and suggesting strategies for resolving problems. A research study conducted in a pharmaceutical firm demonstrated the validity of this common-sense view; 'helicopter' managers were seen as being better at their job than 'non-helicopter' managers.

The problem with researching the 'helicopter' aptitude is measuring it. The closest psychological construct to it is called 'field independence' or the 'capacity to differentiate psychologically'. At the other end of the continuum is 'field dependence', which is characterized by poor conceptual skills, the inability to isolate issues, and dependence on the situation rather than being independent of it.

Research on field independence in a wide sample of people has shown that it reaches its peak at fifteen years of age, remains on a plateau until the mid-thirties and thereafter declines. This may mean we need younger managers, if we are to capitalize on the correlation of 'helicopter' ability with managerial performance.

SUMMARY

Abilities do affect performance. Knowing a person's abilities does not allow us to predict performance, only to predict the potential to perform. Among managers of above-average intelligence, the only ability which has been found to have a relationship with performance is the so-called 'helicopter ability'.

Experience

An experienced employee will outperform the novice. Temporary staff suffer inordinately from a lack of experience within the organization—experience of its systems, structure, strategies, etc. (by experience we mean knowledge, skills and practice, and situational familiarity). Performance will increase with experience wherever knowledge, skill and practice are relevant to the job. Performance also increases if an individual 'knows the scene'. However, we cannot predict people's actual performance from their level of experience. It may contribute to performance but it is, like ability, merely a guide to potential. The practical advantage of experience is the effect it has on confidence. Knowing that one can do the job provides an excellent foundation.

Goals and values

While abilities and experience give us clues about current, and possibly future, performance, the most useful information comes from an individual's goals and the values and beliefs they represent.

Motivation results from arousal and choice in the individual—a desire to allocate time and energy to a particular goal in exchange for some expected result or reward. More generally, motivation is the degree to which an individual chooses to engage in certain behaviours. This involves:

- Goals
- Arousal
- Choice
- Persistence

The most popular arousal theories with managers have been need theories. These theories collect goals, aspirations, values and behaviour into motives and call them drives, wants or needs, as though each need is a psychological construct buried in the individual's head and capable of independent analysis. Some writers (e.g., Maslow) in the sixties and seventies even proposed that we could rank these needs into a hierarchy and predict the order in which individuals would try to satisfy their needs.

I have great difficulty in accepting this concept of a need as a psychological construct. Nor does my research, or that of others, support the concept of a hierarchy of needs. Yet, like much of the common-sense research, it appears that the early theorists were 'on to something'. People *do* seem to find some goals attractive and will pursue them sometimes with frenetic activity. To avoid the complications of need theories it has become more fashionable to talk about goals, values or even work orientations—i.e., to acknowledge that people have tendencies to return to similar ends or goals that seem to be (sufficiently) important to them to suggest an underlying theme, pattern or goal behind their behaviour.

This concentration on behaviour (as opposed to an inner force) overcomes many of the difficulties of the earlier theories. What research has shown is that these tendencies to behave in certain ways are deeply embedded in past experiences. It is no accident that people who are driven to climb corporate ladders have highly motivated parents for whom hierarchical status is important. Conversely, it is no accident that people who search in their careers for stability, structure and avoidance of risk to a large extent acquire these values in their childhood. Nor is it an accident that the managerial and professional classes reproduce themselves in their own image as do the process and clerical socio-economic groups. Upward job or career mobility occurs for many, but not in quantum leaps.

The more generalized view which I have thus adopted is that we have goals which relate to our work. If we can articulate those goals and their underlying values and beliefs, then we have some picture of what, given the right circumstances, may lead to arousal and potential activity. Moreover, goals relate to situations, so arousal may be as much situational as internal; we may be aroused by the presence of others and the knowledge that other people are evaluating us, thereby linking goals or values important to us to the situation in which we find ourselves. Thus the cues of subordinates, peers, supervisors, family and friends become important triggers to arousal.

CAN WE GENERALIZE ABOUT GOALS?

I believe we can. Human behaviour is always an intricate blend of the universal and factors more specific to the individual. Unfortunately psychologists have become obsessed about individual differences to the exclusion of the universal. I believe we have more in common than separates us. If we are to help managers understand motivation then it is the universal goals, values and beliefs that they need to know about. Indeed, talk to any manager and he or she already has common-sense theories of motivation, often built up over long periods of observing people at work. These theories are usually not very different from those of the theoretician or researcher. However, where the theoretician can help managers is in providing some framework into which they can put their observations about goals. In this sense, labelling is inevitable. We label people all the time as 'ambitious', 'smart', 'quiet', etc. By this process we reduce the complex to manageable simplicity. Occasionally the researcher may show that the common-sense theory of the manager has no empirical evidence to support it; for example, the distance between a person's eyes has *not* been found to correlate with criminality. However, most of the time empirical research merely refines the common-sense of the managers.

Central to my analysis of goals is the proposition that the backgrounds of individuals provide us with themes or patterns which reappear in values, beliefs and goals and then overtly in behaviour.

Identifying those themes is primarily a lateral or intuitive process—bits of data are collected into a theme. One piece of information is on its own interesting, but useless in identifying a theme. For example, we may find that a job applicant was an international athlete in her teens; on its own this piece of data is interesting but provides almost no insight into future performance in a sales function, especially if there is no demand for athletics in the job. However, behind that piece of information will be a myriad of pieces of evidence for the selectors to collect—information about parental values to do with winning and losing, about school attitudes to the athlete's success, about energy, persistence, etc. Add the additional evidence, and a theme of achievement, success and hard work will probably emerge. In this case it will be important to see whether the characteristic of persistence is still present; some athletes exhaust their energy supply and the achievement motivation dies. What does one do after being an international star at the age of 18? Hence we need to ask what evidence we have that the will to achieve, to win approbation and to enjoy the rewards of acclaim is still strong.

For the past 15 years I have been collecting information on background, age, position and culture and the rankings by individuals of particular work goals. This has provided a databank of some 10,600 cases, and it is this body of information on which I draw here.

Selecting an individual for a job involves linking pieces of information together. What my research on work goals has done is to highlight the most common or recurring goals and to link evidence which correlates positively with those recurring goals.

Evidence about goals can be linked into a pattern or a theme. This is primarily an intuitive or 'gut feel' process and those who 'specialize' in intuition may be better at it. For example, if we study the executive-search market we will find most of the consultants who find people for clients use insight, intuition or gut feel rather than elaborate psychometric methods. This is not to suggest that systematic selection is wrong. In most selection processes systematic selection is essential simply to reduce numbers to a manageable level. Most selection is, after all, about elimination not about choice. However, once the interviewing begins it is the intuitive, the curious or those dominated by the right-hand side of their brains (as opposed to the logic of the left-hand side) who are best at identifying patterns about goals. Systems are much better at measuring abilities or aptitudes. But intuition or gut feel allows certain individuals to collect seemingly unrelated information into a theme from which goals can be inferred. And if we want to try to assess motivational potential these themes are vital. Indeed, they are probably the best data we can get.

In the following pages I will describe eight recurring goal categories. This classification draws heavily on previous theories but introduces modifications made as a result of asking people about their work. What is clear is that although the broad category of a goal may remain relatively stable there are subtle shifts of emphasis within that goal. Certainly, the goals are not (as Maslow proposed) static. They shift over time in individuals and more generally between individuals within a culture. And it is the endless modification or elaboration of the values and beliefs which underlie goals which makes research difficult. We might be confident that the goal categories I am describing here are important now but we cannot be certain that these same goal categories will all be the same in 15 years' time. Nor can we assume that the values and beliefs which underlie those goals will be the same. What we do know is that any ranking of their relative importance by an individual *now* will be different from his or her ranking in 15 years' time. Both the precise content of the goal and the order in which goals are ranked are subject to change.

The eight recurring goal categories are:

- Comfort
- Structure
- Relationships
- Recognition and status
- Power
- Autonomy
- Creativity
- Growth

These goals reflect the backgrounds (values, beliefs and experiences) of individuals and do *not* emerge fully formed at 20 years of age; they are acquired over long periods, especially during childhood. Similarly, they do not remain fixed; goals at 20 may be different from those at 30 and 40 years. But some underlying patterning remains, despite the intervening years and the subtle shifts in values and beliefs. Let us examine each category.

COMFORT GOALS

Need theories referred to this group of goals as 'body' or 'primary' needs or drives. Hence goals such as food, drink, shelter and sex were included as basic or primary drives. Most employees in this country are now reasonably certain of their supply of food, drink and shelter, and more subtle forms of comfort have become important goals. These include the physiological comfort of pleasant working conditions and the avoidance of stress caused by illness or shortage of money. These goals are best summarized as the goal of a comfortable lifestyle. Clearly income is an important variable in attempting to satisfy this goal; it is certainly what most people tell you they come to work to get, even though the number of people actually solely motivated by it is very small.

Of all the goal categories, this one includes the largest variability because it reflects an individual's socio-economic background. What is a palace for one person may be a cottage for another. For example, process and clerical employees may have a much greater concern for comfort goals than an average chair of a board; most of the latter have enough wealth to provide the lifestyles they and their families want. Further, discomfort is much more prevalent at the base of an organization than it is at the top, both physically and psychologically. One of the corporate myths of this century is that top managers have a monopoly on stress—the incidence of stress is highest among process, clerical and service personnel.

If people are strongly aroused by opportunities to satisfy these comfort goals then they may seek jobs offering repetitive tasks, regular money and avoidance of stress. In interviewing people for jobs it is possible to get insights into their comfort goals. Unwillingness to move location; unwillingness to play sports (team or individual); lower expectations in return for certainty about remuneration; preoccupation with illness; lower expectations about where they want to live, lifestyle, etc.; all indicate a high priority given to comfort goals. Low priority for comfort is indicated by willingness to endure discomfort—disruptions, stress, energetic sporting activities—and a preoccupation with health not illness.

High achievers (in a career sense) will usually rate comfort goals as a low priority in relation to other goals. They fully expect to satisfy them and do not regard them as the most significant of their goals. Further, whatever obsessions they have about bodily comfort are more likely to be about excitement, physical fitness or 'the body beautiful', rather than comfort. Certainly some high achievers are obsessed about, and primarily aroused by, large sums of money, but the goals behind the indefatigable search to become a millionaire are more related to exhilaration, stimulation and recognition from others than to comfort on a day-to-day basis. Money-seekers such as these are attracted to jobs where money is directly related to performance (e.g., piece-work, consultancy and selling, especially of insurance, property or cars) and where the spoils of war can be displayed in possessions (cars, jewellery, homes, collections, etc.).

Money, especially if paid in cash, is effective in motivating people if the following conditions apply:

- Deprivation; a background in which money was short either because of poverty or because the parents tightly controlled it.
- A strong desire for money which persists despite relatively high standards of living.
- A job in which performance can be measured unequivocally.
- A job where pay can be directly related to performance.
- A job in which the time-lag between doing the work and getting the pay are consistent with the individual's time orientation, i.e., how far he or she thinks ahead. For example, pensions do not motivate on a day-to-day basis because the time-lag between work and reward is far too long.

The number of people and the number of jobs in which all these conditions hold is very small. For most earners of a salary or wage, money has very little effect on motivation unless they perceive it to be too low in relation to what others are receiving, in which case the effect is negative.

If problems arise at home or in the family, most people—even the so-called 'high achievers'—become more preoccupied with comfort goals. Illness, death, relocation, etc., are all disruptive and are followed by a decreased concern for more intangible achievement goals and a concentration on returning to normal.

Background and social mobility affect this set of goals in several ways. Socio-economic background clearly correlates with the expectations a person has about lifestyle. For example, some of the most highly career-motivated individuals begin at the top of the lowest socio-economic group and are motivated to gain the lifestyle and status of the managerial and professional socio-economic groups (many managers in retailing, for example, exhibit this pattern). Conversely, those who begin in the managerial and professional socio-economic groups may seek power rather than status and recognition from their job because they already enjoy status in the community.

Athletic interests are also related to comfort goals. People who are aroused persistently by career goals (high achievers in the organizational sense) are not likely to play team sports, preferring golf, running, swimming or squash. People for whom career is less important than comfort (lower achievers in an organizational sense) are more likely to watch others play sport; their first sexual experiences occur younger and more frequently thereafter. High achievers report less physical illness and spend less time discussing their illnesses. The incidence of nearly every illness (including coronary heart disease) is higher at the bottom of the organizational hierarchy.

Of course, these differences are reinforced by the nature of the work people do. The answer to the question whether motivation arousal patterns derive from one's past or from the situation in which one finds oneself is that they derive from both. However, in selecting people for jobs, it is the *current* profile of goals that provides vital background *and* career history to date. And in every case a perceptive manager should be able to discern a clear pattern.

STRUCTURE GOALS

The second set of work goals can be collectively called structure. Earlier theories of motivation (1930–60) identified financial security as a primary goal. In those times this was probably true. However in the last part of the twentieth century financial security is no longer the problem it was; welfare systems ensure survival. Consequently, there has been a shift in concern away from whether we will survive financially or socially to how much we can reduce financial and other kinds of uncertainty. And at a time of great economic uncertainty, this goal assumes increased importance, especially in an ageing population.

Structure, certainty and security are goals which are closely linked to comfort goals. The two sets are so interwoven that it is difficult to claim they are separate. However, in analysing behaviour in organizations, it is extremely useful to consider the two sets apart—on the one hand the goals relating to the individual's search for a comfortable lifestyle, and on the other those relating to the search by the individual for a definition of what is required of him or her.

Experiences found to correlate positively in individuals who place a high value on structured environments are:

- Insecurity in childhood.
- Being the first or only child.
- Lower socio-economic status.
- A genuine shortage of 'comfort'—in many cases money.
- Over-anxious parents.
- Physical punishment at home and/or school.
- Rejection as a method of discipline (e.g., 'If you don't like living here go somewhere else').
- Direct or indirect experience of periods of deprivation (e.g., depression, redundancy, war, repeated redundancies for a bread-winner, terrorism).
- Repeated failures and/or negative feedback.
- A history of stable, predictable employment, dwellings and/or location.
- Parental career models in large private or public bureaucracies.
- A background of deaths and/or serious or prolonged illness.
- A background of financial collapses, bankruptcies or poor investments.

Organizations have traditionally relied on structure and threats of insecurity to control the behaviour of employees. If employees deviated from the required behaviour patterns then they were threatened with the sack (and insecurity), isolation (and insecurity) or promotional restrictions (failure and insecurity). Control and discipline rest on some form of insecurity, even if the outcome is called self-control. Even the Church threatened its members with the ultimate insecurity of damnation or purgatory (with the added organizational advantage of no feedback loop).

While the strength of this set of goals varies with circumstances during our lifetime, the period when it influences our motivation arousal patterns most powerfully is in childhood. The child-rearing practices of a society lead people to develop expectations about structured or unstructured environments. In Britain there has been a long history of reifying structure almost as an art form—in empires, in social institutions, in organizations of all sorts and in ceremonies. The pursuit of rationality has been basic to British and French history, especially the forcing of Western-style rationality on to others.

This search for rationality, structure and certainty appears to be one of the most enduring of goals. Not surprisingly, in Europe, where rationality is often confused with civilization, there has been a tendency to structure social systems until they 'seize up' and stop. Merger after merger (e.g., Peugeot, British Leyland) has been perceived as a rationalization, without any regard for the fact that size is a vital managerial variable. It is possible to build a monster organization that no amount of structure can control. Moreover, once a structure has been imposed, it is extremely difficult to dismantle it.

A generation with less interest in certainty and structure emerged in the sixties and seventies. The post-war baby-boom generation, brought up in an economically secure world based on a welfare state, benefited to some extent from more liberal theories in education and child-rearing. Insecurity was seen to be less effective as a means of control than positive reinforcement. When this group arrived at the schools, universities and business organizations it came face to face with the bastions of structure. Revolt was inevitable. Consequently, in the seventies we saw a major revision within the social sciences of views about jobs, authority and organization design. This revision has continued. Devolution, direct feedback, performance-based rewards, a looser structure for dress, authority relationships and controls, etc., are developments influenced by this generation. But for those people in the last years of their careers, when it is usual for certainty goals to strengthen, these modern trends can be distressing.

Structure, certainty and security are significant goals in certain jobs. Selecting people for highly programmed jobs means finding people with a high tolerance of structure. Hence, the armed services, banks, insurance companies, and large private and public bureaucracies all attract people with a strong search for structure. And when they find that structured environment they feel more content and more motivated. Throw these same people into the apparent chaos of an advertising agency's creative department and they feel extremely uncomfortable.

What would a 'theme' for a person seeking a highly structured environment look like? A typical example might be:

- First child.
- Parent a middle-level civil servant.
- Child-rearing beliefs based on structure, order and discipline.
- Use of physical punishment, deprivation and delayed gratification.
- Attended a large, highly structured school, perhaps a boarding school.
- Graduated in accounting (or law or engineering).

- Worked for a clearing bank.
- Has been in the same bank all the time.
- At job interviews asks detailed questions about:
  - Salary
  - Pension
  - Work location.

While I have deliberately exaggerated this example to illustrate the emergence of a pattern or theme, there are a large number of people in our society who would satisfy two-thirds of these items and who *are* working in large structured organizations in which their search for predictability is reinforced on a daily basis. Ironically, many of them will spend much of their time complaining about the very rationality they were seeking. Knocking the system is a full-time sport for many people with developmental and career themes resembling that cited above.

Turn to a risk-taking, entrepreneurial company and you are likely to come across the converse of the structure theme:

- Not first child.
- Creative, loosely organized family environment.
- Discipline based on self-direction.
- Progressive school.
- Graduated from university in arts (to avoid being 'locked in').
- Has worked for numerous organizations; will change to get more freedom, autonomy, creativity and direct rewards based on performance.

Again, to illustrate the importance of themes I have taken an extreme. But research shows that it is possible, simply by asking questions at an interview, to establish a person's goals in this area. My critics will say that this is a dangerous business—the wrong evidence may be collected, leading to false assumptions. Of course, one might be wrong, but what other choice do we have? Experience to date and motivational goal data give us our greatest chance of picking a winner. Further, I believe that you can choose any job, identify the people who perform best at it and show that, if you go back over their lives and careers, you will find *themes*, *patterns* and *trends* from which you can develop a selection interview designed to find more of them.

RELATIONSHIP GOALS

Everyone wants to love someone, to be wanted, to have relationships with other people. We grow and develop as a result of those interactions. Yet the degree to which this goal is important to people varies widely.

People who have very strong relationship goals will seek out employment where they can form lasting relationships—deep, warm relationships which will endure over many years. Conversely, some people are introverted, and seek out relationships with very few people and then only on their own terms.

Positions which attract the warm-hearted, people-seeking group of employees are in process and clerical work and some of the caring professions and other people-centred areas (nursing, supervisors, personnel officers, counsellors etc.). Most high achievers do *not* seek these forms of relationships. They have many, varied fleeting relationships with a wide range of acquaintances, often preferring their own company rather than that of others. Conversely, Fred and Myrtle on the factory floor may go to work primarily to form relationships and will continue those relationships in the pub after work has ceased.

Women seem to be currently more prone to seek longer-term, close relationships with other women than men are with other men. In Western societies, men (even those in process work) still tend to be taught to seek relationships with a larger number of people and to control the amount of emotion they invest in these relationships.

In looking for background themes the following have been found to correlate positively with strong motivation-arousal goals for forming lasting relationships with friends and an organization:

- Birth order, i.e., later children in large families.
- Families which frequently and openly demonstrate affection.
- Strong and persistent pattern of close school-friends.
- Frequent interaction in pubs, clubs and societies, families and friendship groups.
- High concern for a job where relationships are 'good' and where co-operation is strong.
- An organization with a well-known name (e.g., IBM, Marks & Spencer).

If we ask people to rank in order the eight goals listed earlier, approximately 60 per cent of the workforce will put their highest value on relationships at work and home and not on advancement or achievement in a career sense, unlike top managers who place relatively much less emphasis on relationships. This 60 per cent will remain at the basc of the hierarchy, forming strong interpersonal relationships with their friends; and, contrary to a common assumption, they do not seek the sorts of ego-gratifying goals that the executive class seeks. They are aroused to activity by others, by friendship, by relating.

Many of our industrial problems have their roots in loner, career-motivated managers designing jobs for people motivated by goals other than career. And the process is two-way; misconceptions about managers abound in the office or factory. We have got into the habit of projecting our own goal profiles on to everyone else; researchers spend a lot of time listening to low career achievers commenting on high career achievers, and vice versa. In both cases one group imposes its values on the other. We thrust our values, goals and beliefs about work on to each other with little regard for whether individuals really conform to our assumptions. For example, there are many people in highly structured jobs who are very satisfied. Similarly, despite the picture painted by some social scientists and the popular press, the majority of executives like what they are doing and are not about to have a nervous crisis of some sort. Further, while it is true that job satisfaction levels decline from the top to the bottom of the hierarchy, some 75 per cent of the bottom level are satisfied, no matter what method is used to assess that satisfaction. People at different levels seek different goal satisfactions. What is important is that we recognize those differences in a non-evaluative way.

Nevertheless, misfits—people whose jobs are designed to satisfy goals which are not theirs—are numerous. People who want to relate are isolated from others; others who want to be alone are pursued by hordes. What we need is to get goals and jobs closer together. Yet a new threat is at hand. As we mechanize more of the work of the bottom 60 per cent of the hierarchy, we will increasingly isolate people from each other. We will introduce more highly skilled career-oriented technicians for whom relationships are less important. The result may be a shift in the pattern of employment among process workers. First, many of their jobs will disappear. Second, more technicians will be imposed. Third, the robots will tend to do the interesting work, leaving the mundane and trivial to the humans. If any of these scenarios is right, we will need to invest more effort in satisfying those relationship goals—if we want to hold the system together. Loneliness in a crowd is already a twentieth-century problem. We should learn from the Japanese manager whose prime function is to develop relationships. In the West the prime function of the manager has been the task, not the relationships between the people. Not surprisingly, those for whom relationships are paramount have sought them elsewhere—in trade unions, pubs, sports and social clubs and football crowds.

RECOGNITION AND STATUS GOALS

Much of the motivation literature has linked these two types of goal together into another 'need' category, but it is clear that there are at least two goal sets here, not one. The sets are:

- Goals which reflect a desire for recognition from others.
- Goals which reflect a desire to manage and control the activities of others.

Political activity in organizations involves both sets of goals and for that reason it may initially be sensible to link them together. However, for our purposes of finding the right sort of profile for a job, separation of the goals is essential.

Part of a child's development is the evolution of a concept called by psychologists the 'self'. In crude terms it is the picture I have of 'me' and is basic to my self-respect. This picture of myself develops from a myriad of experiences, particularly from the feedback I get from other people. For example, it is related to parental love in that the child learns at a very early stage that being 'OK' means he or she gets more affection; being 'not OK' leads to a withdrawal of affection. This use of recognition or positive reinforcement occurs for most of us throughout childhood. 'If you eat your supper you can watch TV.' Perform and you get the reward; no performance, no reward, or, even worse, withdrawal of another reward.

As the child gets older and time orientations lengthen, the reward may be delayed; gratification may occur days, weeks, months or even years later, and this may result in a 'work ethic' style—that is, persistence becomes a sub-goal in itself.

Schools extend this reward and punishment system further. If you fail to achieve the desired standard then you receive lower marks, are demoted, or at worst may be asked to leave. Between parents and school, individuals develop very strong appetites for recognition. This enables organizations to continue the same system with salary increases, titles, superior offices and furnishings, cars, expense allowances, stock options, etc., which are, after all, only more sophisticated examples of the process which began with the child's first jellybean.

Some people particularly develop needs for this sort of recognition and are attracted to jobs which provide them with endless 'jellybeans'; for example, the reward systems of the armed services, higher education and the professions offer substantial opportunities to be recognized and praised for one's performance.

Factors which we have found correlate positively with the emergence of strong goals of recognition, status and praise, and which provide themes for selection, are:

- Parents with childhood backgrounds of middle and upper-middle socio-economic groups.
- Middle and upper-middle socio-economic status achieved by parents.
- Certain occupations of parents (especially professional).
- Use of rewards as opposed to punishments in childhood.
- High expectations of parents for children's performance.
- Parental use of delayed gratification.
- Unwillingness to drop standards even in the face of contrary data.
- High status and power goals of parents.
- Deprivation—insufficient recognition of the child's achievements.

Of all these background themes, the last has been the most powerful in explaining adult goals. It is the deprivation effect which dominates the themes of academics, doctors, judges, salespeople, consultants, etc. By deprivation I mean that the parents or school recognized the child's achievements, but only grudgingly, for example: 'You have done quite well', or 'You've passed this exam, but you've still got the next one to get.' This recognition with a 'bite' appears to lead to an endless search for higher status and/or higher achievement, especially among professionals and sub-professionals in the middle socio-economic groups. It is less prevalent among managers—their goals are very much more concerned with power—but amongst people in sales, entertainers, union officials, academics, service chiefs, doctors, barristers and other public performers this goal appears extremely powerful as an arousal trigger.

The importance of recognition as a goal is that it provides managers with an unlimited opportunity. It appears to be almost impossible to satiate those seeking recognition in large doses. Put crudely, there is little danger of over-use. However, in a society where we tend to reject praise, it is vital to observe whether or not a subordinate accepts the praise when it is given. We have a strong tendency to reject it—'Go on, you say that to all your managers!' Used effectively, though, recognizing performance is one of the manager's most powerful arousal techniques. Behaviour can be transformed by its use.

POWER GOALS

Compared with the public performers mentioned above, the manager usually gives much lower priority to recognition. His or her primary goal is managerial power; i.e., the opportunity to influence, control and reward the behaviour of subordinates. In my research into effective managers it is this background theme which correlates positively with success, *not* the recognition theme. That does not mean that people who have recognition as a high priority should not be managers. All it means is that a preference for managerial power rather than recognition is more likely to be a successful mix for a manager.

One of the difficulties in separating 'power people' from 'recognition people' is that organizations and societies make the separation more difficult simply by mixing power and status together. To reinforce the authority of the position (rather than the person) we attribute status, titles, honours and other props to power, all for the exclusive use of those occupying the position. Hence the judge is dressed in extraordinary clothes; the managing director has a large car and a chauffeur (although the director is the only passenger in the car and is perfectly capable of driving); the pop star has all the glitter and pomp of the medieval monarch. It ought to be noted that radio and television advertising titillate these status expectations by offering (at a price) beauty and recognition, power and recognition, love and recognition.

When managers are being selected, an attempt should be made to separate recognition goals from power goals. Factors which correlate positively with a strong search for power are:

- A power figure as a role model (parent, teacher, coach).
- The aspiration to be powerful.
- Experiences with power (school, college, university, work).
- A succession of managerial roles.
- Confidence and good presentation at interview.
- The desire to manipulate others, to 'run' something.

A power theme might therefore look like this (remember *one* piece of data is useless; a theme is needed):

- Parent a police officer.

- First child; head boy/girl at school.
- Community official.
- On faculty committee at college.
- Captain of a sporting team.
- Supervisor at 25.
- District manager at 30.
- Dominant in very close relationships.

Add to this theme positive appraisals as a manager through the internal appraisal system and you have a strong candidate. Indeed, of all the data available on a potential manager, information on past managerial experience through a series of jobs is the best. Unfortunately, with a commendable shift to shredding appraisals after three or five years, such longitudinal data may be non-existent or very short-term. On the other hand, over how many years *does* one need to assess a person's managerial behaviour?

AUTONOMY, CREATIVITY AND GROWTH GOALS

The 'need' theorists' concept of self-actualization or self-fulfilment has a long history (Jung, Adler, Goldstein, Rogers), yet remains one of the fuzziest and least developed in psychology. For this reason, it will be useful to define it more closely here. It consists of:

- A search for independence rather than dependence, for control over self rather than control by others. (Autonomy)
- A search for opportunities for originality and creativity. This relates to autonomy in that creativity may flourish in freedom, but the two goals are *not* necessarily found in the same person. (Creativity)
- A search for growth and challenge; extending the boundaries of the self, stretching the options, experiencing novelty. (Growth)

It has become clear in the past few years that those who seek autonomy may also seek opportunities to be creative. Others seeks autonomy and believe unquestionably that they *are* creative. Still others seek autonomy but do not seek creativity. However, both the autonomy and creativity groups seek growth.

In the simplest explanation, these goals relate to an ideal that may become real. They relate back to Allport's concept of 'becoming' which, by its very definition, is never-ending. Over time, age and reality catch up with the dreams but, even though the dreams have to be modified, often painfully, the search for an opportunity to stretch oneself, to let the potential emerge, is endless.

Factors which correlate positively with autonomy are:

- Strong goal orientation, even to the point of creating unnecessary hurdles.
- Realizable but challenging goals.
- Expectations of parents for very high standards of performance.
- Long time orientation (three to five years).
- Capacity to modify unachievable goals.
- Strong defence mechanisms to retain confidence.
- Preference for self-regulation and avoidance of controls, systems and rules imposed externally.

For those seeking creativity as well:

- Evidence of creativity—writing, art, design, etc.
- Pattern of lateral thinking, even in conversation.
- History of searching for a 'role' ('What will I be when I grow up?').
- Tendency to seek ideal solutions to problems.

Growth goals reflect the endless striving that other writers have noted:

- Seeks challenge.
- Wants to live life to the full.
- Easily bored with repetition or details.
- Initiates rather than completes.
- Tendency to mania; has highs and lows.
- Sees growth as his or her problem, not the employer's.

Many of these growth-seeking people do manage organizations. Unfortunately, if they have little interest in power they may not be very good managers. Indeed, characteristics of some of the extreme cases are:

- Failure to tell others what the goals are.
- Setting impossible standards for others to follow.
- Tendency to delegate all the trivia.
- Poor communicator—they know what they are doing but have not told anyone else.
- Behaves in a frenetic or disjointed way.

It could be argued that telepathy is a desirable characteristic for the subordinates of such a person! Yet it is these autonomous, creative, challenge-driven people who are responsible for new businesses, new techniques, new insights, new products, new buildings, new research projects and new forms of art.

What jobs attract them? Where both the autonomy and creativity are goals, you have film directors, theoreticians, writers, artists, conceptualizers, architects and research academics. Where there is merely an autonomous goal, with less creativity (loners), you have problem-solvers, consultants, integrators, market researchers, entrepreneurs, advisers, forecasters and corporate planners. It is ironic that the media tend to promote individuals in this last group—the autonomous but less creative—as the superstars of the business world, yet many of them are not actually very productive in our economic system. What is worse is that managers have been downgraded in comparison. We seem determined to produce more and more of these 'butterflies' and, as a result, have enormous difficulties finding general managers to run our corporations.

Organizations can only absorb a small number of people with these work goals. They see themselves as special, and their search for challenge, novelty and change, their intolerance of errors in others and their aversion to formal controls make them difficult to manage.

The easiest way I have found to assess the strength of this group of goals is to give individuals a single sheet of paper and to ask them to write down in five minutes what they hope to achieve in the next five years. People who place great importance on the goals of autonomy, creativity and growth will have no difficulty in filling the paper. They are so goal-directed that they are unlikely ever to suffer from having nothing to do. Conversely, lower achievers who do not segment time into past, present and future (time is now) will write down only one or two goals. They are not lazy, they just do not think in the free-flowing, goal-oriented way that the 'butterflies' do. They seek friendship, fun, love—different sorts of goals. And, what is more important, they may in fact have more satisfying lives than the restless high achievers.

SUMMARY

I have proposed eight goal orientations which have been found important to people at work—comfort, structure, relationships, recognition and status, power, autonomy, creativity and growth. Whether a person will decide to put energy into chasing one or more of these goals involves a choice.

We began this analysis with the proposal that motivation is the degree to which an individual wants and chooses to engage in certain behaviour. For the past few pages we have looked at the goals that recur when analysing people's explanations of their behaviour at work.

Now let's look briefly at the question of choice. Why will person A decide to expend energy in the pursuit of a goal or goals while person B decides not to?

Energy

We have looked at abilities, experience and goals as they might influence behaviour at work. The fourth variable is energy, and there are two issues here. Deciding—consciously or not—to expend energy involves a choice *and* an assessment of the total energy available. Some people simply have more energy than others, while others decide to put a higher *proportion* of their energy into their careers.

Why is it that some people have more energy to give to their careers than others? Like all other factors we have discussed, energy is not easily isolated from goals, rewards, abilities, etc. However, any observer will note that the energy some people are prepared to expend in pursuing organizational goals varies greatly. Yet we tend to assume it is equal in all people. Further, we have difficulties isolating energy from social approval. Are people who work till 10 o'clock of an evening more energetic than those who stop at 5 o'clock? Perhaps the former are slower; or perhaps they are doing it because they want people to say they are working hard.

Assessing overall energy levels in people can be a relatively simple matter. Clues are:

- Activity rate.
- Numbers of hours of activity.
- Hours of rest (sleep).
- Choice of and participation in leisure and sporting activities.

Those people who seem to spend their entire lives in a state of hyperactivity provide a selection interviewer with plenty of information. For example, they seem to survive on a few hours' sleep; they will report waking and getting up early (often to the annoyance of their families); sporting activities include frenetic games (squash) and/or strenuous single-person sports (running, swimming). They will, conversely, be disparaging about inactivity; for example, watching the television is a 'waste of time'. This theme of energy or stamina reappears in their careers as a determination not to go under when the ship hits a storm, a striving to avoid failure.

Beyond these fairly obvious signs, the interviewer has problems. Many people take their careers extremely seriously because it is the only way for them to establish who and what they are. Indeed, the whole of the Western economic system depends on a strong link between personal identity and job, although there are significant cultural differences between the newer societies (the USA, Australia) and the older (the UK, France, Holland). If individuals do not need a job or title or status to know who they are (e.g., in older societies), then the energy they put into their job or career may seem slight to those in the new societies. Yet these same people may have great sources of energy which are only seen in non-career activity.

Guilt also plays a part in the energy expended. If child-rearing practices include guilt and a strong work ethic, then the probability that energy will be expended in work tends to increase. Indeed, the popular myth that the work ethic (by which people mean an emphasis on hard-working, persistent and conscientious behaviour) is dead is *not* supported by research. Work, if not career, remains the primary goal of individuals.

What we know less about is why some people expend energy in short bursts while others sustain much longer bursts. In organizational terms, some employees rise to middle management and fade, while others continue into top management. Some fade at 35, some at 45, some at 55, while others are still highly motivated to achieve at 70. Some researchers believe that this is related to the time orientation of an individual; those with short time orientations will not have the tenacity to hold on, to fight, to be pushed down and still to get up again, simply because their time orientations are too short for the longer-term perspective.

Whatever the reasons for the differences, the range of energy levels is wide. Chapter 2 looks at variations that I and others have noted in orientations at work: goals change; circumstances change; energy levels decline, all with a notable change in career-motivation profiles.

Expected rewards

Organizations offer the individual inducements to work and to work hard. These inducements are both extrinsic and intrinsic.

- *Extrinsic rewards* Those tangible rewards that probably attract most of us into the workforce in the first place. Indeed, they provide a more likely explanation for the level of employment than the work ethic—i.e., necessity is the motivator. Extrinsic rewards include wages, salary, bonuses, commission payments, working conditions, a car, pension, etc.
- *Intrinsic rewards* The goal satisfactions of working—lifestyle, comfort, a sense of achievement, companionship, status, public acclaim, challenge, interesting tasks, etc. These rewards of work are often referred to collectively as job satisfaction.

It is sufficient here to recognize that individuals at work are motivated by the sorts of rewards that are available. Thereafter it is a choice as to whether, with their abilities, experience, goals and energy levels, they will choose to work.

Summary

The behaviour of people at work is influenced by many factors, including their choices, abilities, experience, goals, energy levels and the rewards the organization offers.

Abilities have not been very helpful in predicting performance at work. All that ability tests can tell us is that someone has potential—whether he or she will use that potential is another question.

Experience is clearly related to performance. The individual who has done the job before has an advantage over the novice. However, experience is less predictive where individuals are equally experienced. Hence, what experience a manager has had may or may not tell us something about his or her potential.

The most predictive attributes of individuals are their goals—what is important to them. For this reason most theories of motivation have concentrated on identifying an individual's goals, needs or wants. An extensive analysis of research data has suggested that there are a minimum of eight goal categories—comfort, structure, relationships, recognition and status, power, autonomy, creativity and individual growth. These goals or work orientations are largely determined by a person's background, especially the important influences of parental socio-economic status, family beliefs and values, school, Church and the society in which the individual lives.

To motivate an individual means creating an environment in which his or her goals can be satisfied while at the same time the goals of the organization are met.

Choosing people for jobs ideally involves relating two questions: What does the organization need? What sort of goals in individuals are closest to those corporate goals? Not surprisingly, the highly motivated individual is found in a job where the two goal sets are closest. The demotivated person is found in situations where the goal congruency is worst.

In selecting people for jobs the manager needs a framework for reducing the multitude of individual differences to manageable levels. It has been proposed here that the eight goal sets can provide that framework. Further, I have suggested what background 'themes' correlate with which goals. For example, if we are looking for a person to work in a highly structured job, then we need to find a recruit who *wants* structure. From background themes we can identify how strongly any person seeks structure at work. Themes are the most productive way to examine motivational potential.

Whether a person will expend energy in pursuing a goal depends on many factors—indeed, too many for a selection procedure to capture. Yet the manager does have a record of the individual's experience to date on which to draw. What clues are there that the individual expends energy in sport, leisure activity or lifestyle?

Finally, the rewards the organization offers act as inducements to expend energy in pursuing goals important both to the individual and to the organization. Rewards are intrinsic (recognition, praise, challenge, etc.) and extrinsic (salary, wages, bonuses, etc.). The mix of the two is a complex issue, requiring very careful analysis.

References

ON ABILITIES

Cattell, R. B., *Abilities: Their Structure, Growth and Action*, Houghton Mifflin, Boston, 1971.

Dunnett, M. D. and E. A. Fleishman (eds), *Human Capability Assessment*, Lawrence Erlbaum, Hillsdale, NY, 1982.

ON MOTIVATION

Brown, R., M. Curran, and J. Cousins, *Changing Attitudes to Employment*, Research Paper No. 40, Department of Sociology and Social Policy, University of Durham, May 1983.

Hampshire, S., *How to Realise Your Potential*, Institute of Personnel Management, London, 1981.

Handy, C., *Understanding Organizations*, 2nd edn, Penguin, London, 1985.
Maslow, A., *Motivation and Personality*, Harper & Row, NY, 1970.
Pinder, C. C., 'Concerning the application of human motivation theories in organizational settings', *Academy of Management Review*, **2**, 384–97, 1977.
Pinder, C. C., *Work Motivation Theory: Issues and Applications*, Scott Foresman, Glenview, Ill., 1984.
Robinson, K. R., *A Practical Approach to Employee Motivation*, Cambridge Management Training, Cambridge, 1984.
Steers, R. M. and L. W. Porter (eds), *Motivation and Work Behaviour*, 2nd edn, McGraw-Hill, NY, 1979.

ON REWARDS
Galbraith, J. K., *Organization Design*, Addison-Wesley, Reading, Mass., 1977.

2. Individuals and organizations

Introduction

The first chapter developed a framework for analysing an individual's work goals; I illustrated the patterning process by which work goals are reinforced (or not) by early influences on the individual—home environment, school, social relationships, etc. In this chapter we look at how age, job and culture may affect the importance people place on these goals. For any individual profile, it is impossible to tell how much a ranking choice has been affected by background and how much it is the result of the current situation. However, despite the changes in goals, patterns are much more persistent than many writers on individual differences would care to admit. It is extremely rare to find a person who, other than for short periods of his or her career, is able to reverse patterning which occurred as a result of background or inheritance. Even that popular hero, the rebellious adolescent, is likely to revert to the parental values and beliefs by his or her mid-thirties. Consistent with this patterning is the finding that certain jobs appear to attract people who rank their goals in a particular way. Thereafter, the design of the job, the nature of the supervision and the sort of rewards available reinforce rather than break the goal patterns.

The databank of 10 600 people surveyed by questionnaire which I mentioned in Chapter 1 has also been used in the development of the ideas proposed in this chapter. As most of this chapter is about managers I am drawing on a sample of 3200 European managers: 2700 men and 500 women. Of this sub-sample, 653 have been interviewed about their backgrounds. A separate sample of 674 managers participated in a survey of life stages using both questionnaires and interviews. The survey has thrown up some national norms but for managers only. The method of 'testing' an individual's ranking of goals was to set one goal against another and to ask the individual to rank them through 60 iterations. From earlier discussions in Chapter 1 it will be remembered that updating the questionnaire is continuous because of subtle changes in the meanings people attach to certain goals and to the values and beliefs underlying those goals.

From this databank *three* factors can be identified which may influence the rankings or the shape of an individual's goal profile. These are age, position and culture. And it is these influences which I will discuss in this chapter. However, first some further clarifications.

Ranking one set of goals against another is fraught with problems. What if all the goals are equally important? Do people actually *know* what motivates them? Will the rankings adequately show the subtlety of the differences? Probably not. But in managing people in organizations it is the general rather than the specific which has to guide the systems and structures we design. So it is the general patterns we will discuss here. Only an individual or his or her manager can allow for subtle differences.

CONFLICTS IN GOALS

Throughout this chapter we assume that individuals can isolate their goals and discuss them separately. Of course, in reality this is not the case. We all operate as integrated wholes, not as eight independent goals. Whatever goal I am pursuing, all the others—plus many I may not even recognize—are involved. Hence, I may have great difficulty in answering a relatively simple question like, 'Why do you put so much energy into your career?', and I would have even more difficulty in deciding how much energy I should put into my career and how much into my family. Yet this does point to a dilemma—goals are not necessarily consistent. They often conflict with each other and much of the stress that we experience comes from the conflict of one goal with another: career versus family; structure versus excitement and risk; individual versus collective; autonomy versus team-work; money versus challenge.

Each of us has to make choices, to pursue some goals at the expense of others, and some of these choices are painful. Should we take the job in Paris and disrupt the family or stay where we are and continue to enjoy that community? Shall I take the boss's job and risk spending more and more time in the office? Should I go out on my own and start a business, or would the insecurity be unbearable?

Of all the possible goal conflicts, the two that arise most frequently when we interview managers are:

Relationship goals versus autonomy goals

This is a well-documented conflict, especially among creative people who need isolation at certain times and company at others. The conflict is often hurtful for the family or close friends, who have to predict when the creative member wants company and when he or she does not. Many spouses blame this conflict on the organization, this being reinforced by their partners who similarly blame the organization for separating them from their families. Yet the real conflict occurs within the individual, who *could* decide to spend less time on him- or herself and more with the family. Or priorities could simply be rearranged. But rather than admit that the family is secondary to the pursuit of autonomy, creativity and growth, the company is blamed. 'It is not my fault, the company expects me to be there.' People rationalize by saying there will be time to catch up with important relationships (spouses, children, friends) later. Unfortunately, time lost on relationships cannot be retrieved.

Structure/security goals and power goals

The second most common conflict between managers' goals is between structure/security goals and power goals. The fear of taking risks inhibits the potential for managing larger groups. The familiar comment of, 'Darling, what I could have achieved had I not had to consider my pension and the mortgage', reflects this conflict. Again, the conflict is *within* the individual rather than between the organization and the individual. It is a popular excuse for procrastination and avoiding risks. Two popular fantasy ambitions focus on this conflict: one is to run one's own business and the second is to manage or buy a farm. Both may be escapist, but when pressed the most frequent response is, 'Yes but the farm/business would put my family at risk.' In fact, if the individual chose to realize one of these fantasies the conflict might become unbearable.

Hence we have to adjust our expectations and, rather than blaming others for preventing resolution, accept that some goals are achieved at the expense of others. Now let us look at the three influences on the goal profiles I wish to discuss in this chapter—age, position and culture.

Age

From profiles of all sorts of people in different age groups, it has been possible to develop age profiles—that is, an average for each age group. What these show is that age can lead to subtle changes in the overall rankings of the goals at different stages of a person's life. Findings such as these can be used to support a theory that a person's life has stages, and it is these stages that I want to illustrate for managers.

For the purposes of illustration the figures have emphasized variance

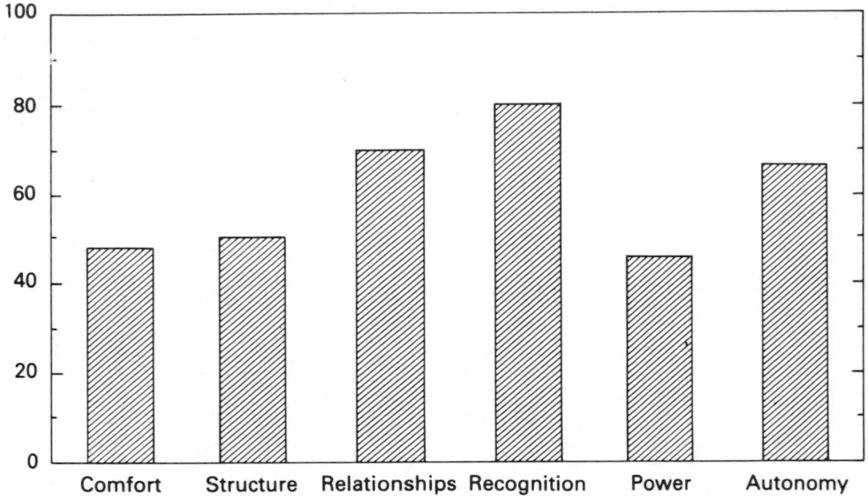

Figure 2.1 Childhood patterning of goal profile, 0–14 years

from the mean. The disadvantage of this is that the resultant profiles illustrate shifts which are more subtle than they appear. In fact, while dramatic re-evaluations of goals do occur in some people (triggered by such stress factors as the death of a spouse, career failure, illness or a change in location) it is usually a much more gradual process related to age, job situation and an individual's financial and emotional position.

On the following pages we look at possible shifts in goal priorities for an average manager. It is important to remember that these shifts do not occur for everyone but they do for a significantly large number to affect the overall shape of the average profile.

STAGE 1: CHILDHOOD PATTERNING (0 TO 14 YEARS)

We do not know how much of the underlying goal pattern is genetic—i.e., how much it is part of the inherited, genetic patterning of the individual. We do know, however, that the early background environment has a very significant effect. By the age of about 14, the goal rankings of the individual start to emerge as stable goal patterns reflecting those of the parents. Whether by inheritance or by reinforcement, the individual's underlying motivational profile has become established.

Fig. 2.1 illustrates the average profile found amongst the children of managerial or executive groups. (Because of the important differences between people's ranking of goals in different sorts of jobs, we will illustrate only the life-stage profile of the children of managers.)

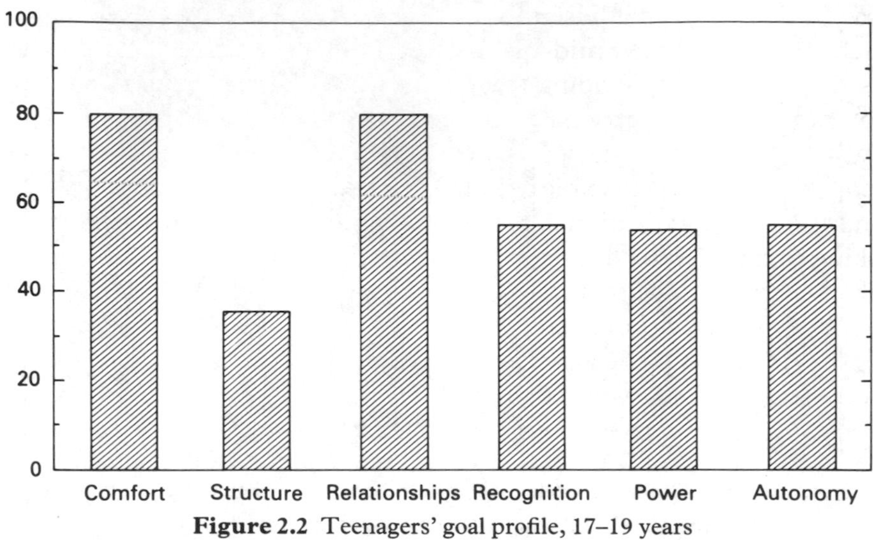

Figure 2.2 Teenagers' goal profile, 17–19 years

STAGE 2: THE TEEN YEARS (17 TO 19 YEARS)

Fig. 2.2 illustrates the average goal rankings of matriculating students aged 17–19 years. The career goals are beginning to emerge strongly, but after puberty the dominant goals are comfort (especially money) and relationships. In contrast, structure and predictability are much less important.

The preoccupation of teenagers with comfort, body and relationship goals may make them difficult to live with, yet the conditioning behind this goal ranking has been powerful. From the time they were born there has been a constant barrage of promises about peer groups, love relationships and sex. Advertisements reinforce the goals, with promises that the teen years are a time for looking beautiful, finding beautiful people and having beautiful relationships.

In contrast to this well-documented profile, the institutions of our society expect teenagers to make some of the most important decisions of their lives. Decisions about vocations, courses and jobs are thrust at them at a time when career achievement should probably be secondary to relating. Not surprisingly, many choose the wrong careers and by the mid-twenties are ready to choose again. Others simply refuse to choose and appear to drift, often to the despair of their parents. By their late thirties, 64 per cent of the managers interviewed say that they would have chosen another career had they known more about themselves at the age of 18.

We would be well advised to let young people make career choices much later, say in their mid-twenties. Indeed, business schools are full of students of that age doing master's degrees, either trying to shift to another career or still trying to discover what they should do.

What the average goal profile in Fig. 2.2 tells us is that teenagers need to experiment, to explore rather than to choose. A general education rather than a vocational one would allow that exploration, without locking them in. This does not deny that some teenagers *do* know what they want to do with their lives. However, most do not and are forced to choose too early. Fortunately for those who join business or government organizations, the variety of jobs available does sometimes permit a second, third and even fourth choice. In this sense the really disadvantaged are those in certain professions from which escape can be difficult (e.g., medicine, law, science and dentistry). The best advice that can be given to someone at this stage is, first, to leave the options open but to base that openness on excellent school, college or university grades which provide tickets of entry to choices later; and second, to try to experience as many tasks (or jobs) as possible. For parents, it should be stressed that drifting is not teenage licence—it is a painful process. Over and over again 'drifters' are asked by concerned adults to justify their existence by answering that inane question, 'What do you want to *be* (or do)?'

STAGE 3: CAREER LAUNCH (MID-TWENTIES TO MID-THIRTIES)

A quite dramatic change in the average rankings of goals occurs with marriage (or the formation of a permanent relationship). The actual age at which the profile changes varies greatly; most people's goal priorities shift very slowly in their twenties but accelerate once a permanent relationship has been formed. Factors which correlate with the age at which a permanent relationship develops are age at onset of puberty (later puberty indicates later relationships), level of sexual interest, parents' marital 'success' or 'failure', opportunity, experience, maturity and social skills. For those unwilling or unable to form a permanent relationship the profile remains weighted towards comfort and relationships. If by the mid-thirties a permanent relationship has not occurred it becomes more unlikely that it will occur at all and a major re-evaluation of goals appears to occur, resulting belatedly in a profile like that in Fig. 2.3.

There is a close connection between identification with a career and/

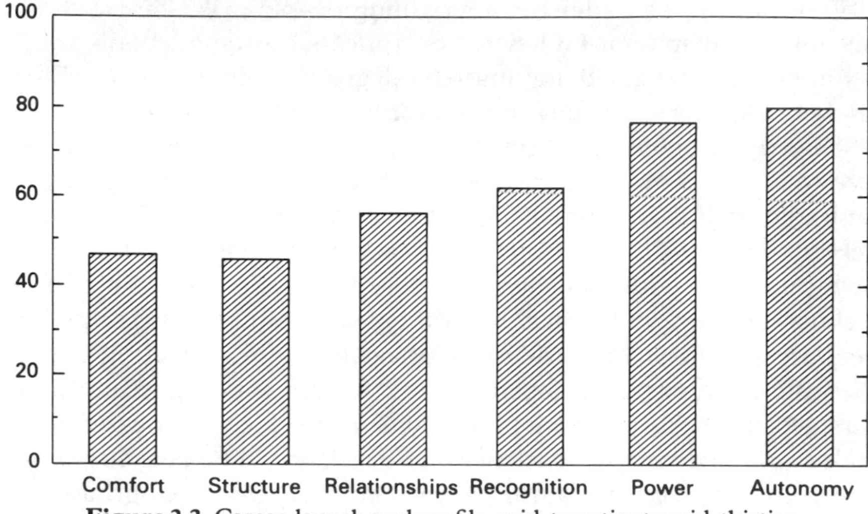

Figure 2.3 Career-launch goal profile, mid-twenties to mid-thirties

or organization and a permanent relationship. In practice the process of deciding upon a career and feeling comfortable with an organizational role usually precedes a permanent relationship; the sequence appears to be 'sort out self' and then 'choose a partner'. Indeed, there may be sense in delaying permanence until the emergence of a clearer picture of what the individual wants to be. Tentative data suggest that hoping a permanent relationship will clarify the career path may impose excessive strains on the relationship.

Once a shared living style has been established, the career profile of the high-flier develops (see Fig. 2.3). It is reinforced by bosses (with recognition and promises of further achievements), by reward systems (with promises of money, status and promotion) and by assignments (which provide power, autonomy or creativity and growth). All the developmental trends established in childhood now begin to consolidate, providing the individual's manager with the first real glimpse of the potential of his or her subordinate. Sometimes this potential may have been clear in an 18- or a 22-year-old, but on average it is clear only after a permanent relationship is established in the early to mid-twenties.

The consequence of this finding is that any attempt to rank the career goals of school-leavers may well be a waste of time. It is not until 5 to 10 years later that recruiters have evidence from which to predict motivational potential. Actual performance is impossible to predict; at best we can predict that there will be potential. But from the mid-twenties onwards, providing a mate has been found, the predictive value of goal ranking increases exponentially. Hence the real problem for recruiters is the school-leaver. Given the level of unemployment and the talent available, recruiters are increasingly using common sense and avoiding school-leavers entirely. Better a graduate in the mid-twenties than an 18-year-old.

If an organization *is* restricted to recruiting school-leavers, then their history to date, especially socio-economic data, remains the best evidence, compiled as the interviewer seeks to establish the inherited and/or trained-in profile the individual adopted at about 14 years. It is still true in the upwardly mobile societies that the executive and professional classes reproduce themselves, and, similarly, the lower-income classes reproduce themselves. The numbers who make major jumps between socio-economic groups are small. However, background both releases and limits potential. Once school-leaver recruits reach their mid-twenties, a much more accurate assessment of potential is possible from the individuals' own ranking of work goals, rather than from an indirect assessment of the goals of their parents.

Not only is it difficult to get a picture of the goal patterns of the 20-year-old employee, but it is also disheartening to learn that on average this is the peak period of dissatisfaction with employment. One simple explanation for this is that the expectations that have developed about work have been wildly exaggerated. Very little time is spent in our education system telling children that work is not an endlessly stimulating activity, that it has its highs and lows. Hence, when young people begin work they are often very disappointed to find organizations depend on repetition, compromise and predictability, rather than the difference, novelty and uncertainty which much of their education seemed to promise. A second explanation for this peak in dissatisfaction levels is that the young people were making a lot of adjustments from adolescence to adulthood and that those adjustments can be distressing, especially if their parents have pushed them out of the family home. One obvious target for aggression (for us all) is an entity identified variously as the employer, the boss, the job, the firm or the company.

STAGE 4: THE CHILD-PRODUCING YEARS (MID-TWENTIES TO EARLY THIRTIES)

The birth of a couple's first child may throw the goal ranking into a

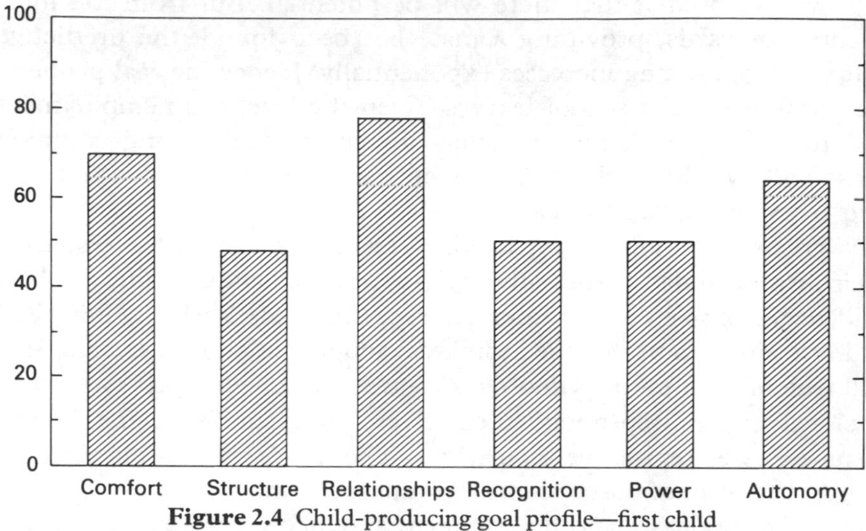

Figure 2.4 Child-producing goal profile—first child

new arrangement of priorities. High-achievement goals may become dampened as the preoccupation with parenthood takes over. Comfort, physiological change and relationships become markedly more significant goals. Fig. 2.4 reflects this change.

We can only speculate on the reasons for this change in the average profile. The birth of the first child is one of the most exciting and rewarding experiences of life. Priorities are certain to be affected. Even before the child is born goal shifts can be detected, and the changes may be even more marked once the child arrives; there will be a 24 hour concern with comfort, security and love. Career goals appear to take second place. How long this goal shift lasts varies, depending on the sex of the individual, how much help there is in the home, the condition of the child, the enthusiasm the individual has for the job, and the strength of the couple's relationship. A couple whose relationship is reinforced by the arrival of the child are likely to adapt more quickly than a couple who had marital problems before the child was born. Whatever the couple's allocation of roles, a family of three is a very different social system from a family of two. A heightened awareness of the importance of relationships is inevitable.

We have identified this child-producing stage for several reasons. First, many managers become disillusioned with their younger staff during the latter's twenties because their goals seem to fluctuate. One very simple explanation for this is that it is generally during this period

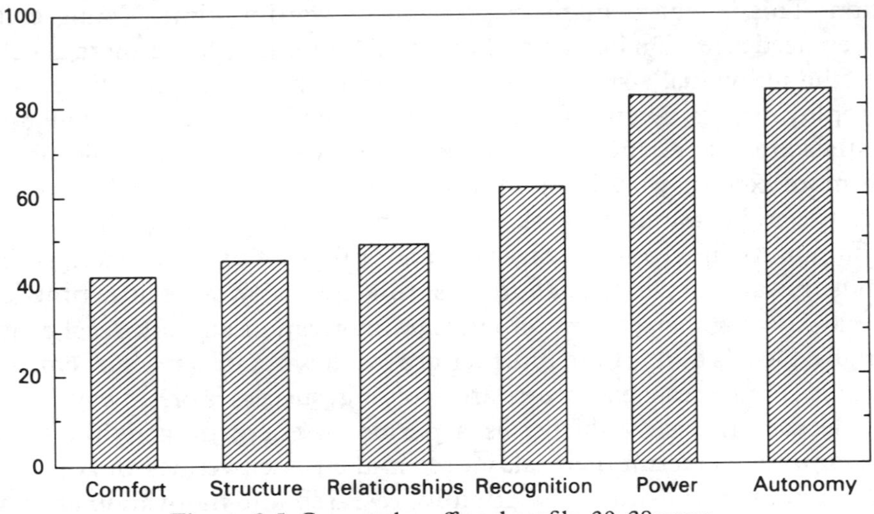

Figure 2.5 Career take-off goal profile, 30–38 years

that pregnancy, birth and child-rearing occur. The second reason for specifying this stage is that once the couple absorb the experience of the birth of their child, the high-achiever profile returns on average stronger than before. Managers are therefore advised to be patient in such matters. The third reason is that subsequent children may not produce the same fluctuations in goal rankings. Indeed, for some very-high-achieving men, the ranking hardly seems to ripple, especially if the spouse is devoting her full attention to the children. On the other hand, for the mother in employment, the goal fluctuations caused by subsequent births will be considerable, depending on the allocation of roles in the family, the provision of domestic help, etc. It is not easy to be mother, wife and employee of a work organization all at the same time. The conflicting expectations mean that very few women actually accommodate the strains. Usually, one or two of these three roles suffers and that is even in the favourable conditions provided by a normal, healthy baby and a sensitive spouse.

On average, six months after the birth of the child the high-achieving father's profile is back in place. The length of time it takes the high-achieving (in a career sense) mother to re-prioritize her goals varies enormously depending on the help she gets, the roles her husband wishes to play and the personnel policies of the employer.

STAGE 5: CAREER TAKE-OFF (30 TO 38 YEARS)

By their thirties most high achievers will reach a peak in career motivation. This is a particularly creative and rewarding time. Young children need attention but are no longer a 24 hour job; either there is help or the individual's spouse has relinquished his or her full-time paid employment in favour of part-time or no paid employment. The dissatisfaction experienced with work in the twenties seems to disappear as more exciting work is found. Improvements to the house, leisure activities and community work begin to bring the rewards of family and community life. In short, this appears for most of us to be amongst the most rewarding periods of our lives, full of activity, with little time for rest. And for that reason, on average, motivation at work reaches its highest levels at this time. Further growth lies before us, achievements have yet to be reached, careers are evolving, success is on its way.

Because the early thirties is a period of energetic activity, some organizations recruit their sales force in their late twenties and dismiss them in their mid-thirties. Certainly, research into motivation arousal shows that energy released does reach a peak at this stage. If we forget questions of morality, a likely trend for this age group will be more fixed-term contracts of employment designed to capitalize on experience and energy.

STAGE 6: MID CAREER (38 TO 43 YEARS)

'Mid-career crisis', 'burn-out', 'alienation', and 'professional suicide' are all terms that have been used with reference to the major shift in the goal profiles of some people in their late thirties. For most of us there are questions in our mid- to late thirties or early forties about what we have achieved, and what we intend to do with the rest of our lives. Some of these arise from affluence—by that time we may have achieved the house, the family, the car and the trips abroad, and a sense of emptiness follows. Others arise from disillusionment with a career: Why are we devoting all this energy to a career? Will moving further up the hierarchy provide more or less satisfaction? Yet other questions come from the inescapable fact that we are no longer young.

Most people seem to cope with these questions fairly well but researchers including myself have found that one-third of managers experience a period of intense and sustained depression which has been variously labelled, most frequently as 'mid-career crisis'. The term 'crisis' is unfortunate as it suggests a short period. In fact, most of the one in three who suffer from a deep sense of frustration do so for much longer periods of time—some from three to five years, with intermittent periods of severe depression.

We do not have the space here to look at this problem in depth. In another book, *Managers in Mid-Career Crisis*, I provide extensive data on the phenomenon. Briefly, there appear to be two forms of the crisis.

The idealists

First, those individuals who are highly aroused by autonomy and creativity appear to suffer an intense feeling of frustration and pain. For them the crisis means being trapped, and therefore changing the rules and changing the organization are logical reactions. This form of the crisis appears to come from an unwillingness to accept that the vision they had of themselves—their potential and their roles in work organizations—may have been wrong.

Organizations are about power, politics and influence, and the autonomy-seekers' naïve view of organizations as maximizing competence is wrong. Idealistic and apolitical, these people differ from others in that they see the situation as unacceptable. Logically, they try to change it. Often this behaviour is inconsistent with previous behaviour—is quite atypical, even destructive. Further, they are almost always doomed to fail as the organization, the collective, is so much more powerful than they are.

The middle managers

A second, and more common, reaction to mid-career comes from those thousands of people in middle-management positions who are forced to realize that they will not make the top. Dominated by a search for status, recognition and power, they are blocked by the people above them in the hierarchy. Desperate to progress, having rehearsed the role(s) above them already, they fail to see that, despite promises of marvellous opportunities, the majority of individuals do *not* get to the top; most must, in this sense, fail. Yet they cannot see that their, and their families', reading of their potential has been wrong; that time, capacity, opportunity, chance have let them down. Unlike the people motivated by autonomy, this group (who are by far the majority of those who suffer from mid-career problems) appear to offer little or no fight but just 'sit down to die'. For them, their career appears to be finished. To a researcher, they present as dependent, believing that they have no control over their careers, or even their lives. Just as senior management is seen to have produced the problem, so it is seen to be senior management's problem to solve. There is no admitting to

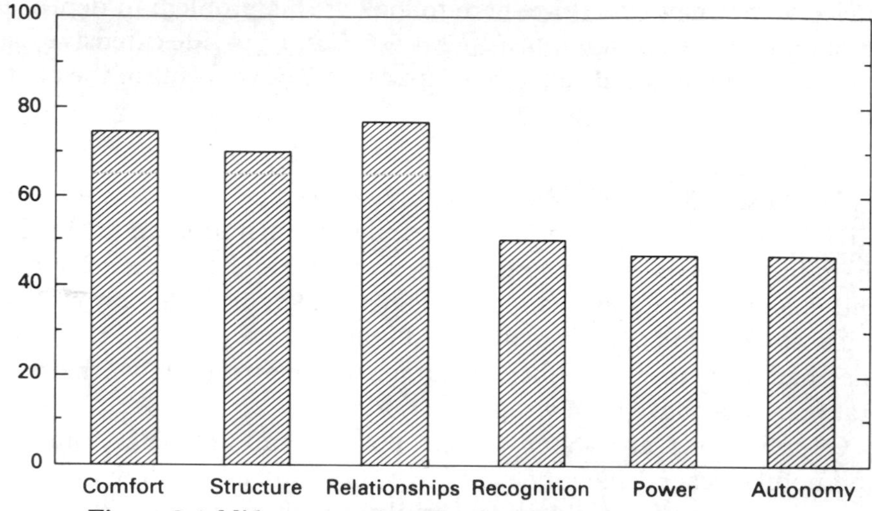

Figure 2.6 Mid-career goal profile, 38–43 years. The crisis profile

ownership of the problem, no acceptance that it has something to do with them. For many people this is the beginning of psychological death. For thousands of them there may be an exit through redundancy or early retirement; others will survive to depress their subordinates with paranoid tales of promises 'the company' or 'they' failed to keep.

The arrival of the post-war baby-boom generation at middle to senior management level has focused researchers' attention on the mid-career problems. A population bulge has arrived on the doorstep of senior management at a time of organizational contraction. By any criterion its timing has been bad and the psychological problems are the result.

The incidence of 'collapsed' profiles (see Fig. 2.6 for an average mid-career crisis profile) is worst in those organizations in which upward mobility has replaced money as the major reward. Hence, clearing banks, insurance companies, multinational corporations, the civil service, higher-education institutions, etc., suffer more than other organizations. The larger the size (number of employees) and the longer the hierarchy (the more stable the market), the more specialized the career paths and the greater the lack of options to shift, then the higher is the incidence of mid-career problems.

Symptoms of mid-career problems are the normal stress symptoms—insomnia, headaches, perspiration, stomach upsets, psychological depression, dissatisfaction and feelings of disillusionment. An inability to focus on cause–effect relationships makes treatment much more difficult. The individual suffering is unable to see that opportunities are limited or that the job he or she wants is not available. Indeed, this lack of focus and a heightened sense of lost control make it difficult to provide help.

One popularly believed reaction to the crisis is personified in the image of Don Juan, seeking an outlet for his aggression and hurt through sexual explorations among the office staff or the neighbours. Studies have shown this is more of a journalists' fantasy than a reflection of reality. Most mid-career-crisis men and women sit back, inactive, ineffective, often drinking too much, and unable to see any escape. Even goal-setting career-oriented training programmes, which theoretically should shift their focus, have proved to be ineffective once the individual becomes inactive.

Fortunately, after a few years most people in mid-career crisis do recover, but for that 7 per cent of middle-to-top executives who do not recover the outlook is bleak. Plagued by psychological and/or psychosomatic disorders, many die before they retire. Many more will be pushed out through redundancy or early retirement. Those who survive to retirement may have a life expectancy of only 18 months.

For those who do suffer a period of depression in their late thirties and early forties the answer is clear. Devote time to activities outside the organization. One of thc problcms of the most severe cases is that they have no other interests, and therefore to fail in their career is to fail in everything. Those who seem least prone to mid-career-crisis depression are those who remain active, seek new challenges and discover new outlets for their energies.

STAGE 7: CAREER PEAK (MID-FORTIES TO MID-FIFTIES)

For the majority of people who have no mid-career problems the profile of the thirties continues into the forties. However, their circumstances are changing. Children are leaving or preparing to leave home, careers will reach their peak, possessions and other signs of success are available. Some realignment of personal goals is inevitable.

Two patterns have emerged. First, there seems to be a shift in outlets for achievement motivation. Whereas previously the career held most interest, other outlets now become attractive. Leisure activities such as golf, sailing, bowls or tasks centred on under-utilized skills such as do-it-yourself home repairs, car maintenance, gardening, etc., take up

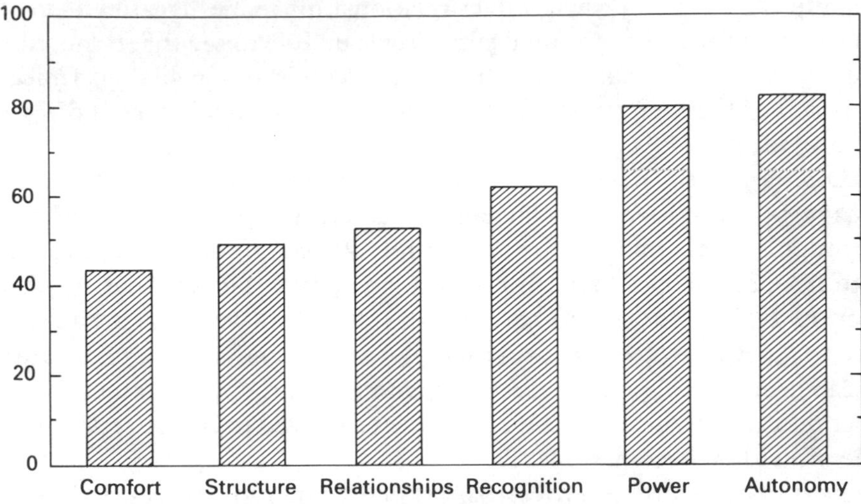

Figure 2.7 Career-peak goal profile, mid-forties to mid-fifties

more of the energy than previously. The second trend is a questioning of relationships. Marriages that have survived appear on average to go through a renegotiation of the 'contract'. What was sought from a partner in one's twenties may be very different from what is sought 20 years later. Together the partners appear, consciously or not, to negotiate a different relationship based on their interests and activities in their forties, turning again to each other, especially as the children withdraw from their lives. This is linked, for some, to a turning into the community to help with welfare or charity work. Sometimes several goals are combined; e.g., the pursuit of a neglected interest in sport is linked to a voluntary contribution to the activities of a club. The friendship patterns which will be important in the fifties and later are settled, faults are forgiven and relationships cemented.

The same trends tend to occur at work. Managers in their late forties begin to see that they are no longer the up-and-coming stars—indeed they may have come as far as they are going to go. Acceptance of this fact often provides a marvellous feeling of relief. To accept what one is and to know that the striving for position, for power, for status is nearly over permits one to accept that others need one's help. As one writer has noted, 'There is a turning from being a star player to being a coach, from being the patronized to becoming a patron, from being totally preoccupied with oneself to being preoccupied with the generation who will take over.' Common-sense observers have long noted

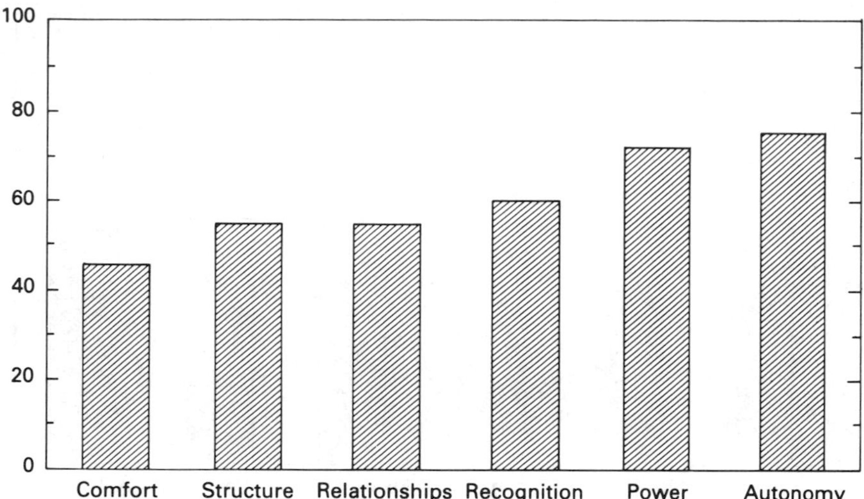

Figure 2.8 Approaching retirement goal profile, mid-fifties to mid-sixties

this mellowing, yet it is only recently that empirical data have demonstrated that concern for relationships does on average increase, that concern for stability and structure also increases, and that enthusiasm for the radical or the different is replaced by conservative views of the world. And this begins a shift which tends to continue until death, as comfort, structure and relationship goals become, very slowly, more and more important.

STAGE 8: APPROACHING RETIREMENT (MID-FIFTIES TO MID-SIXTIES)

On average, the goals are ranked almost equally by the mid-fifties high achiever. Comfort, structure and relationships now warrant as much attention as the high-achievement goals of recognition, power, autonomy, creativity and growth. This appears to be an age of contentment—less stress, less aggravation and the approach of retirement. Yet age has taken its toll.

This is the time of life at which friends and acquaintances begin to die; women have been through the menopause and men can no longer deny that their virility is diminishing. Physiological problems associated with ageing may already have begun to appear (hernia, haemorrhoids, arthritis, heart murmur, etc.). Concern for comfort, health and certainty are inevitable outcomes of this physiological decline.

Retirement forces a reappraisal of relationships. Family, friends and grandchildren must take the place of an organization with whom the

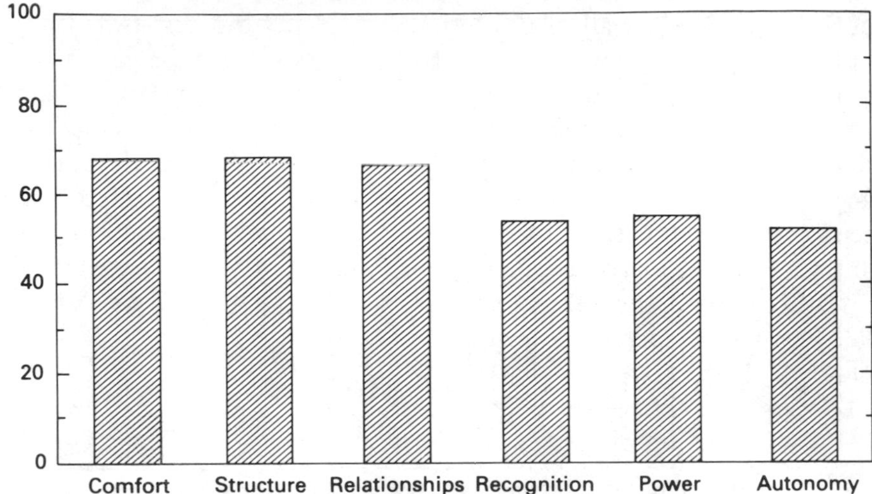

Figure 2.9 Decline goal profile, mid-sixties to mid-seventies

individual has been employed and which for many years gave him or her identity, values and status. This rift in work relationships can be shattering, producing a sense of redundancy at a time when it is too late to retrain or seek another label and identity. Purpose has to be redefined. The potential loneliness of the aged becomes clearer.

Far-sighted high achievers have slowly been transferring their energy from employment to other activities, just to meet this moment. Sport, hobbies, a small business or charity work have been occupying more and more attention through the late fifties, in preparation for retirement. Yet, while we can preach the sanity of this shift, few indeed make the effort. Hence, the shock of retirement is a shock of lost relationships, an abyss of nothingness. Skills and aptitudes required at 60 are rarely learnt in the fifties. Most of those skills, especially the sporting skills, are learnt much earlier. Preparation for retirement remains one of our least developed life stages.

STAGE 9: DECLINE (MID-SIXTIES TO MID-SEVENTIES)

In Europe the age of retirement has been falling. In some industries it is already down to 60 years of age, in others to 55. Hence, generalizing about retirement has become more difficult. As a rule, if one retires early (e.g., from the armed services) one has a greater chance of finding alternative activity. The later one retires, the less energy may be available to find alternative 'work' but the longer a sense of purpose directs our energies. Yet for all of us, retirement is, for the first time in our lives, the chance to do whatever we like, whenever we want.

There is a further shift in goals. For the first time, concern for comfort, structure and certainty, and relationships dominate the high achiever. Achievement is now less important for the average ex-manager. Concern about death and the circumstances in which it will occur increases the shift of focus to security goals. Isolation from family, and particularly from children, produces its own dependence.

If we examine the research literature we find life expectancy is related to several factors:

- The 'right' parents—the effects of genes.
- Activity—having purpose, using energy. The price of being a high achiever is that one cannot stop. To do so eliminates the level of stimulation both brain and body require. Decline is rapid without that stimulation.
- Relationships—enjoying the support of other people.
- Structure—having a routine (this seems to be especially so if the job was highly structured).
- Mission—a wish to help others, to leave a legacy, to pass on knowledge, to serve a purpose.

And even if these are all positive, the end must eventually come. The last life stage will be closed.

SUMMARY

Age is second to background as an influence on the way people rank their work goals. What was important at 25 may be different from what is important at 35 and 45. Furthermore, there are predictable or average patterns or life stages which most career paths appear to traverse and which most career-planning schemes ignore. We need to be much more open in discussing the stage a person has reached. Many problems could be solved if only we were more honest in giving feedback to individuals and in encouraging them to discuss their current goal priorities. So much of a career is an unnecessarily lonely journey.

Finally, the role of the manager as counsellor becomes clearer the more we study individuals at work. Three important periods for counselling have emerged: the twenties, mid-career and pre-retirement.

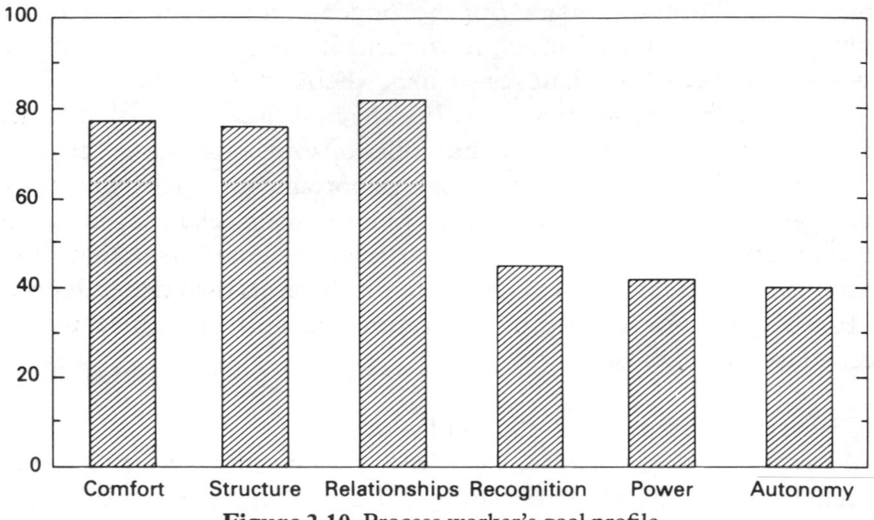

Figure 2.10 Process worker's goal profile

Position

Another factor which may affect one's goal or work priorities is the job one has. Certain combinations of goals appear to attract people to certain jobs, and are rewarded in the job.

THE PROCESS WORKER

Fig. 2.10 illustrates the ranking of goals for an average process worker, maybe working in a manufacturing plant or in a service industry. Notice that in the ranking of goals the most significant are relationships, structure and comfort. The career goals, important to higher achievers (recognition, power and autonomy), are less important to these people. This pattern should *not* be interpreted as being better or worse, but simply as different. These individuals are unlikely to put the energy and time into career that a high achiever (in a career sense) may. For this reason some managers see them as lazy, which is unfair. This is not laziness, but simply a different perception of goals and their importance. Perhaps these individuals have the right view of careers after all, and the so-called achievers are chasing an illusion.

People who rank their goals in this manner are attracted to predictable, repetitive jobs where interpersonal relationships can flourish. Indeed friendship and cooperation are seen as more significant rewards than individuality and autonomy. Yet, ironically, many of the jobs designed for these people are in total contradiction to their personal goals. Where they want to relate they are isolated; where they want certainty, they meet built-in uncertainty.

THE VERY HIGH ACHIEVER

In sharp contrast to the previous example, the profile in Fig. 2.12 reflects the ranking of the very high achiever. Such people may be found in challenging work and will operate best on their own or in a very small team. Comfort, structure and relationships are either unimportant or are already satisfied as goals. In contrast, recognition, power, autonomy, creativity and growth dominate this profile. (It should be pointed out that this extreme profile applies to less than 10 per cent of the population).

People with this sort of profile are generally not attracted to large bureaucracies, possibly because they feel too restricted by them. They are characterized by impatience, challenge and frenetic activity. Managing them can be difficult, yet they are the first ingredient for innovation. We must choose in each situation which is more important, conformity or innovation. For example, if the government makes a grant to an artist who then spends the lot on alcohol, should the grant be withdrawn if the artist, despite his or her condition, produces wonderful art? If an organization employs a creative high achiever who decides to work when he or she feels like it, who fails to follow the most basic of rules of behaviour of that organization, but who produces excellent new product ideas, then does the lack of conformity matter?

People with profiles like this one want to be assessed on their performance not on conformity. For this reason they are often seen to be in conflict with today's organizations, in which conformity and compromise are more common. For example, when we look at a retailing organization, the creative-department employees are very different from the sales personnel; they look different, are more nonconformist, are isolated from the rest and, increasingly, are rewarded in a different way. By such differentiation, creativity is encouraged to flow. Indeed, our current obsession with innovation in organizations may indeed be the product of an earlier obsession with increasing size and structure.

The average profile in Fig. 2.11 is often associated with the entrepreneurial behaviour of independent, unstructured, risk-taking high achievers. The evidence broadly supports that view. There is a qualification to this, however, in that successful entrepreneurs or innovators rarely succeed alone. It may be that the profile of the second or third

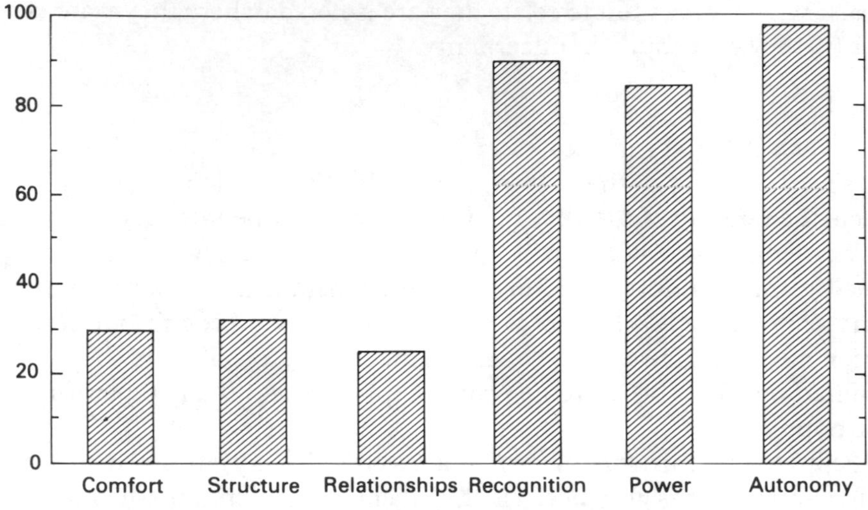

Figure 2.11 The very high achiever goal profile

person that is attached to the entrepreneur provides the clue to his or her success. Put another way, entrepreneurial behaviour is about a minimum of two or maybe more people, rather than the solo performance of the popular myth.

Other jobs which attract this profile are designers, dealers, consultants, systems analysts, architects, managing directors, permanent secretaries and ministers of state.

STAFF FUNCTIONS

The profile in Fig. 2.12 is the average ranking of goals given by a large number of personnel managers—high achievers by any standards, but more concerned with structure, certainty and predictability than are the innovators. Also, power rather than recognition is important to them. A comparable profile is seen in other staff functions such as accountants and some engineers.

THE AVERAGE MANAGER

Fig. 2.13 shows the average profile of a European or American manager aged between 30 and 50 years; that is, this is the most common profile among senior managers, executives and rising stars. As we move down the hierarchy we will find, in general, flatter profiles, with less emphasis on the high and low rankings and more equity between the goals. However, it is difficult to know whether these flatter profiles

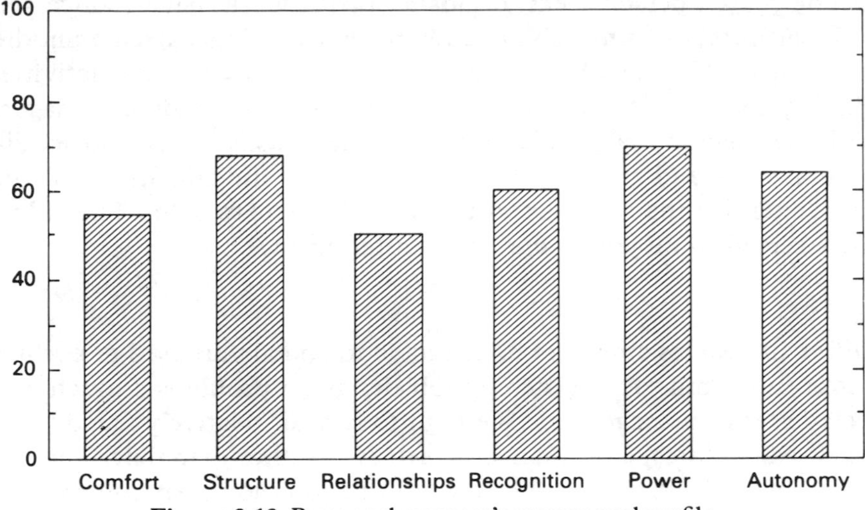

Figure 2.12 Personnel manager's average goal profile

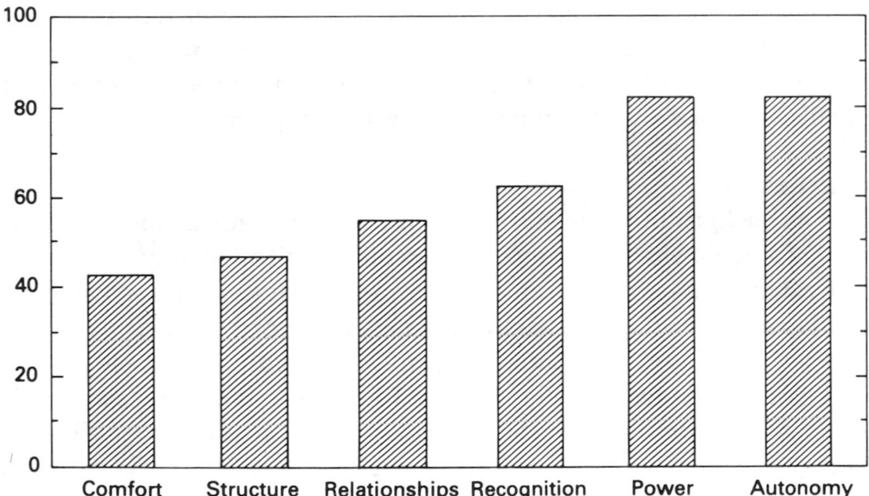

Figure 2.13 Goal profile of average manager in Europe and the USA

are the product of the situation or of background and experience to date. Whatever the reason, middle managers are, on average, not as extreme in their choices as their higher-flying bosses or 'superstars' on the way up. Less energy and less time may be expended on careers or employment.

The goals a person seeks to satisfy outside work may produce very different profiles from those cited here, so these less extreme middle-manager profiles may hide greater involvement in external activities. Having conceded that, most of these first-line to middle managers, with their flatter goal profiles, are simply less easily aroused to activity both at work and at home. Relaxation, family and friends simply get more attention than the 'superstars' would devote to them. The bulk of managers in employment show this flatter profile.

SUMMARY

Different profiles appear to be attracted to and are aroused to perform better in certain jobs. Matching job design to profile is a much neglected area of management. We tend to rely on relatively narrow data (age, sex, abilities, educational record, etc.) rather than delve and find out whether the activities and rewards of a job can satisfy the goals for which a person is striving. Perfect match is well-nigh impossible—even the most notably contented people dislike parts of their jobs. Conversely, the costs of extreme job/profile mismatches can be appalling.

There is not space here to show other than a small selection of different profiles. The major purpose of this outline is to make the point that the first step in motivating people at work is to relate a job to a goal profile, so that arousal to motivation is at least possible.

Culture

Just as background, age and position are important factors affecting a person's goal priorities, so too is the culture of the society in which the individual lives. For example, Fig. 2.14 illustrates an average profile for Japanese managers ranging from supervisors to chief executives. The average European/American profile is given for contrast.

It can be seen from the Japanese profile that relationships are ranked as significantly more important than they are for the average European manager. Indeed, as mentioned, one might propose that a manager's primary task in Japan is maintaining relationships. This is in contrast to the European manager, whose primary task is to get the work done. Note also the lower ranking for autonomy among the Japanese compared with the European average.

Maintaining relationships is also given high priority among managers in South East Asia. However, they differ from the Japanese in that the Chinese South East Asians are very strong on autonomy and entrepreneurial activity, albeit family-based.

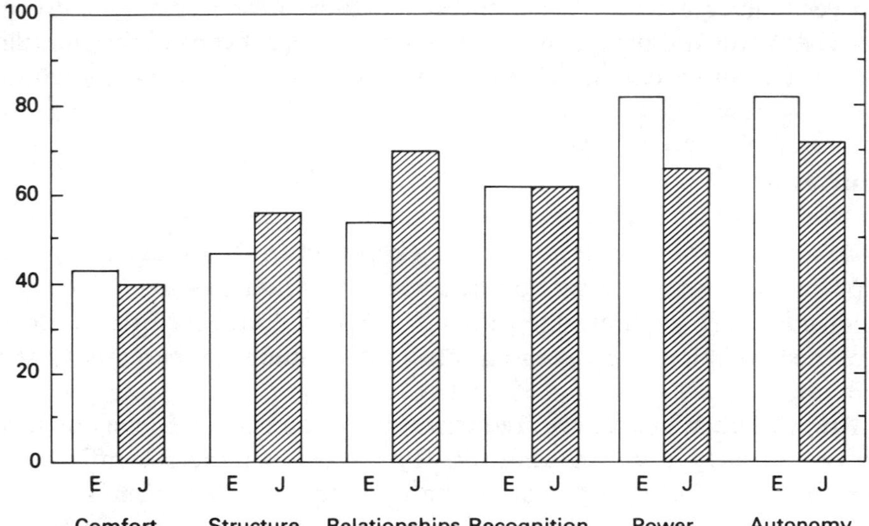

Figure 2.14 Japanese average manager's goal profile compared with European average manager's goal profile

In Europe we can also detect some cultural differences. Indeed, our European profile is a crude aggregate at best. For example, it is not surprising to see that the Swedes, who have put a lot of energy into work groups, report a higher concern for relationships. West German managers also reflect this concern for the collective or group, but differ from their Swedish counterparts by ranking managerial power goals more highly. In contrast, British managers put a very high value on autonomy and creativity (like their French colleagues) but show less interest in power in a managerial sense.

A reference to a study on cultural differences is given at the end of the chapter. It is sufficient here to note that culture does appear to affect the way people rank these goals, with the proviso that these are Western concepts anyway and translating these Western concepts for comparison into certain cultures is fraught with difficulties. What does security and structure mean to a manager in Thailand who believes in predestination based on his or her previous lives? There is no point in feeling insecure if all has been planned already. Similarly, autonomy in Japanese organizations is quite inconsistent with the dependence-producing child-rearing patterns employed by many Japanese parents. We must allow for these cultural differences. Even within our own society, differences do exist; they exist between North and South, between diverse creeds and cultures within the overriding culture, between rural and urban. Where statistically significant differences do *not* exist is between high-achieving men and high-achieving women.

Summary

In this chapter I have shown how individuals' goals or work orientations are determined primarily by background and secondarily by age, type of work and the culture of the society in which they live. The goals I consider here are those identified in Chapter 1 and include comfort, structure, relationships, recognition, power, autonomy, creativity and growth.

An individual's goals are frequently in conflict. To achieve one goal he or she may give up another. The most common conflicts are between the relationship goals and autonomy. The second most common conflict occurs between a desire for security and predictability and the search for power.

Age has a dramatic effect on the way people rank their goals. What was important to the child of 14 years of age will be slightly different from what is important at 25, 35, 45 and so on. In fact, my research and that of others has identified life stages at which certain combinations of goals appear to occur. Profiles of those different stages are given in the main text. The stages I have identified are:

• Childhood patterning	0 to 14 years
• The teenager	17 to 19 years
• Career launch	Mid-twenties to mid-thirties
• Child producing	Mid-twenties to early thirties
• Career take-off	30 to 38 years
• Mid-career	38 to 43 years
• Career peak	Mid-forties to mid-fifties
• Approaching retirement	Mid-fifties to mid-sixties
• Decline	Mid-sixties to mid-seventies

The work a person does in the organization may also influence the importance of different goals. An interesting question this poses is: Does the difference occur within individuals or is the difference the result of the situation they are in? The answer is both. I have found that people with certain combinations of the goals are attracted to certain jobs and professions. However, the fact that like profiles come together has the tendency to reinforce the likeness and reduce differences.

Finally, the culture of the society in which individuals live has a major impact on their goal profiles, simply because it affects background values and beliefs. Several examples are given to illustrate the dangers of assuming Western patterns will occur in other cultures. What this means is that the behaviours of different societies need separate analyses before cross-cultural differences can be assumed.

This brings our analysis of the individuals to an end. Through the rest of this book we will refer to the goal patterns of individuals and the effect these patterns have on jobs, rewards, structures, etc. In the next chapter we take one individual and put him or her with another. This interaction begins the process of building an organization.

References

ON THE IMPACT OF AGE AND LIFESTYLES

Levinson, D., et al., *The Seasons of a Man's Life*, Alfred Knopf, New York, 1978.

Schein, E. H., *Career Dynamics: Matching Individual and Organisational Needs*, Addison Wesley, Reading, Mass., 1978.

ON MID-LIFE PROBLEMS

Farrell, M. P. and S. D. Rosenberg, *Men at Mid Life*, Auburn House, Boston, 1981.

Hunt, J. W. and R. R. Collins, *Managers in Mid-Career Crisis*, Wellington Lane Press, Sydney, 1983.

O'Connor, P., *Understanding the Mid Life Crisis*, Sun Books, Melbourne, 1981.

ON EXECUTIVES AND CAREERS

Cole, D., *Professional Suicide*, McGraw-Hill, New York, 1981.

Cooper, C. L. and L. Thompson, *Public Faces, Private Lives*, Fontana, London, 1984.

Evans, P. and F. Bartolome, *Must Success Cost So Much?* Grant McIntyre, London, 1980.

Melhuish, A., *Executive Health*, Business Books, London, 1978.

ON CULTURAL DIFFERENCES

Hofstede, G., *Culture's Consequences: International Differences in Work Related Values*, Sage, Beverly Hills, Calif., 1981.

3. Individuals and other individuals

Introduction

This chapter looks at the way in which people's perceptions and communications are affected by a whole range of signals which they send one another. It then goes on to trace the process of an individual's joining an organization and acquiring a role within it.

Attitudes and perceptions

Previous chapters looked at the way an individual's abilities, values and goals affect behaviour. Abilities indicate potential performance. Goals and values channel behaviour.

An attitude is a statement of a position that an individual takes about an object, a theory, another person, an event or a belief. Hence, I have attitudes about the importance of your studying organizational behaviour if you wish to be a manager. I also have attitudes about managers, both about managers generally and about the managers I know. Similarly, like you, I have attitudes about foreigners, about stockbrokers, about drop-outs, and so on.

When two people interact, the process of interaction involves their abilities, goals, attitudes and experiences. Even before you and I meet, we have anticipatory expectations and assumptions about what will happen; and in forming those anticipations our own goals, attitudes and experiences are important.

By making assumptions, I am hoping that I can understand your behaviour. The more predictable the behaviour of others, the more secure I feel. The less information I have about you, the more difficult it is to make those assumptions, and the less comfortable our meeting may be, that is until both of us have collected enough data from each other to feel more competent in predicting subsequent behaviour. If I have too little information, I may even start inventing it.

For example, when you go to someone's house for dinner, you may have no information about the other guests. Not unexpectedly, the first half-hour after the guests arrive is stilted, while the hosts assist in the data-collection by introducing guests and 'dropping' data about them, and by serving drinks.

When we meet, we each perceive the other as the determinant of his or her own behaviour. Then we organize our perceptions to make goal–

attitude–behaviour–effect links; that is, I add together clues I see and hear, and form the assumption that you are motivated by X and that this will explain your subsequent behaviour. When bits of information do not fit, we tend to discard them in the interests of preserving our neat logic. Jumping to false conclusions is thus inevitable.

Once we have arranged our experiences of each other into goal–attitude–behaviour–effect links we use adjectives referring to 'traits' to describe each other—e.g., 'ambitious', 'charming', 'easy-going', 'lazy'. Finally, we structure our perceptions further by collecting traits together into wholes, and talk about a personality 'type'. Then we feel much better because we have imposed *our* structure upon the other person.

In establishing interpersonal relationships, what we all concentrate on is not the constantly changing behaviour of the other person, but a series of static pictures which are filed away in a mental album of impressions or snapshots. By this process, we try to comprehend the attitudes, values and likely behaviours of the other person and from there we hope to increase our capacity to predict behaviour. The lower our tolerance of uncertainty, the more readily we produce snapshots of the other person and the more readily we discard contradictory information. The less insecure we feel, or the more developed our capacities to look and listen, the more we seek out patterns or threads rather than snapshots.

Most of the time, we collect very little reliable information about each other. We take the first few minutes of interaction very seriously, and on the basis of these first impressions begin consciously, or more often unconsciously, to link values, goals, attitudes and behaviour together. Even in interviews for jobs, the first four minutes have been found to be vital in the assessment of the applicant's suitability. Data-collection concentrates on appearance, education and experience. Values, goals and beliefs about work (from which one might predict subsequent employee behaviour) usually receive scant attention in job interviews.

The rest of this chapter will look at how we collect data about each other—what signals we use, which are more important, and what happens when someone joins a work organization.

How do we get data about each other?

When you and I interact, we transmit a variety of verbal and non-verbal signals to each other. Some of these signals are intentional, but some are not.

In communicating with you—assuming I am the transmitter and you are the receiver (see Fig. 3.1)—the message is what I send to you,

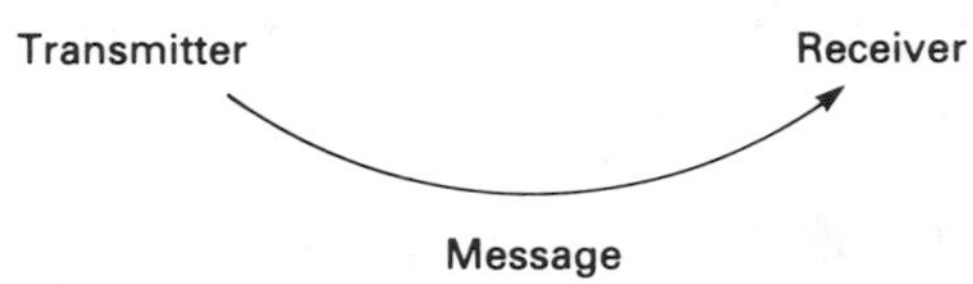

Figure 3.1 Communication—transmitting and receiving messages

but it may not be what you receive. You and I are both restricted to four communication channels in collecting information about each other:

- Visual—using the eyes as receptors.
- Auditory—using the ears as receptors.
- Olfactory—using the nose as receptor.
- Tactile—using the skin surfaces as receptors.

If we meet each other in a work organization, like most other people in that organization, we are restricted initially to the visual and auditory channels. It is not acceptable behaviour in our society to start smelling each other or feeling each other all over. This does not mean that we do not use the olfactory or tactile channels; it just means that there are more restrictions on our use of them. So we talk to each other and pick up data about each other through our eyes and ears.

The olfactory channel *is* used and has been found to be important in making judgements about a person being 'good' or 'bad'! The person who comes to an interview smelling unfavourably may be seen to be a 'bad' applicant. Tactile clues will also be important, but will probably be restricted to shaking hands. This can nevertheless be decisive: the candidate with a limp, damp handshake may well create an insuperably bad impression.

When we know each other better we will use more tactile communications, such as pushing, slapping, stroking and supportive gestures. In intimate relationships olfactory and tactile channels will be used extensively. One touch will convey a wealth of information.

In our work roles we are usually restricted to visual (non-verbal) and auditory (verbal) clues about each other. Let us now look at the non-verbal signals which affect perceptions.

NON-VERBAL SIGNALS

Proximity

Where you stand or sit will affect my perception of you. If the relationship is to be intimate, then we will be close together. If you are applying for a job, then your sitting too close may irritate me because I will be expecting to use visual and auditory rather than tactile or olfactory channels.

Proximity varies with the situation. If we are having a party, then physical proximity, in a confined space with background music and dim lighting, will help in the getting-to-know-each-other phase. However, we are unlikely to see a similar scene in union–management negotiations for new awards. Distance will have replaced proximity, and barriers to tactile communication (e.g., tables and chairs) will inhibit opportunities for touching.

Posture

The way a person stands—e.g., the position of the arms and the leg stance—also gives us clues. Height and good posture are assumed to be 'good' signs for people motivated to succeed in work organizations. As height is genetically determined, it is difficult to see what it has to do with an acquired goal or achievement except where parents or teachers convince tall children that they are achievers.

Physical appearance

The attributes seen as constituting physical attractiveness differ from culture to culture. When I meet you I have in my mind commercialized pictures of attractiveness which have been 'sold' to me from birth. The pictures relate to height, physique, face, hair, hands and so on. On to these pictures we attach behavioural predictions—attractive people are more able, fat people are lazy or jolly, people whose eyes are close together are dishonest, and so on. These stereotypes, too, have been 'sold' to us and we may never question them, despite the considerable evidence disproving them. Physical appearance has become a mass-produced obsession—a search for beautiful people. Indeed, in some jobs, what you are is secondary to how you look.

Clothes, jewellery and other embellishments are only relevant within a particular culture and, within that culture, in the context of particular organizations or professions. For example, if you arrive in my business dressed as a surgeon, a priest or a barrister when I was expecting a banker then we may have initial problems in communicating.

Gestures and facial expressions

Emotions, attitudes and beliefs may be transmitted through facial expressions. Some of these clues have universal significance—weeping, blushing, turning white and pupil dilation all indicate various emotional states. Gestures, however, are much more diverse because of the number of different possibilities; some merely reinforce verbal signals while others convey much more information.

Next to the face, the hands and arms give the most important non-verbal clues, and the functions of these clues are different from those of facial expressions. Hands and arms are used for illustration, for replacing speech, for indicating emotional states, and for grooming oneself; facial expressions may do all these, but in addition may indicate understanding, concentration and attention.

Direction of gaze

Eye movements tell the transmitter something about the receiver. Interaction usually begins with a period of eye contact which appears to signal from me to you (and vice versa) that we are ready to relate. Thereafter, direct eye contact is intermittent (25 to 75 per cent of interaction time) and is longer for the receiver than for the transmitter.

Summary

In summary, proximity, posture, physical appearance, gestures and facial expressions, and direction of gaze are all non-verbal clues picked up through the visual receptors (eyes). From these data the receiver will make assumptions about the transmitter's behaviour.

Fortunately, by using verbal as well as non-verbal signals, we have the chance to test our 'pictures' of each other.

VERBAL SIGNALS

We can classify most speech under five functions:

- Egocentric utterances—'I have just been called to head office.'
- Questions—'On what flight are we booked?'
- Conveying information—'Flight 234 at 11.15, Monday morning.'

- Influencing others—'Don't confirm the tickets until I tell you.'
- Establishing and sustaining relationships—'We must have you over for dinner before we leave.'

We 'dress' the function of conversation with a multitude of verbal signals about ourselves. The words we use, our accents, tone, volume and speech errors give more clues about us. The structure of sentences, the use of repetition, the linking of thoughts or ideas, the variety of words used and the grammatical structure of sentences yield yet more clues.

The use of these verbal clues varies according to the person with whom we are conversing. The training officer conducting a programme for line supervisors will use very different words and sentence structure from those used when he or she is working with top management. Indeed, one of the most damaging behaviours affecting interpersonal relationships can occur if the training officer misjudges the nature of the group and uses inappropriate phraseology. This is particularly so in the use of slang, swear words and inappropriate jokes.

LINKING NON-VERBAL AND VERBAL SIGNALS

Usually our verbal signals are reinforced or supported by non-verbal ones. The non-verbal signals expand or clarify the verbal. Yet in our day-to-day lives, we are witnesses to communication breakdowns, misinterpretations and blockages, where the transmitter's attitudes, values, experiences, language, postures, etc., do not link together in a consistent message, or where the message itself has inaccuracies, or where the receiver's attitudes, values and perceptions make him or her so filter the message that the intended information does not get through—what is heard is what the receiver wanted to hear, not what you said.

Communication breakdowns are the most prevalent symptom of organizational problems. However, they are usually symptomatic of something else; people don't set off for work with the intention of causing a communication bottle-neck. Yet, while other factors (such as structure) cause most of the breakdowns, it is undeniable that your faulty perceptions of what I am saying, and my faulty perceptions of what you are saying, *can* cause a whole chain of problems. Some people are just much more sensitive and perceptive in transmitting or receiving data than others. Fortunately most training programmes designed to help managers 'see' and 'hear' more have moved beyond the 'Look at *that*!' stage to identifying, from verbal and non-verbal clues, the underlying themes or patterns from which behaviours or opinions might be predicted.

We can improve interpersonal communication in the following ways:

- By continuously signalling attentiveness and responsiveness to the signals of the other—it is infuriating to talk to someone who is staring out of the window all the time.
- By continuously sharing speaking and listening—if you are trying to tell someone something, it is very distracting if he or she keeps interrupting you in the middle of a sentence.
- By signalling attitudes and intentions towards one another—it is off-putting to try to communicate honestly with someone who remains totally bland, giving no verbal or non-verbal clues as to agreement or disagreement.
- By checking, over the course of time, on the assumptions about and perceptions of each other's signals—it is confusing if I interpret your expression as annoyance when you are concentrating hard.
- By using gestures which are consistent with speech—it is highly inconsistent if your boss tells you to stay calm, while he or she rushes about, nervously playing with clothes, pens or paper clips.
- By only using gestures to illustrate speech—it is annoying to have to discuss, say, marketing strategy with someone who continuously grooms him- or herself.
- By providing continuous feedback on how the message is being received—if there is no response, no feedback, a dialogue becomes a monologue.

If some of these behaviours in other people annoy you, remember that you are probably guilty of such behaviour as well. Indeed, organizational life encourages us to give incorrect feedback, to be less than honest, to pander to our superiors while neglecting our subordinates, to play a multitude of political games. In a hierarchical structure, where success is seen in terms of promotion but where promotional opportunities are limited (and become even more limited the higher you rise), playing the power game is inevitable. However, games lead to communication breakdowns: I tell you, my boss, what I think you should hear, and leave out much of the rest; and you, in turn, are telling your boss what you think he or she should hear, again leaving out the rest. As long as bosses can influence the careers of subordinates, this filtering or laundering of communication will continue.

Further, we must ask ourselves, do we really want total honesty in communcation? As we are all less than perfect, we actually need laundered messages, filtered feedback, even deliberate lies, to protect ourselves and avoid hurting others. But this dilemma points to the central conflict of organizations—'me' versus 'the system'. 'The system' is designed for unfiltered, open communication; 'me' wants privacy, protection and some filtering in feedback. Finding the balance between 'me' and 'the system' is well-nigh impossible. Conducting more communication-training programmes will do little to help. Only interpersonal trust has been found to reduce the extreme forms of communication-filtering arising from a defensive 'me' fighting 'the system', and even trust rarely reduces filtering to zero—few marriages, even, have totally open communication. We all have our private dreams, fantasies and secrets.

USING VERBAL AND NON-VERBAL SIGNALS TO DEVISE LABELS

You and I receive signals from each other and interpret them. If you have influence over me, I may try to predict what signals you would like to see or hear, and consciously send them to you. If I sent an inconsistent signal, your verbal and/or non-verbal signals will tell me to explain or correct that signal. And while you are collecting and structuring data about me, I am doing the same about you.

We both draw inferences about each other as we order our perceptions into tidy links. Labels are thus slapped on to people with little regard for accuracy. Unfortunately, we need language to communicate, and language needs labels in order to refer to 'things' (objects, people, feelings, events, traits, etc.). Without labels, verbal communication is impossible. However, what is worrying is that, once labelled, we are likely to live up to that label. For example, children who are told they are stupid tend to live up to that expectation. Children who are told they are 'sickly' often actually become sickly. Fathers who tell their boys that they will be engineers may be delighted with their success rate, at least initially (many such sons subsequently flood into business schools to get out of engineering). Managers who see union leaders as aggressive, pig-headed and irrational treat union leaders in such a way that they elicit aggressive, pig-headed and irrational responses. Labels thus become self-fulfilling prophecies.

Similarly the labels we use to point to nationality, race, religion, etc., as in 'Tony is Italian', foster stereotypes. The terms 'Jewish', 'Irish',

'Japanese', 'American', 'Russian', 'Muslim', etc., trigger snapshots of traits.

This passion for stereotyping illustrates yet again our need to structure our perceptions and to reduce the infinite variety of incoming information to manageable levels. Interaction is easier if certain labels, such as those indicating socio-economic status, are established. When we meet people we have at our disposal a series of acceptable ways of establishing minimal data levels: 'Do you live near here?', 'Do you work in the city?' It might be easier if we all presented a résumé of ourselves rather than waited for the questions!

The most blatant stereotyping occurs because of supposed differences between the sexes: 'Men are more intelligent', 'Women are more emotional', 'Men are physically stronger', 'Women are more creative', etc. It is remarkable that this sexist labelling has continued as long as it has, even though most of the research on differences attributable to sex has not supported these labels. In the seventies women—understandably—began to get very angry and attempted to liberate themselves from a whole bag of largely erroneous stereotyped labels.

Factors affecting label accuracy

Certain factors increase the chances of inaccuracy in our perceptions of one another:

- If our work goals are involved, our perceptions of verbal and non-verbal signals become more distorted.
- If you and I are emotionally involved, distortions are greater.
- If I am dependent on you (subordinate–boss), then your perceptions of me are more distorted, and vice versa.
- If our relationship is very aggressive, our perceptions of each other will be more distorted.
- If either of us has a psychological disorder, distortion of our perceptions of each other is increased.

Our perceptions of each other may become more accurate if:

- I have known you well over a long period of time. I can check my assumptions.
- We are peers (rather than boss and subordinate).
- Our interaction is two-way (I talk to you and you talk to me).
- I learn to listen and look and find themes, not instant pictures.

Interpersonal relationships at work

Relationships at work are strengthened by three behaviours:

- Imitation
- Reciprocity
- Reinforcement

- *Imitation* Occurs if I send you verbal or non-verbal signals and you respond with similar signals. For example, we meet and I tell a joke; we both laugh; you respond with a joke; we both laugh.
- *Reciprocity* Occurs when I help you in some way and you reciprocate by helping me.
- *Reinforcement* Occurs when you reward me (respond positively to my signals). I tell my joke and you laugh genuinely and enthusiastically.

In addition to these behaviours, organizations have other ways of forcing and reinforcing relationships. Verbal signals can be controlled, broadcast and edited. Formal devices are designed to reinforce expected behaviours and, where deviations do occur, members employ these devices to correct those deviations.

Joining an organization

I decide to join an organization. It may be a church, a corporation, a hospital, a small business, a tennis club, a multinational company. They are all organizations. So what is an organization?

An organization is an identifiable social entity whose members pursue multiple and shared objectives through their consciously and continuously coordinated actions and relations. Hence, an organization is characterized by:

- People who belong
- Common objectives
- Division of work
- Coordination
- Continuity

When I decide I would like to join, I believe that I have something to contribute—skills, actions, aptitudes, abilities, potential, etc. If I have a free choice, I will seek an organization which I perceive has goals, values and beliefs similar to my own.

The employer buys a contributor to an objective and tasks, but also buys a person, me, even though those tasks only require a part of me—the part that can do the job. The employer's expectations and my expectations will be different, and inevitably compromise will characterize our relationship from the day I join until the day I depart. Indeed, organizations rely on compromise.

Even before I decide to take the job, I develop naïve expectations about what it will be like. If I know very little about the firm or the people in it, then, to reduce my uncertainty, I will invent my own snapshots of what to expect. The disorientation of actually entering the organization shatters some of these naïve expectations. I am confronted by an explosion of non-verbal, verbal, written and tactile clues. I can only reduce the painful uncertainty and bewilderment of those first few days by learning relevant data quickly. But some of the information takes months to emerge, let alone learn, and the pain of joining is the pain of gathering enough written, verbal and non-verbal information to 'learn the ropes'. I know, and the employer knows, that I have a role to play, and I want to learn the role as quickly as possible—in order to reduce my uncertainty to certainty, and to merge myself into the rest of the cast of actors or members.

The process of acquiring the role I have to play can be divided into four stages.

STAGE 1: THE ANTICIPATORY PHASE

This phase occurs before we actually arrive. We take in written and verbal data provided by personnel departments or by interviewers, as well as highly generalized data about the company or department. The more naïve our expectations, the greater the chance of our leaving; therefore employers have a vested interest in telling the truth, or at least not telling untruths, in job interviews, particularly about the less attractive aspects of the organization. But this information still may not get through. Saturday work is usual in the retail trade; however much the social disruption is stressed at interview, keen candidates may nevertheless filter out the information they do not want to hear, resigning six months later to find a Monday-to-Friday job.

STAGE 2: THE FORMAL PHASE

From the moment we enter the organization, verbal and non-verbal signals are being transmitted about required behaviour. Formal signals are often grouped together in an induction programme, and so anxious are we to reduce the total uncertainty to something we can understand that we will swallow the formal induction without even a whimper. The more important security, structure and definition are to us, the more readily we will absorb the formal signals about expected behaviour.

Within hours, the new recruit may have agreed to objectives, tasks to be performed, hours of work, codes of behaviour, boss–subordinate relationships, work territory, and so on, all in exchange for specified rewards, usually monetary, and unspecified promises, such as promotion. The terms for a legal and psychological contract have been established.

STAGE 3: LEARNING THE EXPECTATIONS OF WORK ASSOCIATES

Informal values, norms and expectations are just as important as the formal ones. Through the verbal and non-verbal signals of informal relationships we acquire the social props to our identity. We may be so lonely in the process of entry that we accept the informal group dictates with little evaluation. Group norms about work, work rates, dress, conformity, and so on, are soon added to our concepts of the role we are to play.

STAGE 4: COMPLETION OF THE ENTRY PROCESS

This occurs much later in the entry process. It may be months later, when naïve expectations have become realistic beliefs. By then we feel comfortable. The stress of joining the organization is over; verbal and non-verbal signals are synchronized and ordered; we know the formal and informal expectations; and we are making our contribution to the output of the organization. In return, as agreed on joining, we receive regular payments of money and intrinsic satisfaction from our work. In this pleasant and mostly satisfying environment, the personal stage of role acquisition occurs. We begin to change the role to include our own expectations of what it should be. We may even use our own verbal and non-verbal signals to persuade others to change the formal requirements to bring them closer to our own expectations.

By now, we have fully entered into two contracts—a legal contract and a psychological contract. The legal contract specifies my status in terms of tenure, dismissal, redundancy, discipline, etc. The psychological contract is a contract of expectations between 'them' and 'me'—it links what I expect from 'them' and what they expect from 'me' in the role I am to play. 'Them' includes bosses, peers and subordinates, so it is inevitable that one or more of these sub-groups will be disappointed in me from time to time. Compromise is inevitable.

Roles

A 'role' combines the cumulative formal, technical, informal and personal expectations about a job. It is the link between individual and organization. *Role conception* is how I see the role I am expected to play. *Role performance* is how I actually behave.

An organization is a collective of actors' expectations and behaviours in the pursuit of ends. It is the arena in which occur the processes of verbal, non-verbal, olfactory and tactile signals, of emotions and of decisions. It is an arena where expectations and processes change, some gradually (e.g., formal expectations) others (e.g., personal or informal expectations) quite rapidly. It is the arena where some actors impose their will on others in an endless power game in which the others who are imposed upon allow that imposition to continue for reasons of their own (rewards, money, promotion, love).

It is impossible to describe an organization in behaviour terms (i.e., processes) other than momentarily because the processes are always changing; but when we speak of the processes we freeze that dynamic interaction for a single moment, take a picture, and know that a moment later the picture will be different.

ROLE STRESS

Acquiring a role raises problems for some individuals. Living up to other people's signalled expectations is often a pleasure/pain experience: pleasure in the recognition we receive for satisfying others' expectations, pain in the sense that we lose some of our independence and freedom. For this reason, roles may never be totally satisfying other than for short periods. The result of this conflict between 'them' and 'me' is stress.

- *Role conflict* Occurs where more than one role is required in the same situation.
- *Role ambiguity* Occurs where others' expectations are badly signalled or received and remain unclear.
- *Role overload* Occurs where expectations of others are too high.
- *Role underload* Occurs where expectations of others are too low.

ROLE SETS

When I join an organization I do not have a relationship with everyone. Indeed, I am most likely to have relationships on a day-to-day basis only with a relatively small number of people. These are people such as my boss, his or her boss, my peers and (if I have any) my subordinates. At the most, this may amount to 20 people, and of these there will be fewer than 10 with whom I interact frequently. This small group (within the larger group, the organization) is often called my *role set* or my team, and it is their transmitted expectations which affect my performance most of the time.

Those members of my set who have more power have most influence on my performance. Hence my boss is more likely to produce a change in my role performance than one of my peers. My peers are more tolerant, more willing to accept me for what I am rather than for what I might produce or become in the hierarchy. However, if they decide that I have violated our psychological contract then they, too, have great power to influence my behaviour. Power and influence are what social systems live on. If power is important to me, then I will try to acquire it. The next chapter discusses power and its acquisition and use in organizations.

Summary

When people interact, they emit a range of verbal, visual, olfactory and tactile signals, using the eyes, ears, nose and skin surface as receptors. All these data are channelled through the process of perception. We filter these signals through our own goals, expectations, attitudes and experiences. We structure the data into simplified snapshots, attributes, traits and types, and attempt to give ourselves the understanding we need and to predict the behaviour of others from this process.

Proximity, physical appearance, direction of gaze and gestures and facial expressions all affect our perceptions of one another. Speech patterns, use of words, accent, volume and so on, are verbal clues which we add to our structuring behaviour.

If we take these characteristics of perception into an organizational setting, then the verbal and non-verbal signals still provide data for interpersonal relationships. However, formal induction procedures and the allocation of a job to perform can structure the signals a great deal more rigidly.

New employees join an organization of interacting players, whose perceptions and expectations establish norms of required behaviour. Organizations are behavioural processes which live on influence and power.

References

ON PERCEPTION

Schneider, D. J., A. H. Hastorf and P. C. Ellsworth, *Person Perception*, Addison-Wesley, Reading, Mass., 1979.

ON INTERACTION

Argyle, M., A. Furnham and J. A. Graham (eds), *Social Situations*, Cambridge University Press, Cambridge, 1981.

Handy, C., *Understanding Organizations*, 2nd edn, Penguin, London, 1985.

ON SOCIAL SKILLS

Argyle, M., *Bodily Communications*, Methuen, London, 1976.

Argyle, M. (ed.), *Social Skills and Work*, Methuen, London, 1981.

Pease, A., *Body Language*, Sheldon Press, London, 1983.

ON SOCIALIZATION

Van Maanen, J., 'Breaking in: a consideration of organizational socialization', in *Handbook of Work Organization and Society*, R. Dubin (ed.), Rand-McNally, Chicago, 1975.

4. Power in organizations

Introduction

This chapter sets out to analyse the life-blood of all social systems—social power. I analyse what is meant by social power, where that power arises and how managers use it. Finally I suggest some of the negative aspects of political activity.

There are few words which pose as many problems for the social sciences as the word 'power'. There are currently five popular frameworks for analysing power in organizations. Briefly, these are:

- Power is a personal attribute—'He is big and powerful.' The attribute may not have a purpose.
- Power is a social relationship between two or more people; that is, Mrs X can affect the behaviour of Mrs Y. Power in this sense does have purpose.
- Power is a commodity; like a resource it can be traded for a purpose.
- Power is something that has behaviour as its outcome—it is causal. Power exists because the boss can alter the behaviour of a subordinate to achieve a purpose.
- Power is a philosophical issue—a question of morality or immorality. Purpose is relevant only if ends are relevant.

There is considerable overlap between these views. However, as we are concerned with managers, we will concentrate on those personal and structural characteristics of social power that are relevant to work situations. (References are given at the end of this chapter for the other frameworks.)

Power is the capacity to affect other people's behaviour without their consent. Hence, it is a personal attribute and an interpersonal result, even if the desired outcome is not achieved. Power is the deployment of means to achieve ends.

Power differs from authority in that authority stems, initially, from the resources of the organization (finance, information, people, etc.) but acquires legitimization only if others recognize that authority. Authority is conceded by subordinates. In this sense authority is limited. Power need not be.

A manager may have authority to control resources but may be powerless. Authority does not guarantee power—indeed, it is merely one possible source of power. Authority relates to a position in a hierarchy. If I, as a subordinate, recognize that authority in my boss and, on that basis, allow him or her to exercise authority, then he or she has power based on position. For this reason authority is often called 'positional power'.

What is appealing about power is its importance and its potential. For many people, to possess power is the ultimate ego-trip. For this reason, throughout history individuals have striven to acquire it, usually at the expense of other people. However, unlike authority which is limited, power is not limited, so our opportunities to acquire it are infinite. Your gain is not necessarily my loss.

Three variables determine the amount of power an individual acquires:

- *Capacity* The characteristics of the individual, e.g., knowledge, wealth, beauty, strength, charisma, authority, skill, intelligence, etc.
- *Dependence* Social power exists only in interpersonal situations; others are involved and must be dependent on the skill, knowledge, strength or whatever of the powerful.
- *Scarcity* The rarer the skill, beauty, money, strength or whatever is the basis of power, the greater the power of the individual. For example, international stars in opera, football, art and music acquire power because of their rarity.

What power do you have?

The power you acquire will depend on:

- How motivated you are to have power.
- The power bases you can draw upon.
- The political skills you have to increase your power and influence within an organization.

MOTIVATION TO HAVE POWER

People aroused by the possibilities of social power will seek it more consistently than those who are not aroused by power. In Chapter 1 we analysed power goals in detail; those individuals whose profiles reflect a persistent theme of power will expend more effort and energy in seeking more of it. Unlike many other goals, it is difficult to gratify a strong search for power.

POWER BASES

The second influence on individuals' power is the bases they have to draw on. There are many of these and their usefulness depends on whether other people concede that the individual has them as bases for power. For example, you may be the greatest athlete in the world, but your capacity to influence my behaviour is very small if I do not *know* you are a famous athlete. This process of acknowledging a person's power bases is called legitimization—the recognition by you that you will allow me to affect your behaviour. If a person has a loaded gun we will probably recognize him or her immediately as having power. The power base in this case is physical violence, even death. But if someone claims power merely on the grounds of intelligence, then we may be far less willing initially to concede power.

The following are some of the power bases used in work organizations. They all depend on those with less power conceding to those with more.

Legitimized power

- *Authority* The right to control finance, information, people, equipment, materials, etc., in organizations and to have access to important decision-making processes. (This is sometimes referred to as 'positional power'.)
- *Function* The importance of one's function in the organization provides a power base (I develop this later). Hence the marketing function, the finance function or the establishment function provides a power base for individuals within and without those functions. (See page 73 for more on this.)
- *Personal characteristics* Height, beauty, strength, endurance, achievement.
- *Intellect* A personal characteristic but worthy of separate mention. This is not simply intelligence, but a capacity to diagnose and solve problems; to provide structured solutions for situations of uncertainty.
- *Charisma* A unique combination of personality and behaviour.
- *Interpersonal skills* Empathy, sensitivity, 'sixth sense', social skills (articulateness, listening, observing, etc.).
- *Access* To powerful people—for example, the chief executive officer's chauffeur, the cleaner and the board secretary all have access to powerful people.

- *Wealth* Private funds; financial independence.
- *Connections* Powerful famous friends and acquaintances.
- *Family* Prominent famous family (e.g., Kennedy, Rothschild, Windsor).
- *Performance* Superb performance, outperforming others.
- *Referent power* The use of the power of others is usually based on admiration for another (e.g., gods, famous leaders, rock stars, etc.). More subtle forms of referent power occur when an individual asks others to complete a task because 'the chief executive' or 'the minister' has asked for the work. The power of the chief executive or minister can in this way be used to increase the power of someone else. Internal referent power links one to the internally more powerful. External referent power links to external, e.g., 'The prime minister has asked for this.'
- *Expert power* Expertise is a major source of power. It exists in three forms: expertise from *experience* ('I am the only one who has done this before' or 'She was the best salesperson in 1985'); expertise based on *knowledge*; expertise based on a particular skill (e.g., the surgeon, the programmer, the writer, the foreign exchange dealer).

All of these power bases depend on the perceptions of the less powerful. At any time the less powerful might withdraw their concession of power, in which case legitimacy is lost. For example, the employees who reject their manager's ultimatum and vote for industrial action have withdrawn their concession that the manager can control their behaviour. Similarly, an expert selling obsolete knowledge soon finds power is withdrawn.

Three other power bases depend much more on the capacity of the powerful to affect the perceptions of the less powerful, even when the latter are resisting that influence.

- *Reward power* Managers influence the behaviour of their team members by rewarding them. They have at their disposal two reward groups: financial reward (salary, merit increases, bonuses); and *intrinsic rewards* (a job well done recognized by praise, a better job, promotion, public acclaim, etc.). As we noted in Chapter 1, both forms of reward can have a marked effect on behaviour.
- *Coercive power* Physical coercion is banned in most organizations, yet it does occur. More subtle is psychological coercion: modern organizations are full of 'illegitimate' uses of psychological coercion,

e.g., hints to the less powerful that promotions may be missed, that salaries will not be increased, that redundancy may be necessary.

- *Information power* The release and/or the withholding of information provides an extremely strong power base. For example, why is it that personnel appointments take so long to be announced often when there is no adequate reason for delay? One explanation is that withholding information reinforces a power relationship. Conversely, why is it that finance managers seem to think they have a monopoly on secrets? Indeed, why is so much that is trivial in organizations treated as though it were a state secret?

The power of a function or department

'Systems', 'functions', 'technologies', 'departments' and other groupings of people have power in similar ways to individuals. The more important the function in achieving the objectives of the organization the more power that function will have. Hence, in a finance company the treasury (which raises capital on the market for other functions to lend or invest) can control the behaviour of all other functions. Similarly, in the UK government, Her Majesty's Treasury acts as the finance function and thus has enormous power. Dependence creates power, even when that dependence relates to a function. However, if the important function exercising power can be replaced, i.e., if some other system or group could perform the function, then the power of the first function is reduced.

Also, a function or system may have the capacity to reduce uncertainty. The greater the capacity of the function, group or department to reduce uncertainty, the greater is its power. However, the uncertainty must be central to the organization's objectives or tasks. Coping with uncertainty on a trivial issue will not result in functional power. Similarly, if another function can provide a solution to the uncertainty, then the first function's power will be less.

Studies of power have tended to concentrate on the individuals who have power rather than on the systems or functions that have power. This is probably because individuals are more interesting to study. However, much day-to-day activity in organizations is influenced by functions, technologies, systems and structures rather than by individuals. We complete forms and reports and perform other behaviours merely in response to signals received, all of which often emanate from a computer or similar piece of technology. In this sense the technology acquires authority, in that I concede that I will allow it to affect my behaviour. Some writers have suggested that too much time is given to exploring the interpersonal relationships of power, and too little to studying the influence of structure, technology, systems and plans. This is especially relevant if the structure is based on strong beliefs, values and ideas, which are themselves a major influence on behaviour.

To identify the powerful functions of an organization we must ask two questions of the members:

- Which function has most power in this organization? Is it marketing, finance, service, etc.?
- Which function is in the ascendancy? (That is, which is increasing in power and influence?)

In any organization there will be both a leading function and a function on the rise.

Internal and external power

Power does not only exist around individuals or within functions. It crosses the boundaries of the organization and allows us to differentiate between the power of members (e.g., those employed) and non-members (those external to the organization). So far we have concentrated on the internal distribution of power. Outside sources of power will arise, dependent on individuals, on coalitions of individuals and on structures, particularly legal and government structures.

Sources of power for these externals are similar to those already discussed. The greater the dependence on an external individual, group or organization (e.g., the oil company's dependence on the Middle East for the supply of certain types of crude oil), the more power that external has. The more the external reduces uncertainty, and the less replaceable the external is, then the more power the external will have. The greater the external control, the greater will be the tendency of the internals to centralize power, to standardize and to formalize it within the organization. Conversely, a strong internal power structure with a confident ideology will defend members from external interference, depending of course on the nature of the relationship. If there is no clear focus of power (either external or internal) then internal conflict appears inevitable.

POLITICAL ACTIVITY

A third influence on the power managers have is their political activity. Managers' success in the political arena depends ultimately on their capacity to play the political game. There are three sets of skills which appear to be vital:

- Diagnostic skills
- Tactical skills
- Interpersonal skills

Diagnostic skills
These are the skills used to develop the database necessary for developing tactics. Data-collection, articulateness, listening skills, wandering about, identifying information points, tuning into the informal structure, networking, etc., are all part of this process. Astute politicians do not go off half-cocked; they test the water, collect their facts, identify the support systems, find the coalitions, understand the 'influencers' or the roles that carry weight. Listening, observing and collecting information is a continuous, and mostly face-to-face process.

Tactical skills
These involve predicting the outcomes of different tactics and choosing those tactics likely to produce the results. Outcomes can provide rapid feedback on the effectiveness of tactics.

Both diagnostic and tactical skills depend on what we have traditionally called political acumen—a combination of listening and observational skills, with a heightened capacity to predict likely behavioural outcomes.

Interpersonal skills
These determine the effectiveness of individuals in affecting others, i.e., their ability to influence others. Power is used most effectively when it is used unobtrusively. The greater the legitimacy of what the individual is trying to do, the easier the exercise of power. Most of the time, therefore, managers try to make their use of power less obvious, more rational and more legitimate.

Political activity occurs for a myriad of reasons, but we see it most commonly when individuals or functions of individuals attempt to increase their power. This can be done by using different power bases (more expertise, more use of referent power, more charisma) or by structurally increasing the power of the position or function by making it more central, more vital to reducing uncertainty. Either way, the political process involves the acceptance by other powerful members that the individuals or groups have increased their power.

Pfeffer has noted some of the political techniques people used to expand their power:

- Selective use of objective criteria; the pretence to 'science' and the choice of criteria which support one's position.
- Using the outside expert to legitimize decisions.
- Controlling the agenda such that decisions can be brought forward or, at the other extreme, not arise at all. (A related technique is to order the sequence of decisions on the agenda. Items towards the beginning tend to get much more attention than later items.)
- Formation of coalitions with insiders and/or outsiders who will support one's position.
- Co-option—co-opting external people on a continuing basis in order to influence decisions, e.g., members of committees of enquiry, task forces, outside consultants, non-executive directors.
- Using committees internally to overcome restrictions on information and thereby arrive at a decision.

To which I might add some of my own observations on how individuals increase their power:

- By acquiring, preferably in advance, the expertise the organization requires. (W. H. Auden argued that opera singers and prostitutes survive revolutions because of the scarcity of their skills and the continuing market for those skills.)
- By joining the leading department, and not one which is in decline. In every organization there is a department or division which is 'on the up and up'—one which is seen to be better than others at producing results. Often this reputation depends on technology (e.g., the rapid emergence of data-processing departments and their glamorous image in the sixties) or skill (the current re-emergence of industrial relations).
- By acquiring the values, attitudes and behaviour codes of those with power. Establishments, like any other group, have accepted standards of dress, behaviour and manners. To reduce the distance between oneself and the more powerful, one must learn these codes.
- By performing. Very high performance in a current job is important in securing internal visibility and a more powerful position.

- By increasing people's dependency. You may do this by controlling resources or services, or by listening to the problems of the more powerful.
- By establishing relationships with external but powerful people. This may involve claiming friendship with power figures in society at large, the implication being that one has powerful friends.
- By using the names or positions of the powerful ('I need the information now—for the Minister').
- By inferring the needs of the powerful. This leads to statements like, 'The managing director may need the information', or 'I think she will need that information', or 'The boss is likely to need the information.'
- By entertaining. Wining and dining the powerful is a familiar ploy. Even implying that one entertains the powerful is sufficient ('We had dinner with Sir Leslie last week').
- By increasing external visibility, e.g., by having books and papers published, by appearing and being vocal at conferences and reunion dinners). This is especially important among competitive organizations.
- By oozing self-confidence in speech, dress and manner. Verbal communication can be especially effective in increasing visibility.
- By dropping data about expertise and experience ('When I was marketing director for Europe . . .', 'When I was at Harvard . . .').
- By generating myths and legends based on the past. All power figures are talked about by the less powerful. Myths and legends abound about the boss, the prime minister, the famous musician. Usually admirers generate the myths, but the smart politician, managing director or the person on the make generates his or her own myths and feeds them into the grapevine.
- By acquiring assets and wealth, or just implying that one has acquired assets or wealth ('We have a house in the South of France').
- By working for higher qualifications and thereby increasing expertise, internal and external visibility and scarcity value.
- By developing social skills (e.g., such that you convince even the most boring company director that you are fascinated by his or her endless repetition of anecdotes).
- By using one's spouse and children to multiply one's impact on an organization.
- By recognizing the importance of patronage. Careers need patrons, and choosing the wrong patron can have negative results. The ten-

dency for individual's benevolently to support the up-and-coming younger person is still strong in organizations, despite the much trumpeted fairness of appraisal schemes.

- By broadcasting one's achievements in non-work activities ('I won the race on Saturday. On to the finals now').
- By learning the niceties of political and organizational games.
- By developing skills which are not used in the work organization but which are socially approved. (For example, the champion swimmer's reputation in the organization depends on swimming, not on what he or she is employed to do.)
- By attaching oneself to worthwhile and socially responsible non-work organizations (children's research funds, the blind, the Church).
- By having the right parents. Socio-economic background has been less significant in some countries than in Europe, but in certain industries, class and school are still important.
- By recognizing that most studies of careers show that they do not develop in a carefully planned, logical sequence. Most careers are the product of chance—being in the right place at the right time. Thus the final tactic for those seeking power is to be aware of the fickleness of chance and, when chance makes an offer, to take it.

Kakabadse adds some other strategies in his analysis of power:

- Keep people comfortable. Concentrate on the behaviours, values, attitudes, drives and ideas that the person in question can accept. By this process personal discomfort will not interfere with acceptance of the decision.
- Develop a network of contacts.
- Make deals (a variation on the previous mention of coalitions).
- Withhold and withdraw. Withhold information not consistent with your plan. Withdraw from situations and let those involved sort it out. (For example, government interference in industrial disputes is often seen to lessen the likelihood of a solution rather than compel the factions to resolve their differences.)

All the tactics listed above can be seen in organizations, and those who use them most are either at the top or on the way to the top. Listed as they are, they may appear repellent and exaggerated, but we cannot really blame individuals for using them in a system which promises power and influence to all, and then restricts both to a few. If individuals hope to realize the rewards of the achieving society, then they will use these political tactics as ways to improve their chances of achieving success and power.

Further, we should remember that these games generate conflicts, which in turn energize the system and make it very productive. Without conflict, organizations may well die, just as families and marriages without conflict collapse. However, the conflict can become destructive, and much destructive conflict arises from power games.

The effect of power games on organizational effectiveness can be damaging. In a system where the boss has the power to determine the future careers of subordinates, the filtering of communication upwards through the hierarchy is inevitable. This can lead to a vicious circle, in which important communication is filtered out by power-seekers so that the structure (which causes most of the problems) is reinforced in order to flush out the filtered information, thereby making the filtering worse. It is only in flatter, smaller organizational units that we see a sharp decrease in both the game-playing and the filtering.

Filtering to preserve power

Apart from data required for control, most upward communication in organizations can be categorized into four groups:

- We send up data about ourselves and our problems.
- We send up data about others and their problems.
- We comment on, or suggest refinements to, the procedures, policies and regulations (the structure).
- We suggest strategies for current problems and what needs to be done.

As organizations increase in size, the necessity to predict and control the behaviour of the whole organization inevitably leads to more structure, more controls, more requests for information. Further, the larger the system, the greater the struggle for power and influence. Not unexpectedly, we all learn to filter out data which puts us in a bad light, and we learn to tell the boss what he or she wants to hear. Studies of vertical filtering of information have found four methods used:

- We *put it in writing*, sending written details up the hierarchy in case we have to prove we have fulfilled our role. A multitude of memos circulate in the role system simply to justify our behaviour in the event of a breakdown. If a breakdown does occur, we rush to our files and extract the relevant memo which shows that we *did* tell the boss what was happening—that is, we cover ourselves.

- Because personal power is the promotion of self, we send *positive data on ourselves* up the hierarchy and forget to send the negative data—that is, we tell our superiors how good we are.
- We send in *negative data on our peers*—those who are competing against us for more powerful positions. The 'but syndrome' is a common indicator of negative filtering. It occurs all over the hierarchy, but is seen in its most blatant form at the second level. This form of game-playing begins with praise of a peer, but ends with negative feedback on that peer. Usually the negative feedback begins with 'but'—e.g., 'We were very lucky to get Harry from the opposition because he is the top marketing person in the country—*but* he knows nothing about our products and still has a lot to learn.' Or, even more shattering, 'He means well', the innuendo being, 'but he fails.'
- We try to *reduce the distance* between ourselves and our boss by using first-person-plural pronouns, talking of what 'we' (i.e., the boss and I) will do in the future—'We could always write to head office, and ask them to let us have more data. We could really make this place swing if only they gave us the data to work on, couldn't we?' By implication the use of 'we' attaches the less powerful person to the more powerful, and power is equalized.

Self-promotion and 'covering' oneself occur in all large organizations. The early symptoms occur in organizations with 100 people. The reverse also holds; the smaller the organization, the less prevalent the problems and generally the more constructive the conflict.

Imbalance of power

Organizations depend on a balance of power such that no one individual has dictatorial power. In an age when ownership and management of large corporations are less incestuously linked, if not separate, the balancing of power is possible. However, very costly imbalances still do occur between individuals, between groups, and between management and unions. Work organizations still represent the best example of centralized, concentrated, and largely unopposed, authoritarian power, despite all the movements towards employee participation. In theory, an imbalance of power between individuals can be reduced by withdrawing, by forming new coalitions or by continuous interaction.

By continuous interaction I mean the less powerful interact continuously with the more powerful. By ingratiating themselves with the more powerful, the less powerful may equalize the power. For example, the personal assistant to the managing director, by isolating the boss from the functional heads, can make the latter totally dependent on him or her. Similarly, boards, committees, teams and task forces can act as controls on anyone's attempt to gain absolute power.

In more primitive societies and in totalitarian systems, physical isolation and death are ways of restoring the balance of power. In work organizations, physical punishment and death are not possible. This forces us into some unfortunate psychological games in order to force a redistribution of power. I say unfortunate, because I firmly believe that confronting the problem openly with those involved is, and must be, the most productive technique. Yet my experience is that such a confrontation often takes years to occur. Instead, rumours about individuals' competence, sanity, paranoia, habits or sickness circulate behind their backs. Indeed, our creativity in discovering ways to undermine the person who is 'out of control' or 'destroying the balance', or is 'past her prime' appear to be infinite. Most frequently the imbalance occurs because the wrong person is in the wrong place at the wrong time—what the organization needs now in terms of its leaders may be different from what it needed five years ago. Instead of recognizing this truism, energy is expended in a destructive process. Later someone will ask 'Why didn't we confront this problem years ago and try to solve it?' Honesty may be painful (as anyone who has been involved in a large-scale redundancy programme will know), but undermining a person's confidence until he or she quits is immoral. Managers and leaders do have 'times' and 'places' in organizations, and when person, time and place are no longer congruent we must confront that issue and change the balance of power.

The drama of power

Zaleznik and Kets de Vries have argued that the power struggle in organizations leads to three life dramas. There are other dramas in the power struggle, but these are among the most common:

- *Parricide* The drama of stripping the king (or queen) of power. Subordinates fantasize about what they would do if they were in control. Several people find they enjoy the same fantasy. Add a major organizational setback, and fantasies become possibilities and the power struggle ensues. The struggle results in the 'death' of the ruler. Age is often a reason for parricide—the ageing father figure will not relinquish the reins, so a palace revolt takes them from him (or her). Subsequently, there is likely to be a further power struggle; the potential death of the old ruler has united the second level in a temporary coalition but, once this common enemy is gone, internal struggles occur for the throne.

- *Paranoid thinking* A distortion of thought and perception, of which all humans are capable. This drama follows a coalition which breaks down. It is characterized by jealousy, suspicion and attributing malevolent motives to ex-members of the coalition. Behind the suspicions there are often truths, but they become distorted as the paranoid thinker becomes convinced of his or her own integrity and the dishonesty of the others. Paranoia is second only to depression as the major psychological disorder of executives.
- *Ritualism* The drama of creating and elaborating structures in order to delay decisions, subvert power and/or defend oneself. Sometimes it amounts to no more than an obsession with literacy—putting everything in writing. It may, however, develop into ceremonies, such as imported problem-solving techniques, which delay having to face the issues. Ritualism is an attempt to manifest rationality in a highly emotional, conflict-motivated, power-based environment.

Many of these sorts of organizational problems have been documented over the years. Machiavelli began the process and it has continued ever since. Chris Argyris suggested in the sixties that the pretence of being rational and of following the rituals of the system produced dishonesty, lack of trust and incompetence in interpersonal relationships. Nearly three decades later we can still see in organizations power struggles which are destructive rather than constructive. To some extent this will always be so, simply because power-motivated individuals are attracted to large private and public bureaucracies.

However, there has been progress. Today, many top groups know they must withdraw, as a unit, from the structure and 'let it all hang out', such that petty struggles do not interfere with the real purpose of the organization. Whether such withdrawals are called 'strategy meetings' or, at the other extreme, 'therapy', the message has begun to get through: if childlike political behaviour is induced by the structure, then the team should periodically withdraw from that structure to sort out its priorities and its relationships.

Smaller organizations, decentralized units, dual authority structures and massive redundancy programmes have all left their mark on the balance of power in work organizations. With unemployment running at the level it is, we may even avoid huge, almost unmanageable organizations in which playing power games is a full-time sport.

Limits to power

So far this discussion has treated power as if it could be acquired by anyone, without restrictions. There are in our society, however, increasing limits on the concentration of power. Certainly, concentrated wealth is in the hands of the few, and the separation of ownership and management has been excessively overstated; it is the upper and upper-middle classes who own and manage, if not together, then within a class. One change that *has* occurred in the power game, however, is the awakening of concentrated industrial or union power, which rested like a sleeping giant for nearly a century. Now that the giant has flexed its muscles, management is concerned about the balance of power and the dangers of its concentration in very large organizations. However, this concentration does produce the necessary accumulation of capital to finance more ventures.

What limits the concentration of power?

- *Organizational boundaries* Power is rarely transferable across these. Managing directors and union officers are powerful within their own organizations, but far less powerful in a court of law.
- *Humiliation of those in power* We search diligently for some fault in them, and, having found it, we broadcast our discovery, usually with negligible supporting data. This produces a strange contradiction—lack of respect for those with power, even though we still submissively respond to their commands.
- *Legal restrictions* Restrictive-trade-practices legislation is only one of the multitude of legal restrictions on concentrated power.
- *Limits of time and energy* Few people realize the time and effort involved in being a minister of state, a governor of a prison or a managing director of a business. For most of the people in these positions, work is a seven-days-a-week activity. Of course, most of them thrive on it, but younger people are beginning to wonder if the rewards for having power, and the influence one can have on others,

are worth the costs, especially in terms of family relationships. Are wealth and power more important than love?

- *The individual's search for harmony* Where power imbalances occur, the individual uses one or more of many checks to correct that imbalance. With an increasing awareness among subordinates or union members of their potential power, abuses of power may be prevented.
- *Power exists only if others recognize it* We have had some interesting examples over recent years of power being unceremoniously withdrawn from politicians. Similarly, in work organizations willingness to endure a dictatorial boss or union organizer is diminishing.

Managers and the use of power

Power is vital to organizations; it makes social systems productive. Yet it can be so destructive that managers need to understand rather than decry it. Here are some guidelines for managing power and influence.

BE HONEST WITH OTHERS

There is among animals a *norm of reciprocity*, by which, if A does a good turn to B, B will return that good turn. Among humans I have found a similar tendency: if A is honest with B, in most cases B is honest in return. We need to ask people what they want from organizations, highlight areas of conflict and negotiate compromise solutions. Many individuals are still frightened of honesty, lest it should indicate weakness. Managers can do a great deal to encourage and reward honesty and clarification of personal goals.

AVOID POWER STRUGGLES

Avoid unnecessary power struggles by clearly defining goals and authority rather than functions. Structure is essential for organizations, but invariably designers of structure become involved with controls rather than concentrating on ends.

EXPERIMENT WITH STRUCTURE

Do not be afraid to experiment with structure. People who want power *do* make better managers. Often the wrong people are given management tasks simply because that is the way to move up the hierarchy. Conversely, power struggles run rampant if the structure (particularly the hierarchy) is tampered with continually.

NEGOTIATION IS ESSENTIAL

Explain to people that organizations are compromises of many goals, expectations and attitudes, and that negotiation is essential. For example, taking on a union with the intention of humiliating its officers ('union bashing') does little to help the eventual compromise.

SHARE POWER

Understand that not only senior executives (with powerful egos) want power. Power to influence the behaviour of others is something we all enjoy, yet it is denied to the majority. Two sensible policies are:

- To involve people in decisions that affect them—share power with them.
- To give those who seek power the chance to influence other people's behaviour. The tendency of senior managers to 'hog' power (often on exceedingly trivial issues) does not improve working life for the majority. For example, union delegates are also motivated by the need for power, and management's delusion that one day the union movement will cease to want power is a contradiction of management's own motives. We need to rotate positions of power so that more people who seek it get experience of possessing it.

EXPERTS AND MANAGERS MAY BE DIFFERENT

Recognize that there are, as Anthony Jay has noted, yogis and commissars, philosophers and kings, experts and managers.

In the power struggle, power gained through expertise is different from power gained through authority over resources. Some who seek power through expertise (such as philosophers, yogis, architects, surgeons and academics) may not make very good kings, commissars or managers. Conversely, kings, commissars and managers may make poor philosophers, yogis and experts. Yet in organizations, we promote through a single hierarchy in which philosophers compete with commissars for greater power, recognition and reward. This unnecessary struggle could be avoided by allowing the organizational rewards to relate to performance rather than position in the hierarchy, so that effective philosophers or yogis can be 'promoted' (rewarded) without having to move into the hierarchy of commissars and kings. For example, the advertising industry (and parts of the media) promotes sanity in its midst by separating experts and managers into two hierarchies, thereby avoiding situations where they compete against each other. In contrast, institutions of higher education and most businesses require experts to become managers when they are promoted beyond a certain professional level. Not surprisingly, when those experts become managers, their lack of managerial experience is often blatantly obvious.

DIFFERENT GROUPS HAVE DIFFERENT EXPECTATIONS

Recognize that organizations include different groups with different expectations. Harmony between those groups is temporary—power struggles and conflicts are inevitable and desirable. Organizations are pluralistic, not unitary as so many people want to believe.

Summary

Social power involves a relationship between two or more people. It is the capacity to affect another person's behaviour without his or her consent. Unlike authority, power is not limited; it depends on the willingness of others to allow their behaviour to be influenced.

The power individuals have depends on how much they want power, on the power bases available to them, on the power of the function they perform and their political skills. In Chapter 1 we examined the background themes typically found in people motivated by power. By power bases is meant those personal, structural and interpersonal characteristics of a situation which encourages followers to let their behaviour be influenced. Personal power bases include physical characteristics (attractiveness, strength, etc.); structural power bases include authority and the function one performs; interpersonal power bases refer to the explicit and/or implicit connections one has with others—family, acquaintances, experiences, etc.

Analysts tend to concentrate on the power of individuals, yet functions, technologies and systems within organizations also acquire the capacity to influence the behaviour of others. The centrality of a function, technology or system, and whether or not it can be replaced, will determine its power. Finally, the relevance of that function, technology or system to crisis-resolution also affects its power.

Political skill is the capacity to use power bases and functions in order to affect behaviour. Political acumen is a complex interaction of data-collection and diagnosis, tactics and implementation. In upward communication the power game leads to filtering. At macro levels this sort of political activity may lead to games such as parricide, paranoia and ritualism.

Rather than look at power and politics in organizations in a negative sense we should learn as managers to understand power and to use it effectively. Fortunately, absolute power is rare; there are limits to what a manager can do even if they are often ill defined. Individuals surrounding the manager can use extremely effective informal devices to check the abuse of power.

Organizations and managers of them depend on power. Hence, managers should develop trust, not mistrust, as trust reduces the macro games. They should recognize that conflict is both inevitable and desirable, concede that organizations are political systems, involve people in the decisions that affect them and make sure that in selecting managers they choose individuals who want and understand power. Too often, people who are neither interested in social power nor competent in managing others are asked to be managers.

References

ON POWER IN ORGANIZATIONS

Mumford, E. and A. Pettigrew, *Implementing Strategic Decisions*, Longman, London, 1975.

Pfeffer, J., *Power in Organizations*, Pitman, Marshfield, Mass., 1981.

ON POLITICS IN ORGANIZATIONS

Berne, E., *Games People Play*, Grove Press, NY, 1964.

Jay, A., *Management and Machiavelli*, Hodder and Stoughton, London, 1967.

Kakabadse, A. and C. Parker (eds), *Power, Politics and Organizations*, John Wiley & Sons, Chichester, 1984.

Zaleznik, A. and M. Kets de Vries, *Power and the Corporate Mind*, Houghton Mifflin, Boston, Mass., 1975.

5. Individuals and groups

Introduction

Previous chapters looked at the goals of individuals joining an organization. I explained that, in addition to having personal goals, they arc confronted on arrival by written, verbal and non-verbal signals about the organization's goals and the roles they are expected to play. The relevance of those signals will depend on the power of their source.

One source of power which will affect the entry and subsequent role performance will be the groups that the person works with, drinks with, strikes with, laughs with, connives with, fights with, etc. In this chapter we examine the influence that groups may have on an individual's performance.

Many students of organizational behaviour examine organizations as a multitude of groups, some official and recognized, others unofficial and unrecognized. From my observations, very few people do in fact spend *all* their working day in a group. However, from time to time groups form and then disband, and in that process they influence the behaviour of individuals. And with the current shifts towards smaller organizations, semi-autonomous work groups, power equalization and team-building, a knowledge of group behaviour within organizations has become a major part of a manager's education.

This chapter will draw on research from all over the field—from group dynamics, laboratory groups and organization development groups. Only data which are useful in understanding organizational groups will be cited—a criterion which eliminates much of the available laboratory research. Inevitably, some of the findings are better supported by research than others. Some of my comments come from my experience rather than from formal research, merely because there are areas (e.g., groups and industrial relations) which sadly lack research findings.

What is a group?

A group is any number of people who are able to interact with one another, are psychologically aware of one another, and who perceive and are perceived as being members of a team.

The number of people is usually smaller than 10, and most frequently smaller than 6. To a great extent, tasks determine group size in work organizations. A group is more enduring and supportive than two people interacting socially but is looser or less structured than an organization.

It is useful to examine groups in terms of such characteristics as group norms, roles and structure. An analysis of these characteristics provides highly generalizable observations which will provide a framework by which managers can analyse groups in their own organizations.

Group norms

Work groups differ from free-forming groups outside employment in that they evolve over long periods of time. Hence, they can develop quite rigid codes of behaviour, or group norms, which explicitly or implicitly act to create conformity amongst group members.

The most consistent finding on groups is the emergence of norms concerning shared patterns of behaviour. Norms begin as our own expectations; these then merge or converge with others' expectations to produce 'rules' about required behaviour. Norms thus relate to behaviour, but there is also convergence of expectations, attitudes, beliefs and feelings among members of the group.

The process of norm development in work groups is complex but we do know something about it:

- Norms develop about the task, i.e., the work the people were hired to do.
- Norms develop about non-formal goals of the group, e.g., sport or other types of informal relaxation, outsiders, other groups.
- Norms develop about internal regulation within the group, about interactions, power, language and discipline.
- Norms develop about opinions, attitudes and beliefs—about unions, management, non-members of the group, religion and territory.
- Norms develop about physical appearance—work and non-work dress, use of safety clothing, lockers, etc.

The process of establishing a group norm inevitably means modifying the expectations of some members. However, members will subsequently deny that they changed their own expectations as much as they did. Explaining or rationalizing such changes in order to make them appear rational is a characteristic of us all—we can kid ourselves about anything if (as group members) we need to.

When we enter the group from outside, group norms are already shared by members, and our contribution to those norms is initially negligible. Unlike groups in laboratory studies, the work group is not created and then disbanded permanently, but survives over a long period of time. Consequently, norm development occurs over very long periods, and often very old behaviour patterns are preserved long after they have ceased to be relevant. We may notice these norms when we arrive, and question their relevance, but if group membership is vital to our role acquisition, we will accept the irrelevant norm merely to establish our intention to conform and thereby hasten our acceptance by the group. This sharing of expectations about acceptable behaviour ensures conformity.

The degree to which we will conform to group norms will depend on:

- Our desire for the group to agree to our membership (acceptance).
- Our wish to avoid causing displeasure and possibly inviting isolation or punishment (pleasure).
- Our belief that the norm reflects our own view (congruence).
- Our doubting our capacity to stand alone (isolation).
- Our belief in the group's goals (agreement).

Organizations rely on conformity to group norms. People's performances, including their dress and speech, can in this way be closely controlled. The disadvantage of this control may be the loss of individual initiative and creativity, but we have to weigh that cost against the cost of nonconformity.

Not all norms affecting us at work emerge within the framework described above. Societies also have norms relating to a whole range of acceptable behaviour patterns. These norms arise from the culture of our society and are carried into organizations as well; they relate to universally accepted behaviour patterns—salutations, manners, dress, etc.

Work-group norms are usually more subtle and less universal and relate to behaviour within a part of the organization. However, the purpose of these norms is the same as that of societal norms—to reduce variability in behaviour and to produce conformity, dependability and predictability. Writers on groups who decry conformity but refer to positive or constructive conformity as 'cooperation' are indulging in verbal games. Whether the organization is a church, a car manufacturing plant, a hospital or an army, its existence relies on conformity, predictability and dependability. Shared expectations or norms about what behaviour ought to occur within a group are important in providing that conformity.

Research on conformity has shown that individuals with higher levels of ability conform less to group norms than those with lower levels of ability; individuals with strong relationship goals will identify with group norms more readily than those individuals for whom multiple, close relationships are not important; highly authoritarian individuals conform more than less authoritarian individuals; individuals who find it hard to 'see the wood for the trees' conform more readily than those who find it easy; and individuals with strong structure goals conform more willingly.

Norms provide the base for the structure of any group. They are the structured perceptions or snapshots of interpersonal relationships as members feel they should be. Subsequently, these structured perceptions are elaborated into structured parts or roles which members play within the group. The parts I play in and out of a group are different. If I want group members' approval, I will accept the dictates of the group about my behaviour, even though I might not accept that influence in a one-to-one relationship. I may agree to decisions which are quite contrary to my own standards. I may modify my behaviour to conform to the expectations of the group, and I will do so in a much shorter time than I would in a one-to-one relationship. What has happened to me in the group is that my own perceptions of myself and others have been modified by group norms, which may only marginally be mine.

Too frequently, managers forget the significance of a group as a source of power and influence on individuals. For example, the manager may find it hard to understand how Harry (say), who proudly wears the company's 35 years' service badge, can walk out with his work group in an industrial dispute. The error the manager makes is to try to correlate Harry's performance as an individual employee with his performance in a group—they are two entirely different performances.

Group members' perceptions of expected behaviour are concerned with bits of behaviour ('Can I make jokes in this group?'), rather than with behaviour as a continuing phenomenon ('Do I have a sense of humour?'). On these items of behaviour a structure for behaviour is developed, with norms as the foundations. On top of norms, the group members develop expectations, implicitly or explicitly, about the role that each member is to play. Through interpersonal processes, the group members establish their own psychological contracts (or scripts) with one another.

Group roles

Many behaviours will be performed by members within the group. However, studies of groups have repeatedly found two behaviour patterns which recur:

- Task-centred behaviour
- Socio-emotional or maintenance behaviour

Task-centred behaviour is concentrated in the task-leader role. This is a structuring, organizing, goal-setting and often dominating role. It is generally occupied, at any one time, by one person, but it can sometimes be split between two people—a task manager and a task expert, where the manager does not have the expertise but acquires power through the capacity to get the task done.

The emergence of task-oriented behaviour in the group leads to a second pattern of behaviour—the socio-emotional or maintenance behaviour. This is concerned with avoiding group disintegration through support, seeking consensus, resolving conflicts, and so forth. Like the task-leader role, this may be split between several people. However, the degree to which the maintenance behaviour is absorbed by several people appears to depend on the strength of the task-oriented actor(s); that is, if the group is dominated by one person, then, to restore balance to the group, most other members, for reasons which are difficult to understand, may adopt a consensus-seeking, team-building posture. The less dominant the task-centred actor(s), the less widely spread, or even the less clear, the behaviour of the maintenance actor(s). However, I have seen cases where the reverse holds—the less clear the task-oriented action(s), the clearer the socio-emotional role.

In most work groups, both roles emerge clearly. They may be played by two people; they may be played by more than two people; they may also be played by one person who performs both task and maintenance behaviours. In their own way, and depending on the stresses within the group, the members will almost intuitively sort out a set of relationships which will provide both behaviour patterns and thereby establish a *balance of power*.

Balance occurs when the struggle for power between potential task-centred actors is no longer an issue—the task itself is the issue. Performers of the task and maintenance behaviours find a level of equilibrium, in which case the 'performing' stage of group evolution has been reached.

If the member providing the task-centred behaviour leaves the group, e.g., to go on holiday, then the group members will restructure and the behaviour patterns will be reallocated. The time taken for this balancing of behaviours and influence will depend on the group members, on their perceptions and expectations, on the task, and on the internal stresses. In a work group, a new structure will emerge within one or two weeks. When the original task-centred actor returns, he or she will probably try to get the role back and another week or two will have to pass before the group achieves equilibrium again.

Group structure

Unless there is a high staff turn-over, the structure of work groups in organizations is invariably clearer than that of groups in laboratory studies. Parts for the actors are more finely delineated and other social roles are allocated—the comedian, the best drinker, the union link, the arbitrator, the encourager, the pacifier, etc. Disturbing the group structure has, consequently, more repercussions than most managers realize. The entire fabric and balance of power within the group may be shattered if someone is removed. Certainly, in time, group equilibrium or balance will return, but there are many occasions when the cost of the group's disequilibrium is greater than the cost of not removing that member. Holidays are thus often more expensive than financial statements show.

In *formal* work groups, the structuring process is affected by the hierarchy of authority and the managerial behaviour of the boss. However, just because a person is called, for example, 'leading hand', it does not mean that the task-leader role automatically goes with the title. What it does mean is that, if the leading hand adopts a very warm socio-emotional managerial style, then an informal or unofficial task-leader role may emerge in the work group. Moreover, the balance between the task and maintenance behaviours is central to the output of the whole section. If the section works effectively, we may see the leading hand promoted and the unofficial task leader formally recognized and promoted to the position of leading hand. This strategy assumes that a reciprocal rebalancing of power in the work group will occur through the emergence of maintenance behaviours; in fact, a very different set of relationships may emerge, and not without some intra-group conflict.

How do people acquire task-centred power positions? By the same power strategies discussed in Chapter 4—visibility, muscle, expertise, etc. And unlike temporary social groups, the work group has long periods during which members can check the authenticity of the power bases. For this reason the work group will make fewer mistakes in choosing informal leaders than will a temporary social group.

The emergence of the maintenance-centred (socio-emotional-centred) behaviour pattern is more complex. It appears to depend very much on the emergence of and the strength or dominance of the task-centred member(s). Consequently the strength and number of maintenance actors will vary.

Similar patterns occur in formal relationships. If the chief executive is authoritarian and dominant in managerial style, then the subordinates will move the group into balance by adopting less dominant, more consensus-seeking, maintenance-oriented behaviour patterns. For this reason they are often seen to be weak; yet it is this very willingness of the subordinates to shift their own goals in order to preserve the harmony of the team that makes it possible for the group at the top of the hierarchy to perform at all. The major disadvantage of this form of dictatorial power balance occurs with the death of the chief, which is usually followed by a long, painful period of restructuring whereby the balance is restored. This sometimes means eliminating most of the original actors, and stretching down the hierarchy or even outside to discover a new chief who was not part of the original team.

Group control of members

Informal friendship groups occur most often laterally in the hierarchy—peers, rather than bosses and subordinates, are friends. It is true that in very loose, open hierarchies, people in different hierarchical levels do form friendship groups, but this is still the exception rather than the rule.

The influence of the friendship group is greatest at the base of the hierarchy, where the search for relationships between members is strongest (see Chapter 1). Members at the top of the hierarchy do have informal relationships, but there is little friendship involved; senior managers' informal relationships are based on convenience rather than affection.

Formal groups (e.g., committees, task forces, boards and teams) almost always cross hierarchical levels (boss/subordinate) and often cross functions (finance, marketing). Here relationships are prescribed formally rather than informally, thereby strengthening a manager's capacity to control the behaviour of others. However, in formal groups similar processes of control will emerge as in informal groups, even if there are other, formal techniques as well.

DEVIATION

When a deviation from expected behaviour occurs we can detect definite phases of the control process.

- *Phase 1: initial tolerance* The deviation is noted by members of the group. They may seek an explanation ('Why are you doing that, Harry?') or make excuses ('She hasn't learnt the ropes yet'). Whatever the technique (and it may be total silence), other members of the group have registered the deviation and the implied message is, 'OK, we note the deviation. Now let's be sensible and behave correctly.'
- *Phase 2: attempts to correct* The members have noted the continued deviation from group norms and deliberately attempt to correct the behaviour ('Don't keep doing that', 'Put your clothes back on again', 'You don't have to go home yet', 'Have another drink', etc.). At this stage, members of the group are still tolerant but are signalling, verbally and non-verbally, that the deviation must cease.
- *Phase 3: verbal aggression* Other group members are becoming more annoyed by the deviation. Verbal messages become more hostile, more aggressive, and the threat of rejection may be offered ('If you can't do it this way, don't do it at all'—fail and you must go elsewhere). Verbal aggression is more likely to occur than physical aggression in groups whose members come from middle- or upper-income families. Lower-income groups use more physical aggression.
- *Phase 4: physical aggression* As a control, this is limited by other group norms (e.g., no physical aggression). It is morc likely to be used on the factory floor than in the boardroom (where the process is often more subtle but no less damaging).
- *Phase 5: rejection* 'Get out.' As soon as the individual is rejected (physically or psychologically), the group members will rebalance power and roles, eliminate the deviant's contribution and, if neces-

sary, adjust its norms. Probably the most frequently used rejection is total silence.

In many cases, members of a group ignore all the niceties and reject the deviant immediately. Or the group may start at phase 2 and then go to phase 5. In other words, the phases are sequential but not necessarily consecutive.

The power of the peer group to control a deviant is known and used by both managers and union officials. What is particularly different about work groups, as opposed to others, is that the norms and standards are central to the rewards members receive. If a deviant decides to produce more than the group norm, then all members of the group are threatened. Similarly, if the employees feel industrial action is warranted, they will not tolerate nonconformists, because nonconformists weaken the group's position. Work groups are very much a case of 'one in, all in'.

How powerful is the group?

Power to control behaviour and prevent deviation comes from within a group and depends on many variables. Probably the most important clue to power in a group is the degree of *cohesion*. Cohesion is affected by:

- How often the group meets. If work groups meet every day (as many do), they will represent the second most cohesive group in most people's lives—second only to the family.
- The attractiveness of the group to its members, in terms of objectives, satisfactions and productivity. The attractiveness of a group consists of the interpersonal attractiveness of members of the group for one another. Members may be attracted because the group offers the opportunity for affiliation, recognition, security, etc., or because the goals are significant to the individuals, or because they have expectations that the group will satisfy their personal goals and motives. Group members reinforce the attractiveness of the group by incentives—offers of more love, money, security, fun or affiliation. Research on job satisfaction has consistently shown that the degree of group cohesion is important in predicting the performance of that group, and productivity and satisfaction can be increased, and absenteeism decreased, simply by reinforcing group attractiveness and cohesion.

- The emphasis given to the group's goals. Members of informal groups in work organizations usually have vague objectives, and are less cohesive and behave erratically. Members of formal groups are very goal-oriented and groups are deliberately structured to achieve those goals. The clearer the goals and the shorter the time in which they are to be achieved, then the greater the power of the group to affect members' behaviour.

Other influences on group power include the sort of people in the group, the layout of the office or plant, the boss, the opportunities for interaction and the noise levels.

CLUES TO GROUP POWER

Most laboratory studies of groups analyse the number of verbal signals, assuming that such signals indicate cohesion and structure. This method is not very useful for work groups, especially the informal ones in organizations, as there may be very strong bonds between a group of people even though the verbal signals are very few. Often an informal group will stay near a machine or other work station, even though a canteen is available; in an entire lunch-hour, those same members may produce only half a dozen verbal transactions between them, yet a multitude of non-verbal signals binds them together in a group. After work, at the pub, verbal interactions increase rapidly. It is this bond which the 'achievers' at the top of the hierarchy have great difficulty in understanding, mainly because of their obsession with constant verbal signals. Highly career-motivated people fill silences with socially acceptable noises.

Formal goals also affect cohesiveness and hence group power. Managers seek productivity, but claiming productivity as the only goal of a group may be a mistake. Each current process within a group is the cause of subsequent outcomes, including productivity. Holding only the final outcome to be significant denies the continuous shifts in members' goals, attitudes, satisfactions and interactions. Interactions are continuous and on-going, and it is the interactions *now* that are important for the cohesiveness of the group. It is the social reward of cohesiveness *in the group now* which affects productivity, not the pursuit of productivity itself; productivity is merely the outcome of having a rewarding time in the group. The means to productivity are group cohesiveness and group satisfaction. Conversely, if productivity goals are achieved, this reinforces commitment and the feeling of group cohesiveness.

Performing in groups

Some groups are very decisive, very productive, very creative and very satisfying for their members. Others arc the reverse. As we design more and more committees, task forces, teams and production groups within organizations, we should remember that there are advantages and disadvantages in using groups as decision-making devices.

In their enthusiasm to 'group' people in organizations, managers should ask: 'Is the group the best form?' 'Will the group give the best answer?' Groups have been found to make 'better' decisions in *some* situations. This may be because the group 'averages' its answers, which eliminates the extreme positions some individuals may adopt on their own. Other advantages of groups as decision-making devices are:

- The group has access to a greater variety of experiences and skills than does one person.
- By 'brainstorming', groups can generate far more and better ideas than can individuals working on their own.
- A division of work or effort is possible.
- Groups can generate more information on a problem.
- Members can detect each other's errors.
- Being in on the group decision can arouse the individual's motivation.

On the other side of the argument, groups have been found to make disastrous decisions. Some of the reasons are:

- The members are too alike (homogeneous).
- The group fails to detect the skills and experiences of different members.
- Too large a group (especially with over seven members) leads to restraints on participation.
- Attention is focused on the problem only for short time-spans.
- Tangential discussions are time-consuming.
- The problem is too technical, complex and known only to a few.
- Time is lost because of the social issues (processes) in the group. Individuals working on their own concentrate on the task (content), not the task plus social interactions (content and process).
- One member uses coercion, expertise or position to dominate the

others, and conformity pressures are strong enough to eliminate constructive criticism.
- Conjecture leads the group into irrelevancies and time is wasted.
- Members are so heterogeneous that they could not communicate.
- The group demonstrates what Janis refers to as 'group think'—'a deterioration of mental efficiency, reality testing and moral judgement that results from in-group pressures'.

GROUPTHINK

Janis's concept of 'groupthink' refers to a gross distortion of decision-making by a group. His research leads him to conclude that groupthink is characterized by:

- The group's belief in its own intelligence: 'That information doesn't fit our decision, so let's agree the information is wrong.'
- The group's belief in its own invulnerability: 'If we all work together we can't go wrong.'
- The group's belief in its own morality: 'We are doing this for the benefit of everyone.'
- The group's belief in its own rationalizations: 'We know the unions will agree.'
- The group's belief in its own uncritical thinking: 'Let's not go over it all again. We have thoroughly examined the alternatives.'
- The group's belief in its own unanimity in decisions: 'We have agreed, haven't we, to go ahead?'

To these I might add my own observations on working with groups in programmes of change:

- The group's belief that all persons have expressed views and that the decision is a consensus of divergent views.
- The group's concern for any answer, however bad, rather than no answer.
- The group's failure to identify expertise among its members.

Janis argues that some of humanity's most horrific decisions have been made by groups. To guard against bad group decisions, we can all watch for the characteristics given above. However, drawing them to the attention of the group is likely to lead to instant denial. A much more effective technique is to suggest to the group that it takes a break from the task. This breaks the cohesion and may give individuals time to reconsider.

WHICH TASKS SHOULD BE GIVEN TO A GROUP?

We can also avoid a lot of problems by carefully choosing which tasks are suitable for a group. Here are some of my own guidelines.

Too often groups are selected for tasks with no forethought about benefit to the members or to the organization. So when you are putting the group together, consider the people and the task:

- Choose a task capable of involving all members.
- Give the group a concrete, not an abstract, task.
- Clarify a definite beginning and end for the task, and make clear how the effectiveness of the decision will be assessed.
- Choose people who can 'get along'—balance is essential for performance.
- Give the group sufficient autonomy to carry out the task.
- Reward the group as a whole (rewarding individuals breaks the cohesion in the group).
- Structure the task for the group to include at least:
  - A precise statement of the objective(s).
  - A precise statement on the method of presenting the group decision(s).
  - Time and cost limits.
- Choose a task requiring a variety of skills and experience, not those of an expert (often an expert alone is much more competent than a group).
- Choose a task which needs close coordination, through which people will learn from each other.
- Restrict the size of the group to five or six (although the research data are conflicting on group size).
- Select problems where the administrative costs and time *or* the social benefits support a group solution—that is, justify the choice of a group.
- The more able the members, the better the decision.
- The more aware the members are of group processes, the better the decision.
- Cooperative groups are better problem-solvers than competitive ones.

- Creative groups, where members choose one another, make better decisions.
- Better decisions result where the way the leadership role is filled leads to coordination, thus overcoming the slowness, tangential discussion, loss of focus and other inefficiencies of groups.

DEVELOPMENTAL STAGES

A group's problem-solving capacity is directly related to the interaction within the group. Some writers see free-forming groups moving through identifiable stages. First, the group forms (people meet); second, it storms (as people struggle for power); third, it norms (as behaviour codes emerge explicitly or implicitly); and finally it performs (a function). Hence, *forming*, *storming*, *norming*, *performing*—a useful if simplistic description.

Forming

The various relationships between members have to be worked out. Members are disoriented, not able to solve problems realistically. Questions of roles and power have not been resolved—balance has not been achieved.

The interactive process of the group is brought to bear on the problem. This is the research, data-analysis phase. Roles emerge; task and maintenance role-performances are clearer. Claims for power (based on expertise, experience, etc.) are signalled by members. There is no common definition of the nature of the task. Uncertainty is high, and alternative task definitions are bandied about.

Storming

Individuals formulate their positions. Unfavourable comments are frequent. Polarization of attitudes occurs, as do reactions to the emergent roles and power distribution. Further counter-claims for power are made. Individuals challenge their own and others' membership.

Norming

There is a reduction in the amount of conflict, and fewer unfavourable comments occur. Ambiguous comments permit a shift in ground. Task and maintenance roles are implicitly allocated to individuals, that is, power is distributed and balanced. Ground rules are agreed. The task is defined in a way acceptable to the group.

Performing

This stage is marked by the sharing of honest communications and the development of a degree of trust amongst the members. It is the best phase for problem-solving, when personal animosities (or organizational games) are minimal. Balance has occurred within the group. Role allocations are accepted by role performers, and the group is enabled to tackle the task.

Argument is subsequently minimal as members become aware of the inevitability of the decision they are to make. Balance has been superseded by problem-solving as the focus of attention. Decisions are made. An effective work group is in operation.

These phases of group problem-solving should not be seen as a model to follow but as an analysis of what tends to happen. The pattern may vary widely in specific groups. For example, trust may not occur between the norming and performing phases at all. If trust does occur, however, that is when it is *most likely* to do so. Similarly, conflict may not occur overtly, and after the deliberation phase (forming) the trust phase (norming) may lead straight to a solution (reinforcement of group membership).

Conflict

CONFLICT WITHIN GROUPS

Just as groups depend on the allocation of roles (and power), so they depend also on the consequences of power—conflict/cooperation, trust/mistrust, etc. Conflict is inevitable. It is also highly desirable and constructive in any social system, whether it be an organization, a group, a family or a friendship. Constructive conflict energizes relationships; they might wither and die if we were ever able to eliminate conflict.

This is not to say that *all* conflict is constructive. Destructive conflict is injurious to social systems, and we should aim to eliminate the negative forms of conflict which pervade many work organizations.

*Intra*personal conflict occurs in an individual where there are equally attractive options but only one may be chosen. *Inter*personal conflict occurs between two or more people when attitudes, motives, values, expectations or activities are incompatible and *if those people perceive themselves to be in disagreement*.

Constructive conflict can be very beneficial to a group. For example, conflict may:

- Introduce different solutions to the problem.
- Clearly define the power relationships within the group.
- Encourage creativity and brainstorming activity.
- Focus on individual contributions rather than group decisions.
- Bring emotive, non-rational arguments into the open.
- Provide for catharsis—release of interdepartmental or interpersonal conflicts of long standing.

Conversely, if conflict is destructive, it may:

- Prevent members from 'seeing' the task at all.
- Dislocate the entire group and produce polarizations.
- Subvert the objectives in favour of sub-goals.
- Lead people to use defensive and blocking behaviour in their group.
- Result in the disintegration of the entire group.
- Stimulate win–lose conflicts, where reason is secondary to emotion.

It is difficult in analysing organizations to know when intra-group or inter-group conflict is destructive. Sometimes, what seem to be very heated and destructive conflicts have very positive outcomes; for example, while a strike would normally be seen by managers and union members as destructive conflict, it can provide a focus for attention and an opportunity for catharsis. Or at home, when there is an unresolved issue distorting a relationship, a good row can clear the air, releasing tension and allowing the couple to deal with their differences.

The release of tension in organizations is probably one of the most neglected areas of research. All societies have social mechanisms for the release of tension, such as religious meetings, festivals and rituals. Work organizations are only now beginning to appreciate the need for tension release, for creating regular opportunities to 'let it all out' at seminars, dinners, training courses, rituals, ceremonies, etc.

Most conflict occurs in groups because of differences among members as regards goals, attitudes and feelings. The greater the involvement with those goals, attitudes and feelings, the more difficult it is to change people's perceptions and to resolve the conflict. Personal goals and attitudes about power are usually at the root of conflict, but they do not necessarily cause conflict. Other factors, such as the task, the location of the meeting, the seating plan, the leadership roles and status hierarchies, are all influential in triggering or blocking the release of differences.

Loss of equilibrium within a group may occur because of a variety of behaviours which lead to communication blockages. Some of these behaviours are more often destructive than constructive; how many do you use?

- *Restricting information* A member of the group implies he or she knows the answer to a group problem, but is not telling.
- *Lying* Deliberate distortion of the facts to preserve a position in the group.
- *Pairing* Breaking into sub-groups rather than solving the conflict as a group coalition.
- *Put-downs (of others or of self)* The put-down of others, through verbal or physical aggression, may maintain the structure of the group. Self-put-downs may get sympathy and diffuse the opposition—the 'poor me' game.
- *Fight* Win–lose conflicts which are difficult to resolve.
- *Flight* Running away, sometimes actually leaving the group. More frequently, 'sulk' behaviour, withdrawal (leaving the room, pretending to sleep, sitting back from the table, saying 'I'm not really interested in the question').
- *Making noise* Speaking to be heard rather than to contribute; often very fuzzy, undisciplined. Common in training groups.
- *Expertise* Stopping contrary views by 'dropping' data about your own expertise ('When I was in Paris, the Minister was saying to me . . .'). Using legal or scientific jargon to dazzle.
- *Suppressing emotions* Rather than letting the emotional blockages out, the person demands logic, rationality ('Let's not get emotional' or 'Please let's act like adults'). This is unfortunate, as much of the blockage is emotional and *should* be expressed.
- *Changing the topic* Changing the focus from one topic to another, or from one person to another.

There are many other variations on these tactics. People learn to use the tactics which work for them. Hence, the person who uses the sulk response will continue to use it because it has been successful in the past.

All of us who work regularly in groups should try to identify our own defensive and constructive behaviour. I have found that most people have no idea how they behave in a group, and are upset when they watch their behaviour in groups on video replays. And the closer to the top of the hierarchy, the more surprised they are—high achievers learn to achieve on their own and rarely work in groups.

However, we should not get conflict and defensive behaviour out of perspective. If we need to beware of having too much conflict in a group, we need also beware of the reverse. Too much cooperation and agreement can produce a 'love-in' where completing the task becomes secondary to enjoying interpersonal processes. And members of work organizations do need to produce something or complete a task. The difficult questions for a manager are: How much conflict and how much cooperation? How much love, how much discord? How much process and how much content?

INTER-GROUP CONFLICT

One of the most frequent forms of conflict in organizations is inter-group conflict: sales versus production; personnel versus finance. Much of the inter-group conflict occurs simply because we separate people into functions such as sales, production and personnel. Another cause is the fact that very different people, with very different attitudes, goals and perceptions, are attracted to different functional groups.

The worst form of inter-group conflict is what is called a 'win–lose' conflict, in which the competing groups all seek to win and in which there can in fact only be one winner. Where this occurs, destructive conflict is usually the outcome. What happens in this situation has been well documented:

- Each group becomes more cohesive, as members close ranks.
- Each group alters the leadership roles to strengthen the task-oriented role at the expense of the maintenance role.
- Each group becomes more structured, and demands more loyalty and assurance of solidarity.
- Emotion, rather than reason dictates group decisions.

In looking at its competitor, each group:

- Distorts perceptions of the 'enemy'.
- Distorts perceptions of its own members, minimizing weaknesses within itself and concentrating on strengths.
- Increases its hostility towards and decreases interaction with the enemy.

If one group does win the competition, that group remains cohesive, releasing tension through playful activities, and remains highly co-operative (although it may also become complacent). The losing group tends to splinter; conflicts come to the surface; blame is allocated. Of winner and loser, the loser group is likely to learn more from the experience, and to evaluate its performance for future activity.

RESOLUTION OF CONFLICT

As much conflict is constructive, the goal of a manager is to use it and to allow it to be exorcised. When conflict is dealt with openly, members are stimulated to seek solutions, to resolve differences, to be more searching and creative. Unfortunately, most conflict in organizations is not confronted openly, but is ignored. We can divide responses in handling conflict into the following categories.

Denial/withdrawal

A manager attempts to get rid of the conflict by denying its existence: 'I don't think we have any problems.' If the issue is not critical, then this may be the best way of dealing with the conflict. However, as the causes of the conflict are not identified, denial may result in the conflict growing to a level where it becomes unmanageable. Where neither party can see a solution, both may collude in the pretence that the issue does not exist.

Suppression

The manager smoothes over the conflict: 'We don't really have any major differences, do we?' It is inevitable that organizations do have conflict—some people just dislike one another—and to preserve relationships between managers suppression may often be the only feasible strategy to adopt. But some cracks cannot be papered over.

Dominance

Power and influence may be used to settle the conflict. In a hierarchical structure, the use of dominance or power to resolve differences is inevitable; there will always be a 'last word', if only for the resolution of conflict. The advantage of dominance is that the answer can be found quickly. The disadvantage is that the method divides the members into winners and losers, with all the disadvantages of win–lose conflicts.

Compromise

Negotiation may take place between group members or groups. Organizations depend on compromise; the very act of joining an organization is an act of compromise between what the individual wants and what 'the system' requires. Yet compromise often gets clouded in emotive adjectives, as though it is always a 'good' strategy. Whether we call it bargaining, negotiating or compromising, this style of conflict resolution has disadvantages. For example, individuals tend to inflate their requests to allow for the compromise. Second, compromise is seen by members as a weakening and, hence, commitment to the decisions is less. Nevertheless, in a pluralistic organization compromises are inevitable.

Integration or collaboration
Emphasis is put on the task rather than on defending positions. Everyone expects to modify his or her views. Group effort is seen as superior to individual effort. Differences are acknowledged and respected. In my experience, groups in a hierarchy rarely achieve integration unless they have previously worked consciously to improve their effectiveness as groups.

Improving group effectiveness

As all of us spend time in groups, we can monitor group processes. Two important questions can be asked:

- What contribution do I and other members make to the task (i.e., content)?
- What contribution do I and other members make to group interaction (i.e., process)?

By conducting self-critiques within groups (work teams, boards of directors, etc.), we can eliminate much of the disruptive behaviour in ourselves and others. Unfortunately, too few groups will attempt that sort of critique without the aid of a consultant.

Team-building techniques are now commercially available for conducting group critiques. All groups of individuals who work intermittently together should, from time to time, conduct a group analysis. However, this is rare. More frequently, there is a total preoccupation with task completion—senior executives dominate their groups so that their subordinates make only minimal contributions. In contrast, the preoccupation of eager training officers with the process within their training groups may be just as one-sided, such that the groups degenerate into mini-psychotherapy clinics where solving interpersonal problems becomes more important than the organization task. Somewhere between these extremes is where groups operate best. Just as most parents evaluate their influence on their children, just as most couples spend time analysing their relationship, so, too, do we need to assess regularly what is happening in work groups in organizations. Only in this way can we get the best from work groups, in terms of task completion, problem-solving and decision-making, and avoid the worst outcomes—failure to complete tasks, time-wasting rituals, terrifyingly bad problem-solving and horrendous decisions.

Summary

Very few people spend all their working day in a group. Yet all of us do spend some time interacting with a variety of formal and informal groups. For this reason, insight into group behaviour may be the most important contribution the behavioural sciences have to offer a manager.

Like organizations, groups develop structures based on expected behaviour or norms. The processes involved in gaining commitment to those norms will lead to the emergence of two roles within the group. First, there will always be a task-oriented role, whose player(s) will structure other members, point to goal achievement and control deviation. Second, in response to this first role, a second role, most frequently called a socio-emotional or maintenance role, will emerge. The player(s) of this second role will provide the caring, consensus-seeking, conflict-resolving function essential to group continuity. Balance occurs in a group when both roles have emerged and when the storming or conflict behaviour surrounding their emergence has abated. The group will then be ready to perform its task.

Groups are amazingly powerful influences on behaviour. The control of group members occurs through an informal process which begins with noting that a deviation has occurred, or is about to occur, and ends with rejection. In formal groups the processes can be reinforced by sanctions authorized by the positional power of the players, but the subtleties of the power of the group to affect any member's behaviour are very similar whether or not there are formal sanctions.

A group's power to control its members will depend on many factors. Among these are the sort of people involved, the cohesion of the group, its centrality to the lives of members, the strength of reinforcements, the impact of outsiders, the leadership balance within the group, etc.

Groups can be highly creative problem-solving entities. However they can also be the worst vehicle for making decisions. Effective groups generate trust among members, draw on the different experiences of members, remain loosely structured, have clear objectives and deadlines and have the resources necessary to address their problems and derive solutions to them.

Despite the existence of these basic principles, groups have made some of the worst decisions in our history. This is partly because their behaviour is often erratic, and a lack of trust among members can produce a whole range of childlike behaviours. Janis has studied group decision-making and has identified a phenomenon he calls 'groupthink'. Groupthink is a process which leads to gross distortions of the facts, irrationalities and illusions among the members as they attempt to justify ill-examined decisions. It is true that Janis was concerned most with decisions of governments, but the same processes occur daily in our work organizations as boards, committees and informal groups make extraordinary decisions.

So we need to ask: When should a manager ask a group to make a decision? How will the manager know when the group's processes are such that it is beyond the formative stages and is capable of performing the task given it? Forming, storming, norming and performing are very useful descriptive words for managers to remember.

Signs of relapse or of inter-group or intra-group conflict are not difficult to detect. Observing the behaviour of group members will provide many clues that the level of conflict may be too high and that the group may be incapable of resolving an important issue. First, managers need to assess whether the conflict is constructive or destructive. Conflict is essential to any social system; it energizes, refreshes, brings issues to a climax. However, it is destructive conflict within and between groups that has attracted most attention. Guidelines are given in order to help identify the different forms of conflict, both within and between groups.

Where destructive conflict does occur, managers must decide what tactics they will use to exorcise it. The chapter ends with an analysis of different ways in which conflicts can be resolved. My major conclusion is that confronting destructive conflict—bringing it into the open rather than suppressing it—has more chance than any other method of leading to resolution.

In an age of task forces, project teams, matrix structures, semi-autonomous work groups and decentralized work units, it is imperative that we learn how to harvest the undeniable benefits of positive group activity and minimize the time-wasting, destructive burdens of negative group behaviour.

References

ON GROUPS IN GENERAL

Schein, E., *Organizational Psychology*, 3rd edn, Prentice-Hall, Englewood Cliffs, NJ, 1980, pages 146–53.

Shaw, M. E., *Group Dynamics*, 3rd edn, McGraw-Hill, NY, 1981.

ON ROLES IN GROUPS

Bales, R. F., *Interaction Process Analysis: A Method for the Study of Small Groups*, Addison-Wesley, Reading, Mass., 1950.

Belbin, M., *Management Teams*, Heinemann, London, 1981.

Dunphy, D., *The Primary Group*, Appleton Century Crofts, London, 1972.

Eddy, W. B., *The Manager and the Working Group*, Praeger, NY, 1985.

Hare, A. P., *Creativity in Small Groups*, Sage, Beverly Hills, Calif., 1982.

Janis, I. L., *Groupthink*, 2nd edn, Houghton-Mifflin, Boston, 1982.

6. Organizations as cultures

Introduction

In this chapter I first look at the building of an organization, concentrating on the interactions of individuals. Next I turn to the shared values and beliefs which collectively constitute a culture for that organization. Thereafter, in Chapter 7, I develop a diagnostic model from the shared values and beliefs of members as a way of examining an organization.

The evolution of an organization

THE FIRST TWO PEOPLE

In previous chapters we have looked at individuals and groups. Those same individuals, whether on their own or in a group, are the essential ingredients of an organization. An organization is an identifiable social entity whose members pursue multiple objectives through their coordinated activities and relationships. Hence, all organizations have people, objectives and coordination.

Let me build an organization, beginning with a couple who have decided to live together. At this stage the objectives of the couple are probably implicit rather than explicit and the coordination of the activities of the two—call them Myrtle and Fred—is vague. However, if we assume that they have not lived together before, Fred will develop expectations about Myrtle's behaviour, and Myrtle will develop expectations about Fred's behaviour. Little by little they prescribe roles or positions for themselves.

Without very much debate they fall into a pattern and it is this pattern of shared expectations that will one day constitute the structure of their relationship, in the same way as we saw structure emerge in groups. For example, Fred usually bathes first; Myrtle usually wakes first and gets up first. Fred makes the coffee and Myrtle makes the bed. Fred gets the newspaper and the milk, and Myrtle cooks the toast. After a few weeks these patterns become routine, and after a year an intentional break in the routine may cause the couple some distress. If you were an observer of the couple you could write down descriptions of their roles and produce a manual describing the structure of their relationship.

The same pattern of behaviour occurs in a two-person business.

Initially there may be a vague implicit arrangement that A is the boss and B is the subordinate, but there may be very little more than that. However, after a few weeks of working together both A and B will have implicitly or explicitly prescribed each other's jobs. And if you asked, separately, each of these two people what he or she did and what the partner did, there would be a high level of agreement: A talks to the customers; B orders the supplies. (The analogy with a couple is not misguided; most new businesses are started by married couples.)

What A and B will be doing is drawing some resources from the market-place (finance, materials, equipment, information, energy, ideas) and transforming those resources in some way. And this is true of all organizations; their members transform resources. Sometimes the transformation is a radical one (e.g., turning iron ore into steel) and sometimes it is minor (e.g., buying a garment and merely adding a price label to it). Sometimes the transformation occurs on site (e.g., manufacturing); in other cases A or B has to go to another location to transform a resource (e.g., service industries).

If your two-person business is successful, then more people will be recruited. Each additional person requires the developing organization to adjust; roles already prescribed may be divided and new relationships will emerge. People who do not fit into the developing structure will probably leave without much ceremony (a freedom usually not available in families).

Already, as in families and groups, the two essential behaviours will have emerged. A *task* role and a *maintenance* role, each involving two or more people, will be identifiable. And, as we have found in groups, the small team will continually strive for balance or equilibrium between those roles. In a small business this search for balance may lead to extremely bitter disputes in the actors' external families, who do not recognize that if A is to work with B then he or she may have to shift his or her preferred behaviour patterns and be more accommodating, more relationship-oriented or more maintenance-oriented. Unfortunately, as this realistic shift occurs, A's spouse may see this as weakness, as dominance of A by B; the spouse's 'rational' assessment ignores the apparent irrationality of equilibrium in relationships.

TWO TO TEN PEOPLE

As we add more people to A and B's firm, the parts (or positions) individuals will play become more clearly defined and the constraints on behaviour will increase as more explicitly defined expectations emerge. Rationality (inbred by family, school and society) dominates choices. When C arrives she is told her job is to package the product. D is told that his job is to deliver the package to the customer. This reflects two characteristics of organizations:

- *Functional differentiation* New functions are always emerging as people strive to make the system better, more rational, more efficient, more interesting.
- *Specialization* The economies of scale tell us, at least at this stage, that specialization may be more efficient. Having Bill package all day may be more efficient than having him package for an hour, do the accounts for another hour and sell the products for another hour.

By the time the A & B Company has grown to six people the relationships of A and B will have changed dramatically, just as the relationships within a family change when another family comes to stay—ordering the kitchen arrangements alone requires more definition and control. Amongst six people, separate friendship bonds will develop. It is true that six people can relate to each other successfully, but this is rare. It is more likely that, say, C and E will be closer in their relationships than, say, C and A or C and B. Thus we begin to see two structures developing: one based on expectations about the work that has to be done (the formal or official structure); and a second structure of informal friendship patterns which may have little or no relationship to the official structure.

This dual set of values (formal and informal) becomes even more marked by the time we get to 10 people. It is almost impossible for 10 people to communicate continuously with each other. Even when 10 people are seated round a dining-table at home, the group will divide into sub-groups. Interests, backgrounds, goals, friendships, tasks and the physical layout of the work begin to segment people from each other. And as the segmentation increases, so the informal links become more important. At the same time, more effort is put into defining and redefining the 'official system'. In most cases, informal solutions based on free-wheeling, open discussions are tried out. Subsequently the solution is officially adopted as 'the way to do things around here'. Thus, the informal structure feeds the formal, and vice versa.

FIFTEEN PEOPLE

When the A & B Company has grown to 15 people, it will have more clearly specified roles, rules and controls. The founder boss will have withdrawn from the group and located him- or herself in another room, thereby beginning the 'withdrawal of the chief' process. This is the public manifestation of an emerging general-management function. The reality of the hierarchy is demonstrated; there is a 'him/her' and 'us' dimension, despite all the assurances that we are a team. As the chief surrounds him- or herself with physical and psychological barriers, then the strengthening of the values inherent in the formal structure is inevitable, for the chief must develop formal data systems which bridge the barriers. It is true that chiefs may regret or even fight the emergence of these barriers, but the pressure to withdraw comes from all sides: they cannot see 15 people individually on demand, so secretaries start to schedule their diaries, and to control whether F is favoured or G. The barriers are inevitable.

THIRTY PEOPLE

By the time the organization reaches 30 members, it will have a host of formal structural devices, and the majority of members will have had little to say in their design or implementation; the devices have been emerging from the outset, when most members were not there. Hence the formal structure is already 'the system', the rules. And it is discussed informally with all the fun-making and disrespect that the informal relationships allow. Separate tasks continue to emerge, and similar or like tasks are grouped into functions—accounting, sales, distribution, purchasing. One of these functions will lead; that is, it will have more power, more clout, than any other. This will be true of any organization; one function, be it service, personnel, marketing or finance, is always perceived to be more powerful than any other. Further, there is always a function 'on the make', struggling for recognition and status, the aim being to reach the top of the hierarchy. Most functions fail to make it, but recent high-achieving functions in many organizations are corporate planning, public relations and information systems.

SIXTY TO A THOUSAND PEOPLE

When our small manufacturing business reaches 60 people, it will have formally prescribed production, accounting, sales and purchasing functions. The order of emergence of these groupings of tasks varies, depending on the market pressures and the skills of the founders.

Entrepreneurial founders with selling skills may hold on to that function long after it should have been released to sales personnel. Similarly, as entrepreneurs are risk-takers, they tend to delay developing the functions which inhibit risk (accounting personnel).

The last function to emerge at the top is usually the personnel function. Even though the function has identifiable tasks within an organization from the first day a person is appointed to the founding team (selection, training and rewarding are all tasks that have to be performed) normally it remains with the accountant until a crisis of some sort points to the necessity of having personnel expertise readily available in a senior position. By the time there are 100 people, the demands of employment law guarantee that there will be a well-developed personnel function. However it will probably still be located within the accounting or administration function. It is not until several hundred employees are on the books that a formal appointment of a personnel manager is made, and the personnel function takes its place in the top group of the hierarchy.

A THOUSAND PEOPLE

By the time the A & B Company has reached 1000 people, nearly every structural device ever invented will have been formally introduced. Initially each new idea or concept begins through informal chat, but thereafter the new scheduling system, the new management accounting system or the new appraisal system is given formal blessing by the top team and becomes part of the 'official' or rational structure. And with each new piece of formal control, the informal relationships become stronger and stronger, for it is through the luxurious informal network of relationships that so much of the necessary work actually occurs. Informal relationships oil a rather clumsy rational structure, and if we listen carefully in the canteen we may hear the old hands lament: 'It's not as good here now as it was in the old days.'

And that is true. In the search for rationality and structure the productivity of the organization has been increased dramatically, but at a cost. Something has been lost. The self-regulating small group that began this saga has been superseded by a set of values about how people should behave, which in itself may limit deviation, fun and innovation. Size (number of people) has become a major factor in the design of this organization, and managers whose skill is creating order (rationality) are now in charge.

Culture

By now the A and B Company, like any other organization, has an identifiable culture of its own, in the same way that a society or a nation has an identifiable culture. A culture is the collective of shared values, ideologies and beliefs of members. It includes the transmitting medium (language, stories, symbols, myths, legends) and the manifestations of those values (rituals and ceremonies). This culture evolves from the trial-and-error search of members for ways of coping with common problems and of explaining to themselves what is going on. Subsequently these values and beliefs are transmitted through several media to successive generations. However, culture is not a variable to be manipulated at will by managers. Managers may attempt to strengthen it or change it, but the decision as to whether they will succeed is not in their hands; it is in the minds of the other members.

The culture of an organization is the glue binding together the disparate parts. It is largely covert, invisible. It is the interpretative part of behaviour—explaining, giving direction, sustaining energy, commitment and cohesion. It is based on impressions about what matters. Thus this is a topic many 'rational' managers avoid, for it is not definable or classifiable. Indeed, the obsession this century with rationality neglected culture. This obsession is based on the assumption that structure and bureaucratization must be strengthened if the larger organizations are to survive. One alternative, however, is a coherent culture, based, most often, on the *values* and *beliefs* of the founding fathers.

- *Values* Deep-seated concerns for standards as they should be. Hence, I have values about efficiency, leadership, structures, etc. We reveal our values in our opinions, attitudes and preferences. Values are general; opinions and attitudes are specific.
- *Beliefs* Propositions individuals hold about work/organizations/society. They explain a person's place in the social fabric and partly explain his or her behaviour in that context. Ideologies combine sets of beliefs together to explain cause and effect in work organizations. Hence beliefs about efficiency, structure, leadership, etc., are linked into ideologies (sometimes called philosophies) about how organizations should be managed.

Organization cultures are affected greatly by the culture of a society. Long before people join an organization, parents and schools indoctrinate them with a set of values, some of which may be peculiar to that society. For example, in studies of North American managers 'efficiency', 'high productivity', 'leadership' and 'individuality' are popular. In studies of Japanese managers, 'efficiency', 'high productivity' and 'leadership' are also popular, but individuality is not; 'consensus', on the other hand, is. Many writers (e.g., Hofstede) have demonstrated the importance of understanding a society's culture before transferring one set of managerial techniques from one national culture to another. Yet we can still observe the desperate pursuit by managers of the latest fad in management techniques (e.g., quality circles, organization development, work groups), regardless of the culture in which it developed.

VALUES AND BELIEFS IN ORGANIZATIONS

One way of looking at an organization is to examine shared values and beliefs. If we study that organization we will find that those values and beliefs fall into clusters—values about individuals (the work ethic), the task, rationality, leadership, cooperation and non-members or outsiders.

The individual

In Chapters 1 and 2 we analysed in some detail the values and goals of individuals. The mix of ability, goals and energy levels provides a framework for looking at organizations at the level of individuals. There is no need to reiterate all the details in those chapters here. Of necessity, managers of organizations do develop standardized models or pictures of the people who work for them, and personnel systems are based on common or shared values about work. Inevitably, there are many occasions when the common view is totally irrelevant to the particular problem an individual faces, yet it would be impossible to conduct organizations on the basis of differences between people. 'Sameness' is basic to the design of systems, and in that process individual differences are often discounted.

Common or shared values about work relate to survival, structure, relationships, recognition, power, autonomy, creativity and growth. These shared or recurring values have already been discussed in Chapter 1; it is only important here to remind ourselves of them. Whatever organization we analyse there will be values about the work people do, their goals, their likes and dislikes, what excites them and what does not, what is a fair day's output, what is not, what is central, what is not, what is ethical, what is not. The 'work ethic', despite its critics, remains a dominant cluster of values.

The task

Initially some of A and B's values and beliefs will be absorbed by others. These values explain the purposes of the organization. They also explain what I do, what the person next to me does, what the sales function does, etc. Even if A and B have not stated the objectives formally, members will invent meanings to give purpose to their work. Common beliefs about what the organization is doing become part of the culture. In small organizations the process of sharing values about task is aided by the physical fact that we can all see what everyone else does to achieve the primary task.

In large organizations the shared values and beliefs about task may bear little resemblance to the stated objectives of the chief executive, often for the simple reason that the chief executive has not bothered to communicate his or her view of the objectives to others. This does not mean that the employees will have no objectives. People cannot operate in a vacuum. They rationalize what they do by inventing, creating or stealing objectives.

Rationality

Organizations are permeated by values and beliefs about efficiency and rationality. Order, structure, defined strategy, management by objectives, information systems, models, numbers, all reflect the view that the world would be better if we could conduct our business and government organizations scientifically—i.e., rationally. We could thereby eliminate the inconveniences of emotion, feelings and irrationality. The twentieth century has seen management theoreticians continuously attempting to provide the manager with the latest scientific tool to reduce the irrational to the rational—to control it, measure it and, probably, kill it. Yet behaviour in organizations is also about innovation, creativity, gut feel, emotions, feelings, hunches, love, hate, jealousy, political struggles and ambition, and none of these fits well into a rational model.

Undeniably, rationality has its place. Keeping strategy in the head of one person, the chief executive, does restrict opportunities for collective action. Clarifying objectives and strategies may allow the rest of the workforce to know where they are meant to be headed. Similarly, a defined hierarchy, an adequate information system, well-prescribed personnel systems and effective accounting and control system, all allow the primary task of the organization to be realized on time, within budget, employing the best talent available. For this reason these values are artificially collected together, by theoreticians and managers alike, as the formal structure of the organization, even though the values do not necessarily collect together neatly in the heads of employees.

But just as production and accounting systems represent the outcomes of a set of values based on concepts of rationality, so other functions represent the irrational, the creative, the spontaneous in people. Hence marketing, entrepreneurship, advertising, design and research are not always aided by rational action imposed from above in the name of structure and order. Autonomy, creativity, growth and innovation thrive in less structured environments, and it is these capacities that we may lose in our obsession with order.

Values about rationality are reinforced by technical systems specifically installed to reduce the perceived dangers of irrationality by replacing humans with machines. Into the action system which links inputs to outputs we place typewriters, word processors, computers, factory equipment, plant, buildings, etc. And with each additional piece of equipment, valucs favouring rationality in the culture of the organization are strengthened. However, the machine or computer or whatever has itself incorporated outsiders' or non-members' values and beliefs about work. Whole sets of beliefs and values are incorporated, by external designers, programmers and analysts, into the machines we import into the organization: for example, the word processor contributes to the action system but subliminally it injects values into the culture itself; typewritten material is no longer good enough—it must be word processed. Early management theorists proposed that the technical system determined the values incorporated in the formal structure of the organization. Subsequent work has shown that this relationship is not so simple—the market, the people and the industry also affect the impact that the technical system can have on the formal structure.

Leadership

We will discuss this topic in more detail in Chapter 10. It is sufficient here to say that people have beliefs about their leaders, and their leaders' strengths and weaknesses. Further, they will have values and beliefs about what constitutes good leadership.

All of us create gods and heroes from idealized models, often combining male and female characteristics together in one magnificent god. Through this process, in a democracy, we all concede that some individuals will have more power than we have. A further belief of our society is that we are born equal; hence 'leader' is itself a word that we attach only sparingly to those who consistently have more capacity to influence our behaviour.

In a commercial organization, beliefs about the strengths and weaknesses of the leader often reflect the values and beliefs traceable to the organization's founder. Over time, the founder becomes idealized as an example for the rest. Through this important process, the founder's values contribute to the commitment, energy, integration and cooperation found in the pursuit of an organization's ends. And it is these intangibles, these covert values and beliefs, often hidden in stories of the past, that provide the real clues to differences in the degree of integration and commitment in work organizations. Whether the stories are true or not is largely irrelevant—that is not their purpose; their purpose is cohesion. For example, one value of the Watson family (founders of IBM), that people should not drink alcohol while at work, is itself not profound, but covertly that one belief, as a consistent element in an ideology, reinforces other beliefs like dedication, commitment, abstinence, cooperation, efficiency, etc.

Members will also have beliefs about what leaders should do. The plaints, 'They should tell us more', 'There is no strategy', or 'They should provide more information' are so common in organizations that they represent the converse of the tendency to create leaders. The fact that many managers do not live up to the ideal means that we are left wanting. This is the risk of accepting the top job. Living up to the expectations of others, especially others with a tendency to idealize, is not easy. Members' expectations, based on their beliefs, reflect the would-be leader's dilemma—how close should he or she get to the rest? The closer leaders are to the rest, the greater the risk of their being found to be ordinary; but the greater the distance the more the rest may not know the leader at all. If we look at leaders such as de Gaulle, Churchill and Gandhi, we find that they were both close *and* distant. They understood that an important function of leadership is to provide integration and vision; yet, physically, they remained distanced from the great majority of their followers. They were excellent in their sensitivity in communicating with the mass and in manipulating the stories they wished to have transmitted about themselves.

Cooperation

This is basic to any economic system. It represents a major belief common to all cultures. In work organizations there is a universal belief that cooperation will achieve greater productivity than lack of cooperation—two people will produce a better result than one. And for most tasks this is empirically valid. Cooperation as a set of shared values has a variety of levels. First, there is the clear link to rationality. It is economically demonstrable that, with the exception of creative tasks, four people cooperating on the same task will achieve a better result than one person doing the same task. (Recent research indicates that even creativity draws heavily on relationships with others.)

At the emotive level, cooperation incorporates values about 'us' and 'non-us', insiders versus outsiders, friendship, love and teamwork. And it is a strong belief in relationships which feeds the network of relationships.

Yet although cooperation is central to all economic systems, the degree to which individuals will submit their personalities to the needs of the team varies between national cultures. For example, in the United Kingdom individualism is a major value of the national culture. This exists in conflict with stated organizational views on cooperation. By contrast, Hofstede's studies of the values of the West German, Swedish and Japanese cultures show a much stronger emphasis on cooperation and a much weaker emphasis on individuality. So, even though we can identify cooperation as a cluster of values in work organizations, some societies encourage these values, and the beliefs on which they are based, more than others.

Outsiders

Beliefs about 'us' and 'them' distinguish members from non-members. To differentiate 'us' from 'them', badges, titles, ties, company logos, uniforms and extended surnames—John W. Hunt of XYZ Corporation—are used extensively. And when I meet you at a social function I am likely to ask you (if you have not already told me) what your affiliation is: 'Where do you work?' or 'What do you do?'

Members share beliefs about mastery, control, winning over outsiders such as suppliers, competitors and clients or customers. In government organizations, members have values about other government organizations, and about ministers, politicians (specifically and generally), political parties, the executive and non-executive functions of civil servants, the Treasury, the private sector, etc. While the foci of values in government organizations may be slightly different from those in the private sector, the consequence of ignoring non-members can be extremely humiliating for senior civil servants. A parliamentary question can stimulate breathtaking activity within a ministry, when the 'outside' breaks 'in'.

Values and beliefs about outsiders also operate at the macro level. Members will have shared views of 'the competition', 'the industry', the government and the national and international economies. Indeed, as it becomes more difficult to predict the performance of a firm, there is a tendency to abstract larger and larger models of the world to reduce uncertainty to rational or acceptable levels. Through this process, managers' confidence may be increased and the day-to-day realities of managing may be addressed without panic. This phenomenon has bred a whole panoply of economic and social gurus who attempt to reduce a collective uncertainty by providing predictions about those external to 'us' on a regular basis.

Continuity

Linking present into past and future produces values and beliefs about overriding purpose—the moral imperative. Hence, the past becomes the supplier of the beliefs for the present and the future. Through this process continuity is embedded in the system. Threats of failure or death are suppressed and, with the confidence born of a past and a future, managers and others make decisions based on accumulated experience. 'Social responsibility' and 'making a contribution to the country' become extensions of this justification for existence. The longer the history, the more continuity and tradition dominate the values and beliefs; the longer the history, the greater the tendencies for values and beliefs to become sanctified. Change is easiest in the organization created this morning; it is more difficult in those with long histories and articulated values and beliefs drawn from past experiences. Indeed, the histories of large corporations are dominated by continuity—of structures, systems and power relations—not by change.

Summary

I have looked at some of the values and beliefs that are shared by members in different organizations. Other shared values do exist, but tend to be peculiar to a particular organization. For example, in some organizations there is a collective view that those who 'get on' are of a particular religious persuasion. In others there are values about doing good deeds in the community. In yet others there are views about family life, or shared values about specific political parties. Yet, despite these differences, there are more values and beliefs held in common than not. We can group most of them loosely under the headings I have used above—the individual, the task, rationality, leadership, cooperation, outsiders and continuity. Next we look at how these values and beliefs are transmitted.

TRANSMITTING VALUES AND BELIEFS

The culture of an organization is transmitted through the interactions of people. It enables us to make inferences from or refine, and thereby make sense of, actions, events and communications. Important mechanisms for the transfer are language, jargon, stories, gossip, examples and symbols. As with all other communication networks, only some of this process can be controlled.

Hence, while certain linguistic features, symbols and pieces of jargon may have official approval, other concepts, words, expressions, etc., creep in unawares. And this is one of the exciting characteristics of a corporate culture—it is a living dynamic process which managers may *influence*, especially informally and through example. Culture is not a variable that managers simply control; it is too covert, too intangible, to permit control. However, once there is agreement about the language, the use of symbols, jargon, graphics, etc., communication is possible. Transmitters of communications can transmit and, much of the time, their messages will be received. Other mechanisms (stories, myths, legends, rituals, rites and ceremonies) of the culture have more specific functions and managers should learn to understand those functions.

Stories

These are based on fact, and are used to transmit values and beliefs in an attractive, entertaining and, above all, repeatable way. For example, the values of the founders of the organization are transmitted indirectly through stories about the 'early days'. In the civil service, stories abound about the new minister or the new permanent secretary. Indeed, the announcement of a new minister immediately begins a search for stories about his or her past.

Stories are important, not just for the story or the values central to the story. They are important because of a multiplier effect; for example, stories about an impressive leader of a nationalized industry may centre on the idea that he or she is different, conservatively deviant. On their own the values are rarely profound, but the multiplier effect of the stories *can* be profound. For example, 'being different' might mean always being on time, up to date, efficient, punctual and sharp, so that no trivial details will impair the *real* purpose of innovation, the risk-taking, the 'stretch' to new things. And taken together it is this second set of values which appears to dominate that culture.

Myths

These are explanations of past events which carry powerful cultural messages. They may be true or invented. It really does not matter, as truth is not their function. Certainly they will be true to those who want to believe them; outsiders may find them unbelievable.

Myths are shorthand versions of reality. They centre on a theme, illustrated through several short stories about people and events. For example, myths surround the period Lord Sieff spent as chairman of Marks & Spencer; these myths provide detailed examples (stories) of store visits, of personal help to individuals, of a belief in seconding executives to help worthy causes. The central theme is caring, a responsibility to individuals and a concern for human relations.

Myths perform important functions. They can explain or conceal paradox, block off searches for further explanations, mask contradictions, reconcile opposing forces, uplift a relatively unexciting event to the dramatic, and excite a sense of reality acceptable both emotionally and rationally. They centre on individuals and reconcile the conflicting evidence. Around history's most insensitive leaders there are myths about their sensitivity; how else could a follower reconcile the fact that he or she followed them? We will also find myths surrounding products which are known to be dangerous (cigarettes, alcohol, munitions). Stories of the good 'the company' has done the world (support for sporting events, medical research, opera, ballet, etc.) enable the employee to reconcile doubts about what he or she is doing. Similarly, myths—regarding national security, defence, surveillance—abound in government and secret organizations simply to present a palatable version of reality to employees.

It is the function of myths, not their source or validity, which is important. They bind, link us together, provide us with a sense of adventure, an explanation of the unexplainable. Unlike day-to-day stories, they are not bound by time or space. They link us now to our past, often through romanticized versions of our history, and point us towards our future.

Myths arise in work organizations when there is a distance between the managers and their groups; when the stated intentions of managers and their actual behaviour are incompatible; when the recorded beliefs of, say, the founders and the reality of today are contradictory; or when present circumstances demand an explanation for what was (from today's viewpoint) a very strange decision in the past. Myths emerge around people very distant in time, space or social position (e.g., about the royal family) or around transitory people (the director of overseas operations who visits his or her domain rarely), or around events which fit badly into the history of the organization. To believers they are myths; to the rest of us they are like fairy-tales. To the organization they are part of the covert but oral glue which binds people together.

Legends

These are popular stories with (usually) an historical relevance. Again, they centre on one person or one group. Legends are likely to be based partly on truth and partly on a liberal and emotive interpretation of the facts. Legends depend on projection from those in a hierarchically lower position—their emotive interpretations elevate the legendary figure(s). Distance (social, chronological or geographical) is again an advantage, as reality incorporates the risk of shattering illusions.

Rituals

These are repeated activities which reinforce beliefs and values. They are most often created in order to reflect a belief in rationality and order (e.g., committees) although some of the most impressive rituals are poor reflections of rationality, in that they are loose, informal gatherings of people unrestricted by formalities, able to express their views openly, bound together by one common ingredient—their work.

Good ritual *does* reinforce the values. Bad ritual merely wastes time. For example, examining bodies in universities go through ritualistic processes debating who should and who should not pass, even though the decisions, in the main, have been taken even before the meeting occurs. This is often bad ritual; time is wasted. Good ritual occurs when the same examining board automatically passes the majority and concerns itself (as the arbiter of standards) with the few who failed or who surpassed the rest.

Committees, boards of directors, supervisory bodies, professional institutes, all develop highly ritualistic processes in order to reinforce certain beliefs and values. Over time, these rituals may become so elaborate that they prevent solutions emerging for the very problems for which the committee or board was established. For example, ritualistic behaviour of members of a board may mean that the same item appears on the agenda meeting after meeting, simply because the required behaviour rituals prevent the sort of emotional discussion which could lead to the problem being resolved. Not surprisingly, around most boards there is a vast amount of informal lobbying which oils the work of the board and allows progress to be made.

Monday-morning meetings, annual appraisals, job-interview schedules, presentations by suppliers, search processes for 'new blood', safety committees, have all been targets for ritualistic processes. In government organizations and large private bureaucracies, favourite areas for rituals are budget committees, task forces and commissions of enquiry. Bad ritual occurs in these groups when the ritual becomes so elaborate that the issues are lost from public gaze.

Managers can create good ritual simply by minimizing the amount of prescribed behaviour they impose on subordinates. The user of informal gatherings in a pub, lunches without agendas, coffee breaks without a specific purpose and working lunches to 'chew the rag' can be good examples of management using ritual to good effect.

Social events, annual conferences (with plenty of time to enjoy yourself) and sales conferences can also become enjoyable and valuable rituals, provided they are not over-structured. One managing director of a British company takes his managers and their spouses on an annual conference in some exotic, warm location every year, regardless of the performance of the company. The conference lasts four days, with plenty of time left for sightseeing, sitting in the sun, relaxing, etc. Magical events dominate the evenings—eight-course formal dinners, firework displays, opportunities to 'dress up' in a setting and location most of them could not afford. Very little time is allocated to corporate affairs—indeed, the two or three lectures at the conference are usually only vaguely related to the company. Yet the myths and legends that have been generated from these conferences are endless. Some day, the accountants will have their way; the conference will be moved to a cheaper site, an agenda will fill in every minute, the spouses will be left at home and a formidable list of company-related matters will be discussed—and good ritual will be transformed into bad. The irony of this eventuality is that more time will have been spent informally on company matters in the original conference—work is, after all, what binds the individuals together. Thrusting it down their throats is likely to weaken the bond and reduce the time spent informally on corporate matters. Rational values will have triumphed.

Rites

A rite is a relatively regular set of activities designed to consolidate various forms of cultural expression in one prescribed event. Most frequently, rites are conducted before an audience and provide for reward and recognition of achievement. Annual dinners, annual salesperson awards, sales conferences and assessment centres are all examples of rites. Their most important function is authenticity.

Often when a rite which has been authentic for the participants ceases to be so, the rite continues none the less. Powerful rites emphasize differences in status and make it acceptable to obey senior people, but, once institutionalized, rites (e.g., linking standards of office furniture to salary grade), become the subject of informal ridicule.

Ceremonies

These combine a series of rites and rituals into an event. Ceremony has always been an important social mechanism, especially in traditional organizations like the Church. It performs a vital function in reinforcing certain specific beliefs, at the same time as it provides opportunities for individuals to release their feelings. The use of royal ceremony or such occasions as presidential inaugurations has in some countries almost superseded the activity of the Church in its role of providing an opportunity for a restatement of fundamental beliefs and values.

In work organizations, the shift in an individual's dependence, from community, family and Church to work organization, has made it inevitable that the use of ceremony—both as a reinforcing and a cathartic force—has increased significantly. The average residential management-development programme is more about ceremony than education. Residential training centres, owned and manned by corporations, process thousands of employees in a year through a mixture of stories, ritual, rites and confessions. 'Religious' festivals will be found as frequently in the training centres of banks, insurance companies and government departments as in religious organizations. And for programme participants, the experience is rewarding and stimulating, especially the opportunity for informal, frank discussions about the corporation and their place in it.

Work organizations have recently begun to follow the historical lead of the Church and State in approaching ceremony in a more organized manner. For centuries, Church and State have understood that ceremony is vital on a planned and continuing basis. Hence weekly reinforcement was backed up by elaborate festivals every three months. Academic institutions adopted this pattern from their religious origins—there was nothing educationally sacrosanct about three terms over nine months.

The sales function was probably the first to realize the importance of planned ceremony. The practice of weekly sales conferences (rites) was extended into quarterly 'festivals' and annual ceremonial celebrations of several linked rites. Expensive and visible rewards were attached to each stage of the reinforcement (salesperson of the week, of the quarter, of the year, etc.) and people attending cried out for more. Yet many managers are sceptical of these trends. Planning the ceremony and the 'fun' of work organizations remains largely undiscussed—there is still a great deal we can learn from the open, predictable pattern of events on the Church or State calendar. Ceremony both fosters the continuity of the organization and provides a measure of release, fun and emotional involvement for its members.

Managers and cultures

Managers in positions of power deliberately construct and maintain ideologies. Sometimes these are no more than inferred from their behaviour—subordinates form the belief that their manager values creativity, accuracy, tidiness or whatever. In other instances managers have developed unequivocal statements of the beliefs and values they admire and, with all the enthusiasm of a new-product launch, have pushed these values and ideologies through the organization, hoping to win the 'hearts and minds' of their employees. Indeed, it has become popular among managers to think that, by articulating and communicating the approved dogma, they will focus the attention of employees on to productivity, profit or service. Unfortunately there is very little empirical evidence to support this theory. Culture takes years to develop; it is done covertly rather than overtly, by example rather than by prescription, informally rather than formally. Therefore, to decide to promulgate a new mix of values and beliefs as a counter-culture takes up an enormous amount of time and energy (as the manager of a turn-around environment knows only too well) even if all the available media (TV, video, journals, symbols, myths, songs, uniforms) and all the cultural practices (rites, rituals and ceremonies) are used.

If the top managers do invest the energy needed to communicate their values and beliefs (as a philosophy or creed), those values and beliefs will only be absorbed into the minds of the rest of the organization so long as they do not contradict those of the followers. It is the capacity to link the values and beliefs of the leader with the needs, goals, values and beliefs of the followers that is the magic of leadership. Without that, no behaviour by example, no video tapes, journals, songs, visuals, creeds or statements of strategy will penetrate the values and beliefs already inherent in the corporate culture.

CONFLICT AND VALUES

The most protracted conflicts in organizations occur over basic values. Conversely, the more uniform the values expressed by management, the more they can reduce conflict. It is relatively easy to manage different perceptions of a problem or different proposed courses of action. However, when the difference is over a basic value, egos become involved and defensiveness clouds judgement. For example, there are different perceptions among people about the sharing of profit, the allocation of rewards, the distribution of authority, the rights of employees, etc., and it is these basic differences in values that lead to much industrial-relations conflict, especially in societies where individualism (not collectivism) is admired. Individualism fits badly with a collective decision on, say, salaries or wages. Certain societal values guarantee that Britain, America, Canada, Australia, etc., will have more industrial disputes over values than will those cultures (Sweden, Norway, Japan) based on collective, as opposed to individualistic, values. Indeed, when managers in Britain produce statements of ideologies praising togetherness, team-work and cooperation, they do so in the face of a national culture which prizes individual difference, liberty, deviation and innovation extremely highly.

MANAGERS AND THE CORPORATE CULTURE

Managers have a choice; they can *note* the powerful impact of organizational culture or they can decide to *influence* that culture. Recently there has been more interest in the latter. Developing and communicating a basic set of values or beliefs has almost replaced clarifying strategy as a top-management obsession. First, the message must be distinguished from the medium. To do this means identifying—at a conceptual level—the values central to the firm. The greater the number of core values, the greater the problem of communicating those values. Conversely, most corporations with clearly communicated managerial values (e.g., Marks & Spencer, IBM, MacDonalds, GEC) have extremely simplistic, brief statements of those values. But, if brevity succeeds, do not all companies achieving it end up putting out the same message? One might expect one organization's basic beliefs and values to differ from those of all other organizations. The cultures of the different firms using brief, succinct messages certainly do. Yet the overt or stated beliefs do not. Indeed it is inevitable that profit or service organizations are going to have remarkably similar broad values *if one looks at the values that can be documented.* In reality, the values and beliefs that are transmitted informally and covertly are far more subtle. Nuances, signals and interpretations accumulate in a continuous daily stream in people's minds, giving relevance and significance to what, in a statement of the corporate creed, may look like the same set of values and beliefs as any other organization has. So if we compare the approved statements of five companies in the same industry we will find that the statements are embarrassingly similar and almost banal. However, if we study the cultures of those five companies we will find them radically different.

The real art of documenting the approved set of values is to make it different. An undifferentiated statement may be the recipe for instant rejection. As promulgating an approved statement is an overt process, it will be less effective than the covert processes on which cultures thrive. Topics we might find in the overt statements of corporate philosophy or credo will include the purposes of the firm, its major strategies, and beliefs about individuals, managers, stakeholders and the future. However, taking this list of ingredients as a model in preparing your own credo is still a risky business. Culture depends on *not* being prescribed. Prescribing a set of values is no guarantee that those values will be absorbed.

TRANSMITTING THE MESSAGE

Once an agreed message has been articulated and differentiated from those of other organizations it needs to be transmitted orally. If any influence on the organizational culture is to be achieved, the message and the medium must match the goals and expectations of the members. Transmission should begin with the chief executive, as he or she has the greatest power to influence the culture of the organization. Chief executives can model the types of behaviour subordinates should exhibit. Model incidents may be transmitted in story form and eventually gain the status of legend. As mentioned earlier, the history of the company and the values of the founders may also be a rich source of stories. Similarly chief executives can use new language, invent new jargon, create new rituals, reinstate old ones, approve ceremonial events and invest the reward systems with fresh symbolic meaning tied to the values they are espousing.

The medium for transmission will be personal communication, but television, video, the staff magazine, 'royal tours' and repetition at every opportunity of the values in catch-phrases or slogans ('We try harder') may be useful. Constant repetition of the same simple message is essential—repetition by example, and through actions, demonstrations, speech and visual representation. Personnel departments can assist by linking the induction process, the training programmes, the appraisal system and the reward system to the same statement of core values. By integrating what are usually totally unrelated personnel practices (e.g., induction, appraisal and reward) the set of core values may be reinforced. Wherever people go in the organization, they should find the same statement of values—whether it be on the letterhead, in the training manual, in the staff journal, on the video tape of the chief executive, or on the slogan board. 'Selling' a set of values is no different from selling anything else; it is essentially an interpersonal, oral process. The hurdle for many managers is accepting the need for a message in the first place; a culture exists already, and overt tampering may upset it.

IS IT WORTH IT?

Meddling with cultures is a risky business. Even if the expense and energy required are invested in the attempt to modify a culture, there is no guarantee of success. Indeed, if the development of a counter-culture were easy we could easily reverse an otherwise inevitable organizational decline. The organization would simply find a new set of values and a person to transmit them.

Several important questions arise in any discussion of counter-cultures. First, is this conscious attempt to affect values tantamount to blatant manipulation and propaganda? Any effort to influence an organization's culture is manipulative—but then, so is most of the managerial task. Second, there is no guarantee that successfully identifying, transmitting and selling a set of core values and beliefs as *the* doctrine will improve performance. On the other hand, the most successful commercial organizations *do* have clearly enunciated and communicated values and beliefs. Finally, there is no guarantee that a new set of values will be acceptable to the members, and if they are not, the members will reject them. However, presenting a set of values which turns out to be unacceptable to members indicates a poor assessment of acceptability and/or poor communicating. On the positive side, the satisfaction of members is higher in organizations which have an internalized set of corporate values. It may be manipulative, but those working in them like it.

SUB-CULTURES

Another practical question is whether managers should aim to influence one culture or several. This arises in divisionalized structures and in geographically dispersed units. If managers decide to integrate the organizational parts by identifying a common set of core values and injecting them into the corporate culture, they may find that the sub-units reject those values. A culture exists in all organizations, including the sub-units. If managers want to increase coordination between the parts, they must ask themselves why. If there is no synergy to be gained from that integration, then they would be well advised to let the sub-units identify their own core values and promulgate these themselves; in most cases the culture of the sub-unit is far stronger than that of a loose federation of dispersed parts. What the manager can be sure of is that the basic, core values of the units are probably similar. The subtleties are what differentiate them.

If there is a case for greater integration, then an articulated set of corporate values *may* be useful, depending on the strength of the sub-unit cultures. If closer integration is desirable, involving the chiefs of the sub-units in the process of developing the message is sensible. Thereafter, a centralized 'selling' campaign, maintained for a very long period (5 to 10 years), is essential, while the managers link the parts covertly together. And even then the desired shift in the sub-unit cultures may be extremely expensive, for no quantifiable return. There have been numerous examples throughout history of nation states where people resisted the values their conquerors forced on them overtly. The values that did stick were invariably communicated by example (e.g., justice), by demonstration (e.g., government), by speech, by music and by drama. And even then the conquerors had long time-spans in which to transmit their values. In work organizations we should check that the energy and expense is warranted before attempts are made to alter sub-cultures.

Summary

As two or more people begin working together in cooperative activity they begin explicitly and implicitly to share values and beliefs about their work, their efficiency, their customers, etc. Over time, these shared values and beliefs form the culture of that organization. They will include values and beliefs about the individual, the task, the work ethic, rationality, leadership, cooperation, outsiders and continuity. As more people join, they adopt those values and beliefs or leave. With more and more people, new tasks emerge, new jobs are developed and new functions evolve, the dynamic nature of the social system that is evolving being reflected in the process of functional differentiation common to social systems.

The culture of an organization is the collective of shared values, ideologies and beliefs of members including the transmitting media of language, stories, symbols, myths and legends, and the manifestations of those values in rituals, rites and ceremonies. Culture is the corporate glue that links diverse and often strangely different individuals together into a productive collective. To understand the culture, we need to observe the behaviour of the members. Culture exists independently of managers; it is not a biddable tool in the hands of managers. Managers wishing to affect the culture should be warned that this is a long-term and tricky business. Values and beliefs only become embedded in the culture of an organization if members want to accept those values and beliefs.

Managers should note the vital role of culture in affecting cooperative behaviour. Culture produces cohesion, team-work and loyalty, by giving people a sense of who and what they are.

The important components of a corporate culture are language, jargon, stories, myths, legends and symbols. Reinforcing these oral processes are rituals, rites and ceremonies. Managers can ensure that the rituals they impose on people are good rituals; that the rites that persist are those that reinforce the important values and beliefs of the culture; that the ceremonies that top managers revere have relevance to the people involved. Finally, managers can arrange the organization's calendar in such a way that the opportunities for the exchanges which strengthen cultures are sufficiently frequent for adequate reinforcement to occur. What managers should not try to do is push a set of documented values and beliefs on to members. By all means document the approved values, but it is example, speech and behaviour which reinforce culture, not pieces of paper.

References

Terrence, A. and A. E. Kennedy, *Corporate Cultures*, Addison-Wesley, Reading, Mass., 1982.

Pondy, L. R., P. J. Frost, G. Morgan and T. Dandridge (eds), *Organizational Symbolism*, JAI Press, Greenwich, Conn., 1984.

ON EXAMPLES OF CORPORATE CULTURES

Peters, T. J. and R. H. Waterman, *In Search of Excellence*, Harper and Row, NY, 1982.

Pettigrew, A., *The Awakening Giant: Continuity and Change in ICI*, Basil Blackwell, Oxford, 1985.

ON DIFFERENCES BETWEEN NATIONS

Hofstede, G., *Culture's Consequences: International Differences in Work Related Values*, Sage Publications, Beverly Hills, Calif., 1984.

7. Analysing organizations

Introduction

We have now looked at organizations at three levels of analysis.

- The individual level
- The interpersonal level
- The organizational level

In Chapters 1 and 2, I concentrated on analysing behaviour at the individual level. This approach to analysis is extremely useful in attempting to answer questions like 'What is affecting Fred today?' or 'Why is the shop steward behaving as she is?' However, this view has very little more to contribute to strategy, policy and organization design than giving us generalized models of behaviour which we can link into our design of a hierarchy, system or control mechanism (see Chapter 8).

In Chapters 3, 4 and 5, I concentrated on the *processes* that go on in organizations as individuals interact with each other. This interpersonal level of analysis tells us what is happening *now*: why group A does not like group B; what is going on in division X or in head office. For day-to-day management this is probably the most useful approach—most of a manager's day is about processes.

In Chapter 6, I attempted to shift slowly from the interpersonal processes which go on day in, day out, to a macro view. I used a cultural perspective based on an analysis of the processes or behaviours of members. This approach (a process view) is vital in understanding how any one organization got to where it is. It is the starting-point of any attempt to understand a firm, a department or any other organization; it is central to every case study a student manager considers. Unfortunately, this view merely provides us with a unique *story*—the story of Firm X so far. It gives us very little insight into what happens next or, more significantly, what has caused the situation.

To understand cause and effect and where, therefore, we might go next (i.e., to make some predictions), we need a view of organizations that looks *across* them and finds common variables. This approach is called *variance theory* and it is this approach that I use in this chapter.

The manager as analyst

Of course, managers do not wait for academics to invent new theories before they analyse problems. Managers move, often unawares, from an individual level of analysis to an interpersonal level, and then to a macro level, within minutes, sometimes with dazzling speed. In fact, really effective top managers can conceptualize at three levels almost concurrently. But they are very rare people. Most of us have preferences for one level or another and our problems and solutions are reflections of that bias.

Amongst researchers and academics, the fights about whether a cultural perspective, a process analysis, a variance analysis, or a systems theory or action theory approach is most appropriate are fast and furious (see references). My view is that managers should take what suits them from each approach and let the academics do the fighting. From my experience, the good analyst floats from one level or one theory to another, with little regard for academic purity. This may explain why we know so little about how the successful diagnostician's mind operates. All we know is that such people are rarely limited by one view—they are scavengers.

My purpose in this chapter is, first, to conclude the ways we analyse organizations by presenting a variance analysis. This approach looks at different organizations and draws conclusions about how the parts of the whole interact. Second, I ask the question: How will we know if the combination of these macro variables is effective? To answer that question I examine *end-result variables.*

Finally, I reintroduce the process variables as intervening between the current macro variables and the results. A simple diagnostic checklist concludes the chapter.

Variance analysis

From observing actors' behaviour, a view of the organization's culture emerges. From this analysis, we can group together values and beliefs into 'variables'. For example, as we saw in the previous chapter, there are values relating to the task, rationality, structure and order. These values can be collected into a variable called the *formal structure*. However, it is also clear that there are values about interpersonal relationships based on fun, affection, power and influence. Values surrounding these 'non-rational' behaviours can be collected together as the *informal structure*. Actors also have views on, and are influenced by, the plant, the equipment, the computer, the telephone, the word processor, the buildings, etc.—that is, the physical environment has a major influence on an actor's behaviour. All these physical influences

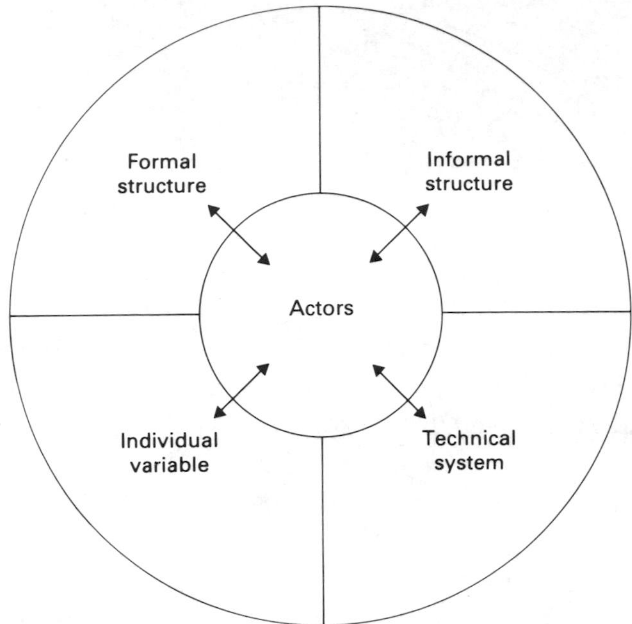

Figure 7.1 Influence of insiders' values on behaviour in a work organization

and the values inherent in them are collected into a third variable, the *technical system*. Finally, there are strongly shared values about individuals, goals, what excites people, and careers, and we link these together into an *individual variable*.

We can represent the influence of these values on the actors performing in the plant, the workshop, the department, etc., as in Fig. 7.1. Note that the illustration includes arrows in both directions. Actors both influence and are influenced by, for example, the formal values about rationality.

Just as there is an internal social system of actors, so too we can conceptualize, at the macro level, the influence of external non-members (suppliers, governments, competitors, customers). In Fig. 7.2, we add the influence of the outsiders or non-members to the framework, and thereby complete the list of major recurring influences on the behaviour of the actors in any work organization.

Let me examine each of these organizational variables from a variance-theory perspective.

THE FORMAL STRUCTURE

Values and beliefs about rationality produce a collective 'law'. It is this

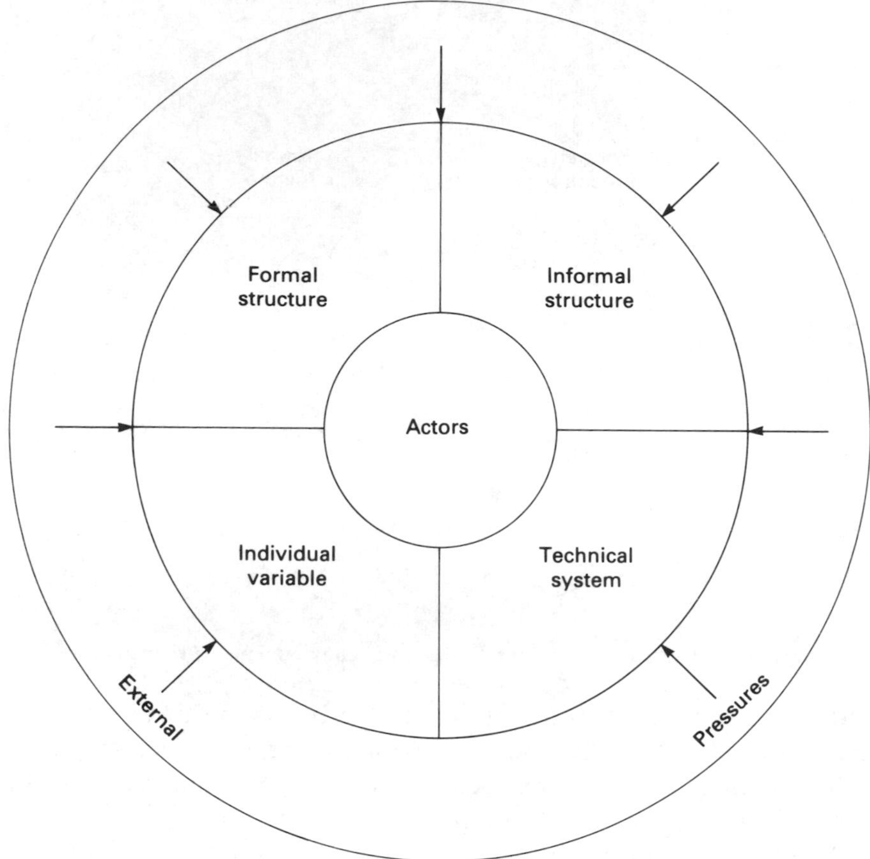

Figure 7.2 Influence of outsiders' or non-members' values on behaviour in a work organization

law which we indentify as the formal structure. In simple terms the variable includes the following:

- Corporate strategies including:
  - Primary purpose, function or mission
  - The multiple objectives and articulated strategies
- Policies
- Approved tasks
- Jobs
- Hierarchy
- Information systems
- Resource procurement systems

- Product or service distribution or delivery systems
- Personnel systems
- Production systems
- Vertical and horizontal integrative mechanisms

In Chapter 8 we look at the way the objectives and strategies lead to the choice of structural devices from a wide variety of possibilities. For the moment, we need to acknowledge that it is this set of devices, collectively called the *formal structure*, and the values inherent in those devices that have attracted most attention in the management literature. After nearly a century of writing, we remain obsessed with finding rational processes of work.

THE INFORMAL STRUCTURE

There is a long history in management literature of separating formal and informal structures, yet the separation is more one of diagnostic convenience than of fact. There is considerable debate as to when a structure is formal or informal. Some new organizations (e.g., a new political party) might begin with a carefully formulated formal structure designed by the founders. Others begin with almost no clear idea of how work is to be completed, so that the structure develops through the trial-and-error basis that I described in Chapter 6. I see a structure as formal when the values about rationality have been sufficiently articulated to be shared by most members.

An informal structure represents values and beliefs about day-to-day relationships, but there is no need for agreement or even articulation among a majority of members.

Another way to understand the informal–formal link is to see one structure as 'latent' and the other as 'manifest'. What is not helpful is to attempt to classify *behaviour* as formal or informal. The method we use here allows us to extract formal and informal *values* as variables and then examine how they affect the behaviour of members.

The values collected together here as informal structure relate to unofficial relationships, peer-group norms, and task and maintenance relationships outside the formal requirements of the hierarchy. Unlike the formal structure, the informal structure is very rarely a unified set of values. Instead it represents a collection of values and interpersonal links relating to a multitude of relationships between groups of two, three, four, people. Very rarely do these values become sufficiently articulated or shared to unite the entire informal structure of all actors into a *single* influence on behaviour. The structure is a kaleidoscope of sub-groups, endlessly changing, reflecting the changing patterns of relationships between people. Some relationships continue relatively unchanged for years, while others are much more fleeting and transient.

Most of the time the behaviour influenced by the values of the informal structure is erratic and relatively unpredictable. Yet it is through these informal links that problems are solved, new solutions to difficult issues are devised, and innovation and creativity are encouraged. Once solutions are found informally, they may be locked into the formal structure, thereby institutionalizing the solution. Thus informal structures generate formal structures, and vice versa.

The most famous characteristic of the informal structure is the grapevine—that remarkable communication channel which links actors across towns, across counties, across nations. Yet the grapevine is not a single, continuously operating communication link between people. Instead it is a multitude of tiny, group-based communication networks that occasionally link together into a single 'vine'. For this to happen, the information must be vital to all the sub-units of the informal relationships. If the chief executive dies, then the linkages between his or her friends, acquaintances and colleagues have a common interest and the grapevine unites. Thereafter the temporary links between sections, departments or groups collapse and the segmented sub-group-based, face-to-face communication networks dominate once more.

Within the hundreds or thousands of sub-groups which make up the informal structure of any organization, the same structuring processes will occur as we saw in small organizations and other groups. Group leaders emerge, norms about expected behaviour develop, controls are exercised. Yet, because the goals of the groups making up the informal structure are usually multiple and less clear, the group structure is less explicit. Leadership roles shift with the task and with the goals of the group members at that time. Hence, there may well be one leader for one task and a second leader for another task. Muhammad is the best person on taxation matters, Beryl is the comedienne, Winston is the person who confronts 'them' (the outsiders).

Only if specific issues which affect all actors arise, and only if all actors can be collected into one place, will the many small units cohere as a crowd. This is the mechanism of industrial disputes; the capacity of shop stewards to mobilize the informal linkages determines their capacity to maintain a strike. A good shop steward knows this and reinforces cohesion during a strike by instigating crowd behaviour every three or four days. Conversely, unions with widely spread members are less cohesive and less able to maintain industrial action (e.g., teachers, civil servants and engineers).

Informal structures are not 'manageable', only observable. The moment informal relationships are analysed at a macro level they are likely to disappear and go 'underground'. Similarly, it is impossible to stop the informal structure—relationships will continue, even if every member is isolated from every other member (e.g., in a prison). If communication is possible, then a rich, informal structure will develop simply because the values of that structure allow me to be myself, to be non-rational and to have fun.

THE TECHNICAL SYSTEM

In the transformation of inputs into outputs, machines, buildings, telephones, computers, etc., are introduced into the formal action system in order to increase efficiency. Values about those buildings, machines, tools, etc., *and* the actual physical environments are collected here as a major influence on the behaviour of members.

We define the technical system as the collective of instruments introduced into the action system, including all physical influences which operate in conjunction with members but which are themselves independent of members and represent some values or beliefs of their designers.

Technical systems are used to reduce uncertainty. Various attempts have been made by writers to categorize them (e.g., into sequential, batch and intensive) or to rank them in terms of their complexity. More important to diagnosticians is the degree of control over members' behaviour that the technical system exerts. The more the technical system determines the method, rate and sequence of task performance, the greater the complexity of that system and the fewer options we have to vary that system. For example, the highly automated plant provides few opportunities for actors to vary the production systems or to redesign the total process. Indeed, in such plants we are in danger of leaving only the most trivial activities to the humans and providing the machine with the most interesting tasks. Conversely, the large office full of designers illustrates the control that the designers have over their technical system in that their system is simple rather than complex, comprising drawing-boards, pencils, rulers, etc., the method, rate and sequence of activities being determined by the designer rather than by the technical system.

The impact of the technical system on variables such as the formal structure can be great. Indeed, there is a confusing research literature which implies that the technical system is the major influence on structure. My experience indicates that the effect also depends on the external pressures and the people employed. Even more contentious is the impact that microtechnology will have on organizations. This recent addition to technical systems greatly improves the transmission, storage, accessibility and manipulation of information. Further, there appears to be a clear link between this technology and the size of the organization, in that microtechnology replaces clerical and middle-management personnel. Small may be beautiful after all. Additionally, the immediacy of information may allow for performance measures to affect behaviour and thus to make a direct reward for performance the major control. On the other hand, this recent addition to technical systems offers the potential for highly centralized organizations at a time when the behavioural scientists argue that we should reduce size, increase autonomy and devolve power. Probably the most important question for those designing organizations in the future is whether we will take the opportunity offered by the new technology to create the sorts of structures we have found to correlate positively with job satisfaction. Certainly (see Chapter 1) all our research on motivation goals shows that a desire for independence and autonomy is driving actors away from large centralized organizations. In contrast, my experience so far has been that major organizations are using the new technology to control more and more centrally.

Whatever the outcomes of the explosive changes in electronic technical systems, their importance to the behaviour of individuals and groups in work organizations is already apparent. The office landscape is undergoing a revolution.

THE INDIVIDUAL VARIABLE

Diagnosing the behaviour of actors in organizations depends on identifying goal patterns or themes. While it has been fashionable for the past 40 years to emphasize each member's individuality, the systems of organizations are in fact based on generalized models of behaviour. Hence, the design of the appraisal system assumes that we all like to have feedback on our performance in the same format, at the same time and from the same person. In spite of the fact that this is obviously not true, managers of organizations are only able to accommodate the idiosyncrasies of individuals in minor ways. A whole range of formal controls, from recruitment techniques to training programmes, from job design to performance assessment and rewards, are based on generalized models of humans. It is not surprising that any one generalized model is consistently found wanting. However, the alternative (designing a separate system for each individual, based on his or her preferences) does not bear contemplating. Further, whilst it is comforting to talk about individual differences, this tends to ignore the fact that we have more in common than we have that is different—that is, the generalized model of a human being is based on more reliable data than many of the attempts (e.g., job design and industrial democracy) to accommodate individual differences.

By classifying our generalized model as the individual variable, we take the discussion of individuals from Chapters 1 and 2 into an organization. Abilities, goals, aspirations and capacities are collected together to form a generalized view of an individual. The developmental influences of family, home, parents, school, college and leisure are added to the egocentric view given earlier. From this position, as diagnosticians, we can discover that individuals seeking high levels of structure are attracted not just to highly structured organizations but more specifically to functions like accounting and production, and not to functions like marketing, advertising or investing. Indeed, when we begin to look at the sorts of hierarchical structures available to managers (see Chapter 8) we will find that the generalized pictures of individuals are highly significant to the choices on offer.

External pressures

Just as managers are likely to see the group or system to which they belong as *the* section, *the* firm or *the* company, so they perceive the external world in terms of *the* market, *the* government, *the* competition, *the* ministry, etc.—that is, a larger system, external to the organization exists.

Outsiders transmit messages to insiders (actors) across the boundaries of an organization; they ask for orders, information, accounts, etc. The two-way flow of these messages gives insights into the extent to which a firm is exposed to uncertainty, to dependence on outsiders, to competition, to harassment, etc.

In proposing one variable as external pressures, we combine the values of outsiders or externals and the value-laden messages they transmit to internals. Hence, suppliers, government agencies, competitors, customers, clients, etc., form the major sources of external pressure on any organization. Furthermore, they are also essential to survival. Cut off this supply line and the organization will atrophy—no more resources will flow in to feed the transformation process. Even a very closed organization like a religious order has to go outside to find new members; without new members it will die.

The power of externals arises from the internals' dependence on them. Monopolistic suppliers of services can operate relatively freely because they have no competition (e.g., electricity and gas). Conversely, the highly competitive company (e.g., the stockbroker, real-estate agent or used-car dealer) will be subject to frequent and unpredictable internal changes, stimulated by the behaviour of externals. The greater an organization's dependence on outsiders, the more central that external is to the firm; and the scarcer the possible substitutes for the external's resources, then the greater the power of the external to control and even manage the internals (e.g., single suppliers to chain stores).

PROTECTING THE FIRM

Analysing the impact of external pressures means tracing communications from non-members (outsiders) to members (actors). If the number of transmissions and the number of transmitters is very great (e.g., as with the Inland Revenue) the more difficult the tracing becomes. The more transmissions are predictable, routine or repetitive, the simpler the internal's operation becomes (e.g., selling newspapers). The more varied, the less predictable, and the more hostile, competitive or aggressive the external transmissions, the more people or firms outside begin to shape the pattern of internal interactions (e.g., in an advertising agency or consulting company).

Managers can reduce the possibility of unpredictable, external influence by adopting strategies such as forming oligopolies (e.g., the glass industry), cartels (e.g., banking) or trade associations (e.g., the steel industry, pharmaceutical industry and trade unions); by insisting on long-term contracts (e.g., Japanese raw-materials buyers); by merging (e.g., retailers); by owning suppliers (e.g., oil companies); and by seeking government protection (e.g., European farmers).

It has become popular to envisage organizations as tossed about in turbulent market-places, but it is also true that many organizations do *not* exist like flotsam on a turbulent sea. They defuse external pressures through power lobbies or monopolies that can influence market patterns, trade barriers and government-guaranteed tariffs. Yet others have such control over central resources that they dictate to other organizations (e.g., the Treasury's influence on government ministries and departments).

Most members of organizations do not try to anticipate, react to or adapt to external pressures. Instead they focus on their jobs and act out their parts. Only if changes occur in their jobs or in the conditions of their jobs (e.g., promotion) do they scan the external environment to identify sources of pressure. Not surprisingly, such isolated reactions by individual actors are unlikely to result in a clear overall strategy for adaptation. For this reason organizational death from a failure to adapt is as prevalent now as it was 50 years ago.

Furthermore, external pressures are not perceived in the same guise by all actors. Some actors (e.g., marketing or sales) are very exposed to the incoming messages; others are protected from exposure and are much slower to react to the incoming message (e.g., accounts or personnel officers). Therefore, when we identify a single variable and call it 'external pressures', we are undeniably over-simplifying a complex process. Pressures come as messages from a variety of often unconnected sources. Some are received, others are lost. Recognition and articulation of a threat from outside may thus take months, even years, to occur. Yet to the casual observer the threat was obvious—actors inside could not or would not see it. This gives some support to the life-cycle theory of organizations—inability to adapt guarantees death.

THE ADAPTIVE PROCESS

The reactions of actors to external threats appear to depend on their perceptiveness, their goals and the vertical and horizontal links between them. Where they are tightly linked into a team (e.g., a football team) and where the links between teams are strong (e.g., a nation at war), the capacity of members to adapt is better than where they are only loosely coupled together (e.g., partners in a bank). Similarly the capacity to learn to adapt varies widely. Those who have handled uncertainty before (risk-takers) are more likely to adapt than those facing uncertainty for the first time (risk-averse). Other influences are age, goals, dependencies, history, experience, etc.

When external pressures are recognized by the actors, there is a multitude of possible reactions, but some patterns can be identified:

- The actors may conclude that they cannot predict the rate or direction of change, and remain inactive even in a state of shock (an *avoidance* response).
- They may accept the evidence of uncertainty and react on whatever information they have (the *reactive* response); information not available is ignored.
- They may adopt a *proactive* stance; they take all the information they can get and make plans to deal with it.
- They may take the information and interact with the environment, trying to clarify the uncertainty about what is happening so as to influence their environment (*interactive* behaviour).

These reactions will have an impact on both the formal and informal structures of the firm. As external pressures start to threaten the primary task, members will begin to perform their roles differently. Their jobs will be modified, tasks will be altered. Initially this shift appears in structural ('safe') change—a tightening of controls (especially cost controls), a reallocation of tasks. Most of these structural changes occur as the result of informal problem-solving 'huddles'; questions of power are addressed by rearranging authority. If hostile pressures continue, then the search for structural solutions is dropped. Structural change is too slow, so standards are altered, new priorities are adopted and attempts are made to confront the sources of power, regardless of authority. In short, altering the structure has failed, 'So let's short-circuit it.'

If significant pressures still bombard the actors, then loosening the structure may be seen as the only way to survive, not because the structure is perceived to be wrong but simply because it is too slow. Members thus move into the interactive phase. As the proactive or survival phase is reached, the primary focus switches to positive actions to affect the external environment. Ironically, the looser the structure becomes, the more excessive external pressures are essential to sustain it. Without that clear identifiable threat, focus is lost and internal conflict may be the result. Over time, new members with a tolerance of uncertainty will replace the 'old guard' and the looser structure will then be less dependent on outside pressures to sustain it. However, the shift may take years.

The degree to which members will change their behaviour depends on their goals and on how stressful they perceive the external pressures to be. If the marketing department is seen, as part of its function, to have external pressures on it, and if the market is friendly, relatively certain and predictable, then the level of stress within the marketing department (and elsewhere) will be tolerable. If pressures from externals suddenly increase—becoming uncertain, hostile, unpredictable, critical—then the reaction and proaction phases would probably precede the adaptive phase, simply because insufficient actors would feel the stress or pressure to adapt: 'It is a marketing problem, they should solve it.'

THE FOCUS OF POWER—INTERNAL OR EXTERNAL?

External influences come in many forms. One dominant external (either an individual or a group in agreement) may hold the balance of power (e.g., the Inland Revenue, the Bank of England). Alternatively, the externals may be divided, perhaps even widely dispersed. The larger the number of externals and the more dispersed they are, the more likely it is that they will be perceived as passive (as with the customers of a monopolistic service organization, e.g., the Railways). If an external does dominate an organization, then internal centralization through a tight, formal structure appears certain. If powerful externals encourage divisions within the organization, the internal actors look outwards for support, and internal political activity thrives. A strong internal leadership and ideology can strengthen the resolve of the actors to erect defences against, and thereby neutralize, outside influence. Finally, the absence of a single, external focus of power tends to encourage internal conflict. As in war, a common enemy focuses attention and resolve; without war the armed services spend more and more time inventing powerful externals to reduce internal disintegration; that is, they have mock wars and hope the troops will take them seriously.

These, then, are the major organizational (or macro) variables—formal structure, informal structure, technical systems, the individual variable and external pressures. Our next question, after we have analysed these, is how we can know whether the combination is an effective one or not. To answer that question the diagnostician must look at the performance of the total system. What does it achieve? Produce? Sell? Invest? For what return?

End-result variables

Organizations exist to achieve objectives. Most of these objectives are measurable, either qualitatively or quantitatively. From these objectives we are able to assess whether or not the organization is successful.

In some organizations with multiple, complex and long-term objectives, the actors will resist attempts to measure performance individually or collectively. For example, it is much more difficult to get agreement among the actors on the criteria of evaluation when assessing a university than it is when assessing a business. Similarly, it is much more difficult to get agreement about the criteria for a research establishment than for a netball team. Yet, as organizations exist for a purpose, it is vital to know whether they are achieving that purpose or not, if the actors are to feel motivated.

Because measuring performance can be difficult, some actors postpone the introduction of performance measures, arguing that such measures will limit creativity or individuality. Contrary to their fears, human performance increases with measurement rather than declines.

Possible end-result variables or performance variables for a business might include the following, all of which can be assessed at the end of a specific period of time (monthly, quarterly, half-yearly or annually):

- Profitability
- Share of target market
- Growth
- Productivity
- Customer satisfaction
- Employee turn-over
- Absenteeism and sickness
- Image

Research in organizational behaviour has largely failed to relate the organizational variables (formal structure, informal structure, the individual variable, technical systems and external pressures) to these end-result variables. This may help to explain the tendency of managers and diagnosticians to run back to process analysis—an historical analysis of the processes that got us here may teach us why we have achieved what we have. Unfortunately, this provides little insight into what we should do next. Historically, a shift, among consultants, academics and managers, from variance analysis to process analysis has been the result. However, since the mid-seventies, organizational and end-result variables have been linked successfully through a third set of variables called intervening or moderating variables. And through that link, the impact of, say, formal structure on the end results (e.g., productivity) has become clearer, largely because the moderating variables are indicators in a relatively short time-span, whereas structure, strategy, technical systems, etc., may remain stable for long periods of time.

Measuring a person's or a unit's performance is, increasingly, replacing other attempts to structure the behaviour of members. Rather than having numerous behaviour rules, it is far better to concentrate on what outputs are wanted and let individuals work out their own way of getting there. For this reason, and because some people are asking for less direction and more evaluation, let us look briefly at some typical end-result variables. However, we must remember that generalizing about them is difficult as they are specific to a particular organization. More importantly, they are useful only if we can measure them quantitatively or qualitatively.

ECONOMIC MEASURES

Profitability

This can be expressed in terms of profits (before or after tax return) on investment; earnings per share; profit-to-sales ratios; etc. It is the central measure of performance in a business. By having a central measure, businesses have a much easier task in relating organizational, intervening and end-result variables than a government department does, where there is no single, universally recognized measure of performance. Profit has the further advantage that it is readily understood, even by the least gifted of employees—it may not mean very much in terms of motivation, but everybody understands roughly what profit means, even if they do not know what it is for. Even non-profit organizations resort to profit (euphemistically described as 'surplus') as a viable end-result variable.

As profit is expressed numerically, it is possible, in establishing objectives, to express this end result specifically (e.g., 'an increase in group profit of 12 per cent after taxes within five years').

Share of the target market

This end-result variable may be expressed in financial terms, unit volume or market standing. However it is described, it has the advantage that it, too, is readily understood. If we have 49 per cent of the target market, then we know a great deal more about our potential and relative competitive position than if we have no idea what our market share is.

Productivity

This is probably the most controversial measure of results because of the emotional overtones it has for management and employees. Where units are produced in short time-spans, the motivational advantage of this end-result criterion is clear—feedback is available. People need to know where they stand and what they have produced.

Where possible, productivity should be expressed as a ratio of inputs to outputs (e.g., 30 units per worker per 8 hour day). Beware of false cross-cultural comparisons; with different markets and technological under-utilization, such international comparisons may not stand statistical scrutiny.

Productivity measures (as performance criteria) are appearing more and more in government agencies, although there are many civil servants for whom performance criteria are difficult to establish. I would not accept that as an excuse. We will not be able to liberate people from a lot of trivial behaviour controls until our information systems reliably assess their performance in terms of 'outputs' or 'ends'.

Physical and financial resources

Financial results may be expressed in a variety of ways, depending on the company—capital structure, new issues of shares, cash-flow, working capital, dividend payments, debtors, creditors, etc.

Physical resources may be described in terms of square metres, fixed costs, units of production, etc.

HUMAN AND SOCIETAL MEASURES

End results for the human and societal ambitions of an organization have had an uninspiring history. To some extent, this is because the relationship between indicators such as employee satisfaction and the 'hard' data such as profit, surplus, and productivity or service level has been difficult to establish. Hence, the human measures have led to a 'So what?' effect—'We did have a turn-over of staff of 25 per cent in the same period, but we produced a profit of 30 per cent after tax anyway.'

More recently, by linking organizational, intervening and end-result variables, the importance of the human variables has been established empirically. For example, formal reward systems (formal structure) that underpay staff lead to increased dissatisfaction (intervening variable) and good people leave (end result). (We return to this in the next section.)

Traditionally, the information collected in order to assess the human condition has been end-of-period or end-result data. This includes turn-over of staff, sickness rates, absenteeism, days lost in industrial disputes, etc. Most of these data point to a need for shorter-term indicators (intervening variables). Attitude surveys, surveys of managers and quarterly statistics on turn-over, etc., reduce the time-span between the end result and the intervening variables so that corrective action can begin earlier.

Market-research surveys, with sub-categories of public responsibility, public awareness, etc., can provide data on the corporate image. Image data are important to organizations selling consumer products or providing a service. Not surprisingly, consumer-durable manufacturers spend vast sums each year assessing and promoting various parts of their image and that of their products.

Public responsibility has been more difficult to assess—scholarships supported, sponsorship of the arts, donations to charities, secondments of personnel, are all common indicators of what an organization is doing for society. Ironically, most government organizations are assumed to be doing something for society already and we tend not to assess them on these criteria. Conversely, most corporations are assumed to be living off society and therefore must establish that they are responsible 'citizens'. And it is usually forgotten that private companies do provide most employment.

Intervening variables

By taking the organizational, intervening and end-result variables together, we can overcome many of the previous problems faced by the diagnostician. The three sets of variables provide a check-list by which the processes which have occurred to date in any organization may be understood and compared with the experience of other organizations.

Intervening variables introduce time into the analysis because they are concerned with the *now* of interpersonal and intrapersonal factors which affect collective behaviour.

What are the possible intervening variables? The most frequently cited fall into three groups:

- Managerial
- Interpersonal
- Intrapersonal

MANAGERIAL INTERVENING VARIABLES

- Leadership
- Managerial style
- Power
- The balance between task and maintenance orientations
- Philosophies—values and beliefs
- Decisions
- Communications

These variables attempt to encapsulate the *exemplary* behaviours of managers, and hence their influence (on the actors) throughout the organization. Not all managers are leaders; indeed very few are leaders in the sense in which I use the term in Chapter 10. Most of the managerial influence derives from the way they behave day to day, the way task and maintenance are balanced, the way power is used (or not), and the way decisions are made (or not), strategies clarified, and values and beliefs (philosophies) articulated, demonstrated and communicated.

One important influence on behaviour in organizations is its culture. This represents values, beliefs, customs and the media by which values and beliefs are communicated and reinforced. All organizations have a culture, which is the sociological product of *all* the variables I have discussed in this chapter. As stated earlier, it is erroneous to assume that culture is a variable that managers can manipulate at will (see Chapter 6).

However, the managerial intervening variables do include managers' attempts to articulate *their* preferred values, philosophies and beliefs. And because these values and beliefs do have the potential to influence the culture of the organization, it is sensible to articulate what they are. Put another way, as mentioned earlier, successful organizations do seem to have clearly articulated values and beliefs. Thus it is the degree to which those values and beliefs are articulated and communicated that I am isolating here as an intervening variable, *not* the culture of the firm. The culture of the firm clearly is important in explaining the overall behaviour of that firm, but it has limited diagnostic value in comparative analyses because, by definition, it is peculiar to that firm.

INTERPERSONAL INTERVENING VARIABLES

Cooperation is the only variable that has consistently been shown to relate to performance positively. The degree of perceived 'teamwork', the degree of assistance one group of actors gives to another, is encapsulated in this concept. The opposite would be the degree of destructive conflict or non-team-work.

All social systems depend on cooperation. They also depend on conflict. Constructive conflict energizes activity and stimulates creativity or action. Destructive conflict, by definition, destroys. This variable assesses cooperation and conflict in a positive sense. High levels of destructive conflict are seen as low levels of cooperation.

INTRAPERSONAL INTERVENING VARIABLES

- Satisfaction with work, challenge, recognition, achievement, performance
- Dissatisfaction with boss, working conditions, peers, security, salary

In any organization, there will be positive and negative information on how the actors feel *now*. At any time some 15 to 20 per cent will be feeling low, or dissatisfied with the organization—sometimes over specific issues but usually because of a vague feeling that all is not well in the land. Similarly, at any time most of the actors will feel satisfied, challenged, rewarded and stretched, but a certain number of them will feel let down by the lack of excitement in their work. These feelings about work *now* can directly link to end-result variables both now and in the longer term.

There is a massive literature on what satisfies a person at work and what does not. One persistent approach is that satisfaction is an overall feeling that I have about my work. This overall feeling is often called 'morale'. A second, and more popular, theory is that specific characteristics (e.g., challenge, recognition, growth, autonomy) of the situation and job produce satisfaction (or non-satisfaction); thus one set of characteristics make me happy and enthusiastic about my work, while a second set of specific characteristics (e.g., boss, structure, peer group, job security, salary, working conditions) make me dissatisfied or unhappy about my work. This two-factor theory is highly controversial but, like many controversial theories, is extremely useful in practice.

My own view is that satisfaction must relate to the goals of the individuals involved. I therefore go back to Chapter 1 and to the profiles of individuals; if individuals have very strong power goals, then they will be dissatisfied while these goals are frustrated. Similarly, while it is clear that satisfaction is closely related to group cohesion for many people, it is clearly not closely related for those who do not rate relationships highly in ranking their goals.

In addition to these intervening variables, each organization will have other variables that an analyst needs to assess. For example, in some organizations the weather is a variable; in others, one family is itself a major intervening variable. For a comprehensive analysis, diagnosticians need to add whatever variables their data-collection indicates are important. For the present, I have listed below those that recur sufficiently often to warrant a generalized list of both variance and process views.

Organizational	Intervening (process)	End result
Formal structure (strategies, hierarchy, systems, etc.)	Leadership style, power (philosophies, decisions, communications, etc.)	Profitability
		Share of target market
		Growth
Informal structure	Satisfaction	Productivity
Technical system	Dissatisfaction	Customer satisfaction
Individual variable	Cooperation	Employee turn-over
External pressures		Absenteeism and sickness
		Image

Figure 7.3 Variables for analysing an organization

The whole

Fig. 7.3 tabulates the different variables we have discussed. For the person trying to diagnose what is what in an organization, this figure provides a check-list. For each organization, some variables will be more important than others—indeed, very rarely do we need them all to explain the situation we are in. In Chapter 8 (on organization design) I look at different combinations of these variables.

We are much less competent in predicting what will happen if we want to change one of the variables. This is a complex question. I will address it further in Chapter 11 on changing organizations. What we need to recall here is that intervening variables can shift far more quickly than either organizational or end-result variables.

This completes our analysis of how actors come together in organizations. We have analysed individuals, groups and organizations as social systems. Goals, values and beliefs have been collected together into a diagnostic check-list to enable managers to look at the important influences on the actors' behaviours. Organizations are highly complex and managers, through their 'gut' feel and common-sense view of the world, learn to analyse their environment. What I hope this analysis will do is provide clues to the links between the different parts by providing a diagnostic list of possible influences.

Analysis in practice

An analytical exercise always begins with a process approach: How did we get here? Through interviews, examination of documents (organization charts, annual reports, staff journals, sales statistics, industry data) and observing people at work, the analyst begins to get a 'feel' for the situation. Included in this analysis are the end-result data which show a deviation; something is going or has gone wrong—sales have fallen, clients have left, staff have resigned, profits have fallen, etc.

This phase is dominated by the traditional management-consultant approach. Most consultants operate from a model or check-list in order to ensure that they cover all the major influences on the firm. All analysts have biases, and their models reflect those biases; for some, the model is extremely tight and they follow it religiously; for others, thc model is an unarticulated idea distilled from years of experience of what makes an effective organization. What is important at this stage is that analysts try to remain objective—they are collecting information not making a diagnosis. Unfortunately, unlike in the physical sciences, for most of the variables we have no objective measure. Even the end-result variables (profit, productivity, absenteeism, etc.) suffer from subjective inputs.

Initially the analyst's ignorance is dominant. He or she is trying to get a grip on a complex system, so the tendency is to adopt the prevailing view, to become seduced by the views of interviewees. I find it vital to recognize this tendency and to learn to withdraw, to escape from the site for several days. Working with a task force or with another consultant can act as a check on becoming too involved too early. It is vital at this stage to collect information, and not to make judgements.

Of course, it is impossible to remain completely objective. Indeed, some analysts would argue that it is the capacity to live with the situation and become embroiled in it that allows them to sense what is happening. I find I need to refer back to a check-list and to distance myself from the client as the information-gathering phase proceeds. Analysis and diagnosis are primarily intuitive, based on experience and confidence. All that science has provided is the model or check-list, against which comparisons can be made. Yet it is surprising how these models have dominated the analyst's work, to the extent that many analysts talk as though the model *is* reality.

Concurrent with the information gathering is the comparison with other organizations. How does this firm compare with others in the industry? Are others also experiencing the market as threatening? Which firms have grown and/or survived? Which firms dominate the market? Can we get data on them? Is the structure radically different in other firms? And so on. Again I compare against a framework of the organizational, intervening and end-result variables.

It becomes clearer as one proceeds that not all the variables I have discussed in this and other chapters are equally important in explaining the process in a specific case. For example, if we compare the branches of a bank, then the formal structure is likely to be very similar in all branches and may not, therefore, explain the many differences between them. Indeed, in a study of 80 branches of a clearing bank, I found that it was the managerial style of the branch manager and his or her capacity to enthuse, allied to strong informal linkages, that differentiated the branches that performed the best from those that did not do as well.

Reference can also be made to the latest research findings. What are the current theories on inter-variable relationships? While it is important for an academic to keep abreast of the academic journals, it is much easier for the practising manager simply to keep up to date with one popular management journal—the useful research material is eventually distilled from the academic journals to become common property.

Surveys of the employees can provide an extremely valuable snapshot of how they currently feel. Standardized questions will allow important comparison between the focal organization and others; that is, we will be able to see readily whether more people report they are dissatisfied in the firm being analysed than in other organizations. Similarly, we can see whether the employees feel they are more structured and controlled in their behaviour than is normal for this industry. Such comparisons are helpful in retaining a balanced view. It is so easy to fall for interviewee statements like, 'Everyone is fed up with working here', or, 'Head office never lets us do anything', or 'We have the best teamwork in the business.' Climate survey data can be used to check other information against and to facilitate a comparison with other organizations.

Analysts who have worked with such survey data will know the traps:

- The range of responses will be wide, varying not only between different parts of the company but also within the same section.
- Survey data make any attempt to talk about the whole firm difficult. Organizations are loosely linked groups of individuals and the survey data show quite clearly that what is perceived to be happening in the accounts section is radically different from what is perceived to be happening in Fred's group on the factory floor.
- These data are useless unless they can be traced to a unit or a section. Knowing that 30 per cent of the respondents are dissatisfied is interesting but useless information. We need to know where the 30 per cent are.
- It is the stable variables (formal structure, technical system) which provide the background to analysis.

The perception of external pressure will vary enormously from one section to another. Indeed, talking about market pressures as though they impact uniformly on a company (as strategists or economists tend to do) is misleading. There are wide variations in the perceptions of people in different units and even within the same unit. Similarly, satisfaction, dissatisfaction and the influences of the informal structure will be very situational. Here the analyst is looking for the highs and the lows rather than a consistent pattern. For example, the informal cohesion of a group of clerks in an office will look like a 'love-in' compared with the apparent lack of cohesion of a group of staff specialists, yet both levels of cohesion could be perceived by the analyst as positive data.

The linking of the stable and consistent information with the largely situational requires detailed analysis. But such analysis pays dividends; from it, the subtle inter-variable relationships can emerge in a way which is much more difficult to assess from interview data.

The second form of survey data is market-research data. Rarely do we have the luxury of knowing how externals perceive the structure, say, of our firm. Usually we are restricted to product, service or image data. Opinion surveys designed just for the local firm can provide more pertinent data on how customers, suppliers, clients, etc., see the overall management of the firm. But this is rarely an option. Interviews within the industry are the most frequent source of externals' views. As with all other parts of the data-collection, these interviews will be based on what are perceived by the analyst to be the major influences on behaviour.

In the next chapter I look at different combinations of the organizational and intervening variables and attempt to show that different combinations lead to different structures. What should be clear by now is that the combination of the variables in any one organization will be different from that in any other. This has led to what is called a contingency view; that is, there is no one, best way to combine the major influences on the actors but a myriad of possible combinations. The art of good organization design is to choose the design which will best combine these influences so as to produce the most effective results.

Summary

The objective of this chapter has been to bring together the major influences on the behaviour of the firm. There are two major approaches to analysing organizations—process and variance. As most of the earlier parts of this book adopt a process approach, this chapter has concentrated on a variance approach.

When we examine an organization we can bring together the values, beliefs and practices present, and the evidence of those practices, into variables. Using these variables we can examine the same factor in different organizations or within the same organization at different times. The major variables fall into three categories—organizational, intervening and end-result.

The organizational variables are formal structure, informal structure, the technical system, the individual variable and external pressures. As most of these variables have been addressed in earlier chapters the emphasis here has been on the impact of the marketplace—i.e., on external pressures.

To decide whether an organization is effective or not, we need to look at what it produces, what are the outcomes. These are called end-result variables. They include indicators of performance at the end of a fixed period, most frequently the fiscal year. Hence, profitability, productivity, share of target market, return on invested capital, customer satisfaction, image and evidence of industrial harmony (or disharmony) are common end-result variables. These variables tell us how the firm is performing compared with others. Linking the organizational variables to the end-result variables has not been a very productive area of research. For example, what sort of formal structure does lead to greater profit? Put plainly, we do not know. Nor can we say that a very cohesive informal structure will reduce industrial disputes.

However, in recent years, valuable insights have been gained from a third set of variables which return us to the process analysis. These variables moderate, or intervene between, the organizational and the end-result variables. They fall into three groups—managerial, interpersonal and intrapersonal. By combining all sets of variables we can detect important linkages between certain organizational variables, certain moderating or intervening variables and the end results.

The chapter ends with a check-list of the major variables research has shown do occur when we compare organizations. The check-list provides the framework for analysing organizations and for designing relevant structures (see Chapter 8).

References

ON ANALYSING ORGANIZATIONS

Child, J., *Organisation: A Guide to Problems and Practice*, Harper and Row, NY, 1984.

Handy, C., *Understanding Organizations*, 2nd edn, Penguin, London, 1985.

Katz, D. and R. L. Kahn, *The Social Psychology of Organizations*, John Wiley & Sons, NY, 1966.

Mintzberg, H., *Structure in Fives: Designing Effective Organisations*, Prentice-Hall, Englewood Cliffs, NJ, 1983.

FOR A DISCUSSION OF PROCESS AND VARIANCE THEORIES

Mohr, L. B., *Explaining Organizational Behaviour*, Jossey Bass Publishers, San Francisco, 1982.

FOR EXAMPLES OF VARIANCE THEORY

Hunt, J. W., *The Restless Organization*, John Wiley & Sons, Sydney, 1972

Tichy, N. M., *Managing Strategic Change*, John Wiley & Sons, NY, 1983.

FOR EXAMPLES OF PROCESS THEORY

Kanter, R. M., *Men and Women of the Corporation*, Basic Books, NY, 1977.

Pettigrew, A., *The Awakening Giant: Continuity and Change in ICI*, Basil Blackwell, Oxford, 1985.

8. Designing organizations

Introduction

The design of an organization can be derived from an examination of the purposes, objectives and goals for which the organization exists, the patterns and grouping of tasks, the coordination of those tasks, their relationship with the external world and the expectations of the people who do the work.

In this chapter we look at the design of organizations as though it was a rational process. In fact it is a behavioural process, sometimes approaching rationality but mostly moving forwards rather erratically, responding to changes in the expectations of members and of externals in the market. Whatever the design we choose, it is out of date before the ink is dry. The environment for which we designed it and the people who will operate it are dynamic and do not conveniently 'freeze' for designers. The reality is that parts of the design are up to date, others out of date, some clear, some unclear, some supporting each other, some in conflict with the very goals of another system.

Nor surprisingly, good organization design is messy. However, having said that I will look at the major design components on the assumption that they do support each other and that we do have choices; that is, I will ignore the sort of limitations that occur in reality. For example, it may be clear to the designers that a simpler structure could be more effective, yet the owner/manager has theories of his or her own and wants a complex structure. Conversely, it might be clear to an outsider that the company would be more easily managed if it were divisionalized, but the board is power-hungry and wants to maintain control over detail. Or, in the multinational company, it may be clear to a designer that the local firm should be structured another way, but the head office wants uniformity world-wide. In practice, designing organizations is never straightforward. Most have existed for some time and have built-in limitations on what is possible.

Components of structure

The major components of a structure are:

- *Purpose* The reasons (there is nearly always more than one) for the organization's existence.
- *Strategy* Choice of ends.

- *Objectives* The multiple ends of the combination of people, markets, technical systems, managers and administrative systems in a productive whole.
- *Policies* Established (longer-term) guides to action, channels to thinking.
- *Goals* Short-term (e.g., one fiscal term) ends for individuals, teams or units.
- *Tactics* Short-term operating programmes.
- *Tasks* The specific work to be done. Tasks become collected into jobs (e.g., accountant).
- *Functions* The collection of like jobs together into units (e.g., personnel, marketing).
- *Hierarchy* The ranking of functions, jobs and tasks into more and less significant, with an overlay of authority to affect behaviour. Based on control of resources (finance, people, materials, equipment, information, energy).
- *Systems* Required behaviour patterns applied to people, production and information. 'System' refers to a method of proceeding shared by members. It includes rules, regulations and procedures.

Strategy formulation

There is no academically agreed definition of strategy, yet, in the managerial world, the problems with the word seem less divisive. Strategy encompasses long-term objectives, plans of action and the allocation of scarce resources to achieve these objectives. Important strategic questions are: 'What business are we in?', 'What should we be in?', 'What specific actions are necessary to get where we want to go?'

Many of the differences in definitions of strategy centre on time (long, medium or short term) and complexity.

Formulating strategy is a behavioural process by which long-term objectives and the alignment of resources with the environment are determined. This includes the deployment of financial, human, material and informational resources. The major choices are the choice of purpose and the choice of a relationship with the external environment.

Contrary to what is suggested by books on strategy, these choices are rarely neat and sequential but evolve over time in the mind of the founder. Initially he or she may have an idea that, say, selling flowers to commuters would be profitable; strategic choices are flowers, selling, profit, commuters. For the small business, formulating further strategies is unnecessary. It is only after considerable periods of uncertainty or increasing size that a clearer formulation evolves from an imposed rationalizing process. Indeed, research in medium to large firms would support the contention that a rationalization and communication of the formulation does lead to superior performance in terms of profits, sales and the return on assets. However, this is saying little more than that giving meaning to what people are doing is likely to improve performance. Rationality, *per se*, has not been shown to correlate with superior performance, but knowing what we are doing and how we are going to do it does focus the performance of members.

Formulating strategy forces us into a longer-term perspective and a concentration on ends rather than means. Further, it immediately raises the question, 'How will we know if we achieve the long-term objectives?' This means identifying the performance measures, end-result criteria or key result areas as guides to the setting of objectives. A key result area is an identifiable end for which success or failure would have major consequences for the organization. Hence profit, productivity, share of target market, return on assets, earnings per share, standards of service and customer satisfaction are common key result areas in a business.

By emphasizing one or two words (e.g., profitability, quality, service), the key result areas provide a language which focuses attention and effort. So much of the official literature in an organization (such as the statement of long-term objectives) is, for the majority, extremely uninteresting. But the majority can and do focus on the simple and/or single result area and thereby find reasons for their contribution.

LEVELS OF STRATEGY

Strategies will develop at four levels:

- Corporate
  - Purpose, mission
  - Long-term objectives
  - Allocation of resources
  - Organization design
  - Portfolio analysis
- Operating units
  - Divisional plans

  - Strategic business units
  - Business strategy
  - Systems

- Local
  - Departmental plans
  - Product market plans
  - Local personnel plans, etc.

- Personal
  - Career objectives
  - Personal theories, values, beliefs

PURPOSE

The answer to the question, 'What business are we in?', should reveal the purpose or mission of the organization. The answer is important for two reasons. First, it clarifies by over-simplifying. Second, it gives meaning to what members are doing and contributing; therefore its motivational possibilities are great. The statement of purpose is the superordinate, all-encompassing end to which all other objectives are secondary and dependent.

OBJECTIVES

These are future desired states. They transcend standard performance and give direction.

The objectives of a business will usually include some statement about product, some statement about financial obligations (to owners, shareholders, citizens) and some statement of the relationship between the focal organization and the rest of society.

Guidelines in setting objectives are:

- Make them precise, and measurable either quantitatively or qualitatively.
- Keep them few in number (people cannot focus on more than about five).
- Provide more than one; people need a range, so that failure to achieve on one may be compensated for by success on another.
- Remember that objectives inevitably compete against each other, e.g., a productivity objective may compete against an objective of reducing staff turnover by 5 per cent.

- They should stretch performance above the norm (but should not expect the impossible).
- Feedback systems must be designed to let people know how they are doing (key result areas should be linked to each objective).

GOALS AND TARGETS

Objectives usually refer to the end of a period (the calendar year, the financial year, a season). Goals are the intermediate steps to those dates.

The use of the terms 'objectives', 'goals' and 'targets' in management is extremely loose. There are no strict definitions of them. Consistency is the only valid guideline. There are three time dimensions underlying the use of the terms—long, medium and short. Objectives usually refer to longer periods—i.e., 12 months to infinity. Goals are usually medium-term—say quarterly or half-yearly. Targets are short-term—perhaps daily, hourly, weekly or monthly. However, what terminology you use is less important than the fact of indicating to people what is expected of them. Performance that is regularly measured against standards or targets is superior to that where there are no measures.

PROBLEMS OF THE OBJECTIVE-SETTING LOGIC

However, this neat logic breaks down when the objectives, goals and targets shift. The shorter-term (goals and targets) can be more easily modified. Shifts in the objectives tend to reflect the personal objectives of the senior members of the organization; these may shift almost imperceptibly, say from profit to power and prestige, without the change being acknowledged. Yet no comparable shift is made in other parts of the structure.

A second problem for designers arises in those government organizations where objectives are written into Acts of Parliament. Most of the Acts have not been formulated as the vital starting-point for the design of a structure. Instead, legislators have allowed loose, vague, sloppy statements to emerge in order to massage the political processes of Parliament. Objectives such as 'to raise the standard of living', 'to make the environment a better place in which to live' or 'to lift the level of health care in this society' are almost useless for the managers of the relevant public organizations. Rarely is any reliable measure available to the civil servant to test success or failure on these vague poorly designed objectives. The result is that these objectives tend to be ignored and employees in the agencies concerned concentrate on the objectives (e.g., cost) that *can* be assessed. In an ideal world, the government of the day would regularly assess the objectives of its major ministries, departments and agencies to ensure that they remained relevant to government strategy.

A third problem in objective-setting is the clarity (or lack of it) of the objectives. Some organizations exist for rather vague or very long-term objectives. Lack of clarity is probably the most consistent finding on objectives of an external consultant. For example, for reasons which are difficult to understand, the senior management group has not, or will not, clarify and transmit their objectives. This does not mean that people work without objectives—in desperation members lower down the hierarchy will invent objectives of their own. It has always struck me as ironic that some business managers will spend millions on selling their products or services to their consumers or clients, yet spend nothing on selling the objectives of their organization to their employees—i.e., to their best public relations team.

A fourth problem with the logic of determining objectives, goals and targets is that this planning process is a static one imposed on a dynamic system. Inevitably there is a time-lag. The situation changes, yet it takes longer to change the objectives and to communicate that change.

A fifth problem is that some people do not find the objectives, as pronounced by senior managers, very stimulating or uplifting. After all, profit or quality of service are not madly exciting objectives for everyone. It is difficult to formulate statements which will be universally motivational. What excites the top people (e.g., profitability) may have little relevance to the majority, who seek fun, excitement and friendship rather than a dreary concept like the return on invested capital. For this reason, the objectives need to be translated for the audience. The use of statements of beliefs or corporate creeds reflects this problem; they are usually much more compelling documents than statements of objectives.

Finally, there is the theoretical dilemma of what are the *real* objectives of the organization. Do people gathered together in work organizations really have shared objectives, or is there only a motley collection of sub-objectives loosely linked to a sense of purpose such as 'being in the banking business' or 'helping sick people get better'? If this is so, then undeniably the logic of the corporate strategist is naïve in assuming that a tighter linking of purpose to objectives, objectives to goals, goals to targets and targets to performance measures has any relevance to performance.

Organizations do represent loose linkings of individuals' sub-objectives, which may be only vaguely joined in the minds of members to a sense of purpose or 'what we are doing here'. Corporate strategists are naïve if they think that documenting an imposed logic creates order. The neatness of the strategy document is useful only if it is communicated and thereby becomes clear and meaningful to members. This century has been littered with neat statements of vertical logic (purpose, objectives, goals, targets, etc.) which have remained no more than statements gathering dust in office files. The process of making strategic choices is pointless unless those choices are transmitted in order to create purpose for the members. If purpose is clarified, performance can be stimulated.

TACTICS

Objectives require operating plans. The process of planning (e.g., a budget) identifies the key result areas that become the focus of managers. Plans based on budgets delineate the tasks that must be performed to achieve the end results; that is, objectives lead to budgets which lead to plans. A more logical process would be to agree on objectives, devise a plan to achieve them, and finally devise a budget to establish the costs and resources needed to achieve the objectives.

Establishing the tactics and formulating those tactics into plans relies on internally generated data, particularly from the accounting and personnel systems. For this reason, tactical plans are more precise, shorter-term, more time-specific and less value-laden than strategies. Tactical plans are formulated within and in pursuit of goals, and are functional (sales, production, service) rather than corporate.

Many of the tactical plans in organizations are never documented. People pursue their plans through intuition, experience, 'gut feel'. The larger the organization, the greater the tendency for the planning function to be differentiated into a function on its own. Hence corporate planning gained 'star' status in the seventies, but in the less predictable markets of today has suffered some demotion. In contrast, tactical or functional planning continues year in, year out, as individuals establish the tactics they wish to employ to meet their objectives and goals.

TASKS

Linking objectives to tactics involves the identification of what has to occur if objectives are to be reached. This is quite simply the process of establishing what tasks have to be performed, and how those tasks are to be linked or grouped into an action system. Finally, we establish how people are linked into the action system we have designed.

In fact, this never occurs the way logic suggests it should. Most frequently, the trial-and-error processes by which organization members increase their output are driven as much by panic, crises or demanding customers as they are by logic. Tasks which may appear unrelated are linked together simply because Conchita or Bill is 'good' at those tasks. History, markets and individual skills are a more common explanation for the grouping of tasks in small organizations than reason.

However, the rationalization process we all admire ('Let's be efficient!') means that, in time, there *will* be an analysis of tasks in order to determine whether the current task groupings are the most productive. The practical problem is that the logic through which groupings of tasks might occur is not simple. Tasks might be grouped by:

- Expertise
- Function
- Process
- Product
- Time
- Geography
- Customer
- Interdependencies

Tasks are differentiated from one another across these dimensions. The logic of design tells us to link together tasks differentiated by the same factor (e.g., product) to create jobs and functions. Yet tasks are differentiating from one another all the time as people interact. What I do becomes slightly different from what you do simply because we are different people. Further, I will concentrate on those parts of my task which interest me and will tend to concentrate less on the parts that do not interest me. Within weeks, two people doing the same task will show signs of differentiation; that is, the task performancc will be slightly different. Tasks are thus being differentiated continuously in organizations; new tasks are devised, others dropped; new functions are emerging, others are fading. This continuous process of task differentiation is a major influence on the choice of a hierarchy. It is also a reason why an outsider may find the grouping of tasks in an organization rather odd. Groupings are partly based on experience, partly on logic and partly on politics.

JOBS

Tasks become collected into jobs. The process of differentiation means that similarly differentiated jobs do tend to collect together. For example, the mail room gets the packing tasks allocated to it. Subsequently, the delivery function is added, as the delivery is mostly of incoming and outgoing mail and supplies.

The two dominant influences on job design have been *specialization* and *control*. The influence of economists on task specialization led to highly refined jobs, especially at the lowest levels of the hierarchy. Hence, Saleem and Eileen spent their entire day soldering four points on to circuit boards. The consequence of this mania for specialization has been behavioural problems.

The second historical influence on job design has been managerial control. Jobs were designed to minimize the discretionary influence of any individual. Control was seen to be a managerial task.

Nearly half a century's research on job design has led to less restrictive and more motivationally based guidelines for job design. Here is a summary of those guidelines:

- Incorporate variety so that the employee performs a wide range of operations and/or uses a wide range of equipment and procedures (like, for example, the craft worker).
- Create autonomy—powerlessness is a consistent finding in all the studies of poor job design. By autonomy I mean allowing individuals to schedule or have a say in scheduling their work, and in deciding on the way the work is done and quality assessed.
- Ensure that the job is a total piece of work not a sub-set; that is, the job should have a beginning and an end, such that tangible evidence of achievement occurs.
- Design a job in such a way that there are opportunities to learn, grow and develop.
- Provide feedback on performance. Individuals performing the job need to know how they have performed.

For those individuals motivated by a direct link between performance and tangible reward, we could add a fifth guideline:

- Link performance to reward.

One of the risks of writing about job design is the tendency we all have to transfer our own values and goals to everyone else. There are some individuals who like highly programmed jobs. They are individuals who do not want a direct link between their performance and their income. Hence, the final guideline in job designing is to talk to those performing the jobs. Find out what they would like, so that any redesign incorporates their wants. By that simple process commitment to the new design is partly assured.

Choosing hierarchies

Linking tasks and jobs into functions, departments, authority chains and systems is the territory of *hierarchy* and *control systems*. There is a vast literature on the choice of a hierarchy—i.e., the organization tree, chart or organigram. This literature has dominated management thinking for most of the twentieth century. Ironically, it evolved from two very different sources. The first of these was practising managers who looked for guidelines for good design in the later nineteenth and early to mid twentieth centuries—people like Taylor, the Gilbreths, Mooney, Reiley and Urwick. The inspiration for these so-called traditionalist or classical writers was a 'better way'—practical simple explanations for other managers. The second influence on designing hierarchies was a much more academic one. The German sociologist Max Weber analysed hierarchy from the perspective of authority and power. Writing at the turn of the century, he was to provide the most significant theoretical insights into why and how bureaucratic hierarchies develop.

So important has the influence of these two groups on management practice been that I would like briefly to look at what they proposed. (Of necessity I do both the traditional writers and Weber an injustice, so references for further reading are given at the end of the chapter.) Look at your firm, department, ministry, hospital, school, etc., and you will find that its hierarchy reflects a combination of these two views. This is not because these early writers were prophetic. Rather it is because they saw a process which recurs, and described it. And it recurs so frequently that it still dominates the organizations you and I work in, play in and live in. There are two important consequences of this for designers: first, the choice of hierarchy is limited by the sociological process which is occurring; second, as all of us are familiar with the outcomes of this process, we are also blinded by it. Asking us to design new forms of hierarchies may be asking too much.

THE TRADITIONAL GUIDELINES FOR DESIGN

Collecting together the conclusions of this group of management theorists would give us the following guidelines for designing hierarchies:

- There must be clear lines of authority running from the top to the bottom of the hierarchy (*chain of command*).
- No one in the organization should report to more than one line supervisor. Everyone in the organization should know to whom he or she reports and who reports to him or her (*unity of command*).
- The accountability and authority of each supervisor should be clearly defined, *in writing*.
- Responsibility should always be coupled with corresponding authority.
- The responsibility of higher authorities for the acts of their subordinates is absolute (*absolute accountability* of chief executive).
- Authority should be delegated as far down the line as possible.
- The number of levels of authority should be kept at a minimum.
- The work of every person in the organization should be confined, as far as it can be, to the performance of a single leading function (*specialization*).
- Whenever possible, *line* functions should be separated from *staff* functions, and adequate emphasis should be placed on important staff activities.

Line functions are those which accomplish the main objectives or goals of the organization; for example, the production line departments are often called 'operating' departments. Staff functions are those which aid in, or are auxiliary to, the line functions. Members of staff departments (e.g., personnel, administration) provide service advice and integration for line or operating departments.

- There is a limit (e.g., seven) to the number of positions that should be coordinated by the single executive (*span of control*).
- The organization should be as simple and as flexible as possible so that it can be adjusted to changing conditions.

WEBER ON BUREAUCRACY

Quite independent of this managerial approach to hierarchical design was the work of Max Weber. Where he differed from the management writers was in his superb analysis of authority in hierarchies, an issue the management theorists largely ignored.

Weber's analysis, which looked at a sociological process, *not* the map of a tree, found bureaucracies shared characteristics:

- Official business is conducted on a continuous basis.
- It is conducted in accordance with stipulated rules, characterized in an administrative agency by three interrelated attributes:
  - The duty of each official to do certain types of work is delimited in terms of impersonal criteria.
  - Officials are given the authority necessary to carry out their assigned functions.
  - The means of compulsion at the disposal of officials are strictly limited and the conditions under which the employment of these means is legitimate are clearly defined.
- Every official's responsibility and authority are part of a hierarchy of authority. Higher offices are assigned the duty of supervision; lower offices the duty to obey. However, the extent of supervision and the conditions of legitimate appeal may vary.
- Officials and other administrative employees do not own the resources necessary for the performance of their assigned functions, but are accountable for their use of these resources. Official business and private affairs, and official revenue and private income, are strictly separated.
- Offices cannot be appropriated by their incumbents like private property that can be sold and inherited. (This does not preclude various rights, such as pension claims, regulated conditions of discipline and dismissal, etc., but such rights serve—in principle, at least—as incentives for the better performance of duties. They are not property rights.)
- Official business is conducted on the basis of written documents.

Weber's analytical insight led to a multitude of sociological studies of bureaucracy. His work has become a major reference in any course on design, whether in business or government. Yet he is blamed for promoting 'bureaucratization', which, for some people in the field of organizational behaviour, is like promoting cancer. 'Bureaucratization' is a term often used very loosely, and it is sometimes difficult to know what those using it actually mean. But worse, it points to a poor reading of Weber by his critics. Bureaucracies (private or public) still dominate our lives at work. Some researchers consider them to be the most efficient hierarchical form.

CONTINGENCY THEORY

This approach grew out of attempts to understand why these common characteristics of hierarchies evolve, rather than simply describing them after they have evolved. In brief, hierarchies evolve in response to a multitude of influences. These include the pressures from the market, the choice of product or service, the sort of people involved, the style of the chief executive, etc.; that is, the hierarchy is *the product* of a process involving a variety of internal and external influences. If one wishes to design a hierarchy then one should begin with an analysis of those influences.

The concept of contingency also implies that there is no one, absolute 'best' design; rather, there is a multitude of possibilities and the best or preferred choice will be contingent on the situation being analysed. Universal models designed to suit all situations are therefore rejected. And this is consistent with the fact that most organizations are networks of a variety of bits of design rather than conforming, as one entity, to a particular model. So we might find units of bureaucracy, units of matrix structures, units with project teams, units with extremely loose, almost *ad hoc* structures—and all of these within, say, the same oil company. In this sense, the contingency theorists merely reflected the findings of hundreds of researchers. There are common elements in the hierarchies of different organizations but there are also very many differences peculiar to the local situation.

From this very practical perspective, the first step in choosing a hierarchy is collecting the relevant data. And it is this approach which I will use here. As would-be designers we should begin by analysing those factors or variables which have been found to affect the evolution of a hierarchy.

Design variables for a hierarchy

- History
- Objectives
- Time orientation
- Task differentiation
- People involved (including experience, motives and numbers)
- Size

- Market (or external) pressures
- Technical system
- Possible integrators
- Managerial style

Only after an exhaustive analysis should we consider a design for the overall hierarchy. Let us examine these variables in more detail.

HISTORY

What has happened so far in any business organization gives us insights into the structural possibilities that have survived and those that have been tried and dropped. Organization design does not begin from scratch; 99 times out of 100 the organization exists already and there is a history and a culture which facilitate and limit the choices. Important historical considerations are the managerial style and philosophy so far; the possible influences of family or founders; the geographic locations of the parts of the organization; its segmentation and size; the history of customers/clients, products, services, pricing, marketing, etc.; and the history of support functions, e.g., personnel, accounting, maintenance, etc.

Acquisitions, take-overs, mergers, expansions and contractions all impact on the values and beliefs dominant in the members' minds and thereby influence the design choices. For example, there are a large number of organizations currently attempting to introduce performance measures for the second or third time, largely because the last attempt (was it called management by objectives?) failed. Such experiences shown up by an analysis of the process so far do restrict the possibilities now. On the positive side, though, what structural mechanisms (hierarchical forms, systems) have been successful? What sort of people seem to succeed? What are the values surrounding success?

History is specific to an organization and that is where the designer's analysis begins. However, as it is specific I will not refer to it when looking at hierarchical types: hierarchical types are generalized models of a particular form and generalized models are not based on generalized histories but on generalized product/market linkages. For this reason, the generalized hierarchical models never occur in the forms I discuss here. History makes reality a much more messy (and interesting) subject.

OBJECTIVES

Are the corporate objectives clear, unclear, partly clear? How precisely do other employees know the ends? Vague objectives make design more tentative. Conversely, the clearer the ends, the easier it is to choose the hierarchical form and the integrating systems.

TIME ORIENTATION

What is the time-span necessary for task completion—long (over 12 months), medium (6 months), or short (day to day, week to week, or shift to shift)? The longer the time, the more complex the design.

TASK DIFFERENTIATION

How are the tasks essential for reaching the objectives categorized? (This is traditionally referred to as the *division of work*). Is there a high level of differentiation? The greater the differentiation of tasks, the more complex the integrative mechanisms.

Tasks may be differentiated according to:

- Product (e.g., cars, soap)
- Skill (e.g., surgeon, anaesthetist)
- Territory (e.g., London, Paris, New York, Sydney)
- Process (e.g., polishing, packaging)
- Customer (e.g., retail, wholesale)
- Technology (e.g., batch production, mass production)
- Time (e.g., shift or non-shift workers)

PEOPLE INVOLVED

Different sorts of motivations and skills attract people to different organizations and occupations. Traditionally, design of structure meant *ignoring* the people. What sort of people? How many? What experience? What qualifications and skills? What motivation profiles? The presence of a large proportion with high security goals, or low tolerance of ambiguity, or a large proportion of older employees, may lead to a more defined hierarchy. Low security goals lead to looser hierarchies. High social needs may indicate a group-based hierarchy. Strong power goals may indicate centralized control, etc.

SIZE

Size can be defined by a number of indicators. The most common is the number of employees. Other indicators are net profit, turn-over (of sales, services or fees), fixed assets, total expenditure, surplus, etc.

Size defined in terms of the number of actors has many design implications. The greater the size the more levels of management there are; the more rules and regulations replace managers as controllers of behaviour, the more communication is filtered, and the greater is the consequent development of information systems to extract the information. In very large organizations (over 10 000 people), lines of communication become extended and distorted. Conversely, the smaller organization (under 500) is limited in its options by the resources (financial) it can attract and by the less developed state of its support functions (e.g., personnel, strategy formulation, planning).

Size has a major impact on the type of hierarchy one can design. For example, 4000 employees allow regions or divisions and a well-staffed head office with divisional-office support functions. Thereafter it is possible to consider divisions within divisions and to question the relevance of the head office support functions as more differentiation of day-to-day functions occurs in the divisions (or the regions, strategic business units or subsidiary companies).

The size of the market(s) is also relevant to the choice of hierarchy. For example, in many countries like Canada, Sweden, Australia and South Africa the use of the divisional hierarchical form may be questionable, simply because the size of the local market (number of customers) is relatively small. However, by expanding into exports these local organizations can adopt very different hierarchies.

MARKET (OR EXTERNAL) PRESSURES

Market pressures are the major influence on design. We need to know how strong the market pressures are, and how far the pressures penetrate the organization. For example, sales departments are very exposed to uncertain markets, while a production department may be less exposed. We should look at the following dimensions of the environment:

- *Complexity* How many different activities are there for us to deal with in the environment? How diverse are they? How many markets? What is the industry structure?
- *Certainty* How predictable is the direction of change in the market? How predictable is the rate of change? How predictable is the tone (friendly or hostile) of the market-place?

- *Relations with other organizations* What are the relations between the organization and other organizations? Are requests from others predictable? If so, can routine responses be used to those requests? Are the relations direct or indirect? If indirect, then it is much more difficult to plan the response. How dependent is the organization on other organizations? The more dependent it is, the more tasks will be devoted to maintaining relationships. How much power (size, control of resources, financial links, capital invested, sales, number of employees) are there, compared with other organizations? Are there dominant outsiders or are they powerless? Are outsiders dispersed (e.g., airline passengers) or linked (e.g., stockbrokers, through a trade association)?

TECHNICAL SYSTEM

What plant and equipment is there? Is the influence of the technical system on behaviour very large, average or negligible? What restrictions does the technology place on design? A £40 m paper-making machine places extraordinary restrictions on structural design. One typewriter places very little restriction on the overall organizational design. The more complex the technical system, the more specialization of skills and functions and, subsequently, the greater will be the pressure on integrative mechanisms.

POSSIBLE INTEGRATORS

Having examined the objectives, major tasks, people, technology and market, we need to know what tasks need to be integrated. Some will need close integration, while others may have no bearing on one another at all. Integrative mechanisms are many and varied—from accounting systems to task forces, from liaison officers to industrial spies. Fig. 8.1 lists a range of integrative mechanisms for possible use as either external uncertainty and/or members'/actors' goal expectations change.

MANAGERIAL STYLE

What sort of management style best suits the combination of objectives, tasks, markets and people?

The choice of hierarchy

Having analysed the history, objectives, tasks, people, size, technology

External certainty →					External uncertainty →	
Vertical information system	• Centralized hierarchy • Rules • Sanctions • Resource controls	• Centralized line and staff hierarchy • Rules • Sanctions • Planning • Resource controls • Assistant to . . . • Executive assistants	• Centralized hierarchy • Functional authority • Sanctions • Planning • Resource controls • Training • Cost-reduction programme • Electronic data processing • Centralized records (personnel inventory)	• Divisionalized hierarchy • Planning • Resource controls • Training • Management by objectives • Management information system • Market research • Decentralization of personnel, purchasing, etc.	• Conglomerate hierarchy • Training • MbO • Changed goals • Surplus resources • Management information system • Consolidation of divisions	• Dual-authority hierarchy • Planning • Reduced HQ staff • Financial-resource controls • Training • Short-term end results only • Management information system • Subsidiary companies • Participative consultation
Lateral information system	• Committees	• Committees • Direct informal contact	• Committees • Direct contact • Liaison officers	• Executive committee • Task forces • Liaison officers • MbO assist. • Corporate planning department • Management consultants	• Head-office task forces • Liaison officers • Corporate planning dept. • Management consultants	• Semi-autonomous groups/project teams • Functional teams • Resources management • Project managers, team leaders • Functional internal consulting service
People's expectations		Imposed control High structure goals Medium achievement goals →				Self-control Low security goals High social goals High achievement goals

Figure 8.1 Methods of integration as affected by uncertainty and expectations

and environment, we must avoid the tendency to jump to instant hierarchical solutions. I find it very useful to use a simple *task analysis matrix*—it compels me to look again at the data I have collected and to relate to it analytically.

TASK ANALYSIS MATRIX

I draw a simple task analysis matrix (see Fig. 8.2 for a simplified example). At the top of the matrix I list the major tasks that have to be performed (buy wheat, grind wheat, package flour, for example) in getting the resources in and out of the firm. On the vertical axis I list the design variables. On the matrix itself, I note the data I have acquired about each of the variables and link these to the major tasks. Through this process, I can avoid designing a hierarchy which is incompatible with either the tasks or one of the major influences on the choice of hierarchy. For example, a superb piece of design based on most of the major influences may ignore the fact that the sort of people employed could not implement or operate that design.

After analysing the major tasks, I am able to see which tasks have sufficiently similar reports to allow them (and the people) to be linked together into a function. With additional analyses, functions can be linked to departments, divisions, national units, etc. The final design is thereby built up from the data rather than thrown down from an overview which, of necessity, reduces the variable information. Clearly, whichever approach one uses, compromises are inevitable.

Selecting the form of hierarchy is the most important step in design. There are numerous hierarchical types and even more hybrids. To

	Task 1	Task 2	Task 3	Task 4	Task 5, etc.
Objectives					
Time					
Differentiation					
External pressures					
People					
Technical system					
Size					

Figure 8.2 Task analysis matrix

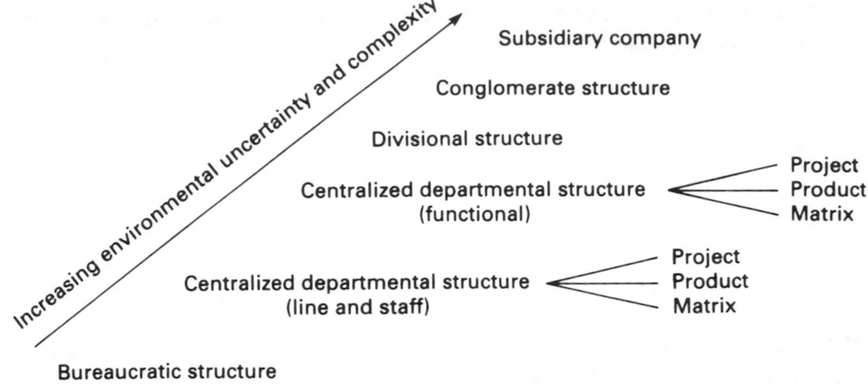

Figure 8.3 A continuum of hierarchical types

make my explanation easier to follow, I have selected six well-known examples of hierarchies. They are presented in Fig. 8.3, positioned on a continuum from market certainty to market uncertainty; that is, the major influence on the relevant type of hierarchy alters with market uncertainty. However, we must remember that there will be examples of different types of hierarchy within any organization, simply because perceived market uncertainty varies from function to function. Fig. 8.1 includes the second major influence, the changing expectations of people and, using both variables (certainty/uncertainty and changing expectations), lists the increasing use of integrative mechanisms as these two important variables change. While the six examples of hierarchical types on Fig. 8.3 are similar to the six columns of Fig. 8.1, they are not intended to be identical.

INTEGRATION

The integrating systems are the second important characteristic of a hierarchy; some (e.g., task forces and liaison functions) are intended to hold the structure together *laterally*; others (authority systems) attempt to hold it together *vertically*. Fig. 8.1 also shows a major redistribution of power from the centralized bureaucratic structure to the team-based structure. However, as I have suggested already, whether power devolves or not is highly contentious. Fig. 8.1 is not meant to indicate exclusive categories. It is very possible that some of the integrative mechanisms will occur in structural forms in which I have not included them. What the table aims to show is the increasing complexity of design issues as size, uncertainty and people's expectations change to less predictable patterns.

Vertical integration

While much has been written on the allocation of work to groups, departments, functions and divisions, less attention has been given to coordinating or integrating those units. There are many vertical and lateral techniques for integration. Among the most common vertical devices are rules, procedures, authority systems and planning.

- *The hierarchy of authority* Limited resources always restrict the decision-making process. For this reason, some managers have the authority to control more resources than others. In this way, managers lower down in the hierarchy are compelled to integrate with their superiors by having to ask their superiors to approve some of their actions. Such requirements result in managerial control.
- *Rules and procedures* These are mechanisms for standard behaviour, what some writers refer to as 'procedural programmes'. A stimulus can induce a programmed response from members of the organization. For example, the blow-off whistle is the stimulus, and stopping work is the behaviour programme. Increased market uncertainty means more processing of information through the hierarchy. There will be more requests from subordinates for guidance, and the traditional exception rule, whereby only deviations from the expected norm are reported, becomes less operative. There are numerous tactics we can adopt to meet this. They fall into two major categories, and the tactics of both categories are integrative.
- *Delegation* This means trying to do the following:
  - Refer fewer decisions upwards for approval.
  - Divisionalize or regionalize by product.
  - Allocate resources to the units so that they will not be found wanting—allow them more people, money and materials than are required immediately, in order to allow the unit to handle the highs in demand (management has to ignore slack resources during low demand).
  - Employ more independent managers who will make decisions on their own.

- *Devise mechanisms for handling more information* It may be possible to introduce the following:

– Management information systems, to improve the vertical flow of information.
– Matrix structures, project teams or *ad hoc* organizations.

- *Systems and planning* By developing standardized systems and plans as behaviour programmes, the integration is made easier. Thus, the railway produces a schedule of train departures in order to integrate its services and the numerous trains at its disposal. The Second World War gave a great impetus to highly intricate methods of assisting the planning process, and the increased complexity of our society has added to these techniques.

Lateral integration

The more complex the structure, the more horizontal differentiation occurs and the more lateral links cannot be left to chance. Formal and informal links are made to hold the differentiated mass together. Sometimes this is well-nigh impossible (often because of size) and those with authority decide to separate the units, to admit the managerial problems are too great and to sell off or separate completely one or more units from the larger mass, e.g., as separate companies or separate government agencies.

- *Formal lateral links* These include committees, task forces, consultants, attitude surveys, liaison officers, planning departments, project teams, matrix structures, training programmes, conferences, sales meetings, annual dinners, etc.
- *Informal lateral links* These are even more numerous simply because most frequently they occur informally between individuals. There is only one constraint on them; that is that the information must pass verbally which makes informal links more difficult between, say, London and Birmingham than within one location.

Direct contact is the most frequent solution to lateral problems. If this fails, formalized solutions appear, usually following a crisis—liaison roles, 'assistants to . . .', task forces, etc. On a larger scale, product managers, divisional units and matrix structures are clues that lateral links have been (or are) a major problem. If they continue to be a major problem, the next step could be to separate the unit or division totally from the rest, to segment that part of the organization, give it all the support functions (accounting, personnel, marketing, purchasing, maintenance, etc.) and run it as a separate business. The product–

market relationship, geography, size (in terms of number of people) and the disadvantages of sharing functions are all important influences on hiving off one part from the total mass.

Encouraging and rewarding positive lateral relations allows the members of the organization to make more decisions and process more information without overloading the vertical information system; that is, decisions can be pushed down to the task force, committee or division, rather than being controlled and taken centrally. In theory, the process improves the quality of the decisions because those 'on the spot', with the necessary knowledge, make the decisions. A bonus is that job satisfaction and motivation are likely to increase.

One flaw in using strong lateral relationships to solve time and market pressures is that it takes a lot of work to convert a collection of laterally linked individuals into an effective decision-making team. Often group and interpersonal skills are poor and the well-planned lateral linking device fails. Effort must be put into facilitating interpersonal processes before the decisions are made. (The failure of so many committees to produce effective lateral thinking is evidence of the importance of interpersonal skills.)

A second problem for the hierarchically flat, but laterally differentiated, organization is how to obtain overall task integration without reducing the inter-group differences that lead to effective group performance. As task uncertainty increases, the departments performing sub-tasks become more differentiated because sub-tasks vary in uncertainty, language, training, goals and people. Hence, at the very time that inter-departmental cooperation is essential, it becomes more difficult to achieve. Clearly, it cannot be left to chance and vertical linking devices may have to be strengthened. It is over issues like these that the loose/tight dichotomy of control is a useful distinction.

The aim of integrating roles is to reduce differences, increase trust and link the separate parts laterally. By its verv nature this violates the 'unity of command' principle of traditional designs. However, there is no evidence that multiple authority (as in many lateral linking or integrating roles, e.g., project managers) or role conflict *does* lead to ineffectiveness.

Combinations of the design variables

Figs 8.4 to 8.13 consider, in each case, one idealized structural form and all the design variables—the nature of objectives, time orientation, task

Objectives	Clear only to the power élite. Functions or duties override objectives as ends.
Time orientation	Long-term, even infinite.
Task differentiation	Low. All tasks are distinct sub-sets of the primary task—e.g., collect taxes, provide health care, supply water and sewerage, administer life assurance.
People	Attracts people with goals of safety and predictability. The highly prescribed rules, regulations and authorities are reinforced and extended by the very people who work there, because they want prescription, definition, etc. This makes it very difficult to change the structure. High achievers are attracted, but risk-taking is low.
Technical system	Traditionally, low influence from plant, equipment and physical constraints. The computer is changing this and affecting the control systems. It is feasible that the computer will become the major control on behaviour.
External pressures	Low. This is one of the important conditions for this structural form. A second condition is a monopolistic position, or at least only two or three suppliers in the market. A third condition is large size. Structural devices (such as complaints departments, inaccessibility of people, form-completion techniques, etc.) are used to 'ricochet' off complaints or threats. The influence of the market is therefore minimized in terms of its penetration.
Managerial style	Highly centralized and task-oriented.
Integration	• The hierarchy collects vertical information. • Committees collect lateral information. • Job descriptions, rules, regulations and formalized procedures ensure that people stick to their prescribed roles. Sanctions may be used to reinforce the rules. Justice is handled through appeals tribunals. Impersonal controls are vital to this structural form.

Figure 8.4 Bureaucratic structure

differentiation, people, technical system and external pressures. They also suggest the integrative mechanisms appropriate to each form, and the managerial style likely to prevail. They suggest a macro-view and a one-structure form which, as I have already said, occurs rarely. However, Figs 8.4 to 8.13 do allow us to look at the different combinations of the variables and to illustrate specific forms from bureaucracy to matrix.

BUREAUCRATIC STRUCTURE

Fig. 8.4 outlines the conditions which lead logically to a bureaucratic structure. If any of the following changes occur, the other variables will get out of kilter:

- The objectives change.

- External pressures increase and penetrate the system.
- People less motivated by structure (or more motivated by risk-taking) are employed.
- The computer changes the control system.

Signs of breakdown in the structure are seen first in a hasty attempt by those in positions of power to reinforce the legitimacy of the structure as it was (e.g., governments use police to suppress violence). A second sign is a search for new integrative mechanisms (e.g., management information systems) to hold together that which is falling apart. A third sign of structural problems is continual cost-reduction campaigns.

The first positive sign that those in power recognize that the structure must be altered is when they begin structural experiments with task forces or project teams. A second sign is when managers realize that the market can be influenced and the marketing function emerges—initially with logos, tentative advertising, and amateurish public relations efforts, but eventually with a fully-fledged department called *marketing* (perhaps replacing an 'enquiries', or 'PR' or 'complaints' function). But by the time this happens, the formal structure is being moved away from a bureaucratic form—it has acquired the characteristics of a centralized departmental structure, in which departmental positions show a greater degree of specialization and differentiation. If pressures for change continue, then the line and staff departmental hierarchy shifts to a functional authority structure.

CENTRAL FUNCTIONAL STRUCTURE

In this form, functional specialization (finance, marketing, personnel, production, etc.) has led to an increase in functional delegation, both laterally and vertically. (By 'functional' I mean that authority is based on the function—c.f. line and staff, where line executives have authority to make decisions and staff advise. In a functional authority structure those with authority for a function can tell others what to do in that function.

Characteristics of the centralized functional structure are:

- A very high degree of centralized decision-making.
- Positions are defined but are more influenced by who occupies them—the structure is less sacrosanct.
- The major difference from the bureaucratic structure is the serious questioning of a whole range of rules, controls and pieces of paper.

Objectives	Much clearer and certain.
Time orientation	Medium-term.
Task differentiation	Increasing task differentiation, leading to all the traditional functions of a business.
People	Structure goals still strong for the majority of employees, but more achievers prepared to take risks. The number of people may be very large, and for this reason the organization is seen as bureaucratic.
Technical system	May be exceedingly complex, but is programmable and repetitive, as in mass production, oil refining, large-scale batch production, computer-based services.
External pressures	Medium to high.
Managerial style	Task-oriented, but more dependent on the style of the chief executive than the climate of the organization.
Integration	• The hierarchy remains the major vertical integrator. • Standardized controls over people, materials, money and equipment, but managers may interpret them for local consumption. • Complex computer-based management information systems have largely replaced hand-written forms. • The increasing breakdowns in lateral information flows have led to more head-office task forces and integrators who visit different locations of the firm.

Figure 8.5 Central functional structure

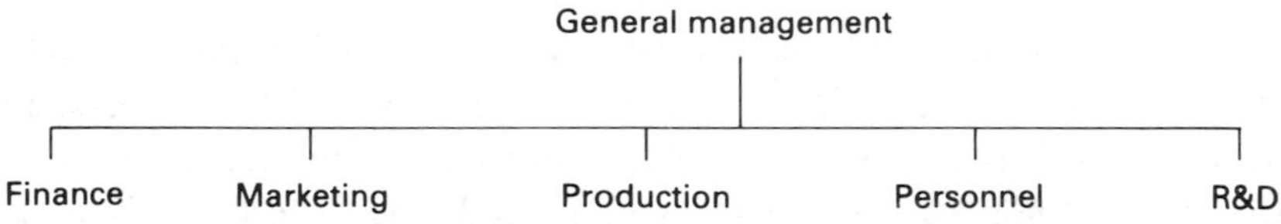

Figure 8.6. Task differentiation in a centralized functional structure

This is a period when structural consultants may be invited to comment on, if not change, the structure.

Fig. 8.6 shows a section of the centralized, highly differentiated hierarchy found in most large business organizations (functions, not positions, are named). Functions which are likely to be differentiated as third-level functions or departments are:

- Cost accounting
- Data processing
- Industrial relations
- Corporate relations (with governments)
- Scheduling
- Training
- Maintenance of plant/office
- Purchasing

If external pressures increase further (clearer objectives but shorter time-spans), the functional model of a hierarchy undergoes periods of breakdown, while members attempt to meet the increased uncertainty through a highly centralized structure. Signs of the increasing inability of the people or inadequacy of the structure to meet the information requirements are:

- The planning of even more elaborate management information systems.
- Increasing use of liaison (integrator) positions (assistants to ..., deputy managers, personal secretaries, task forces, teams).
- Increasing demands for more vertical information, in addition to that required by the management information system (and invariably an inability by those in power to understand why subordinates have not got the data).
- A contraction (centralization) of authority, which worsens the situation as it breaks communication channels and annoys subordinates.
- Recognition that *lateral* information flows need attention.
- Use of project teams, management committees, etc., and a sharp rise in time spent in meetings.
- Increasing evidence of employee dissatisfaction, which is often blamed on the training courses.

The first sign of an offensive attack on a threatening market-place (as opposed to a defensive stand) is a regrouping of tasks on a product or market basis. Divisionalization often follows as the alternative option. However, if the firm is large and diversified, then the functional authority structure may no longer be tenable. The painful result is usually structural change—maybe to a divisional structure, a project structure, or a matrix structure. More likely, the structural change is to a messy-looking hybrid of many structural forms. As a divisional structure is increasingly common, we will look at that form first.

DIVISIONAL STRUCTURE

The appearance of this structure type arises from four major changes in the highly centralized structures:

- Objectives are clearer, quantifiable and directly related to survival.
- Tasks are clearly differentiated, most frequently by products (see Fig. 8.8). Food, property, cars, building materials.
- There are much higher levels of environmental uncertainty.

Objectives	Clear, but multiple and product-based.
Time orientation	Much shorter time dimension, with rapid changes occurring because of innovations of many competitors. Product innovation is a constant activity.
Task differentiation	High, usually (but not always) on a product base. Each division is quite different in product, manufacture, market and usage from others (e.g., soap compared with cars, compared with property). Diversification is now a permanent search for growth. Coordination will become a central issue in this structural form, but products provide logical units to break up the structure (see Fig. 8.8).
People	Much lower concern for structure, safety and security, and more willing to take risks. Achievement goals are stronger among senior executives, demands for involvement greater. The necessity for structural innovation is greater. Psychologically, size has been reduced by collecting people into product groups.
Technical system	High technological component, ideally product-based (this condition is often the major stumbling-block in choosing a divisional form). Product-based means the equipment used for property development is not used in soap manufacture, etc. Divisions *ideally* have their own separate technical systems.
External pressures	High, variable, uncertain. The shift to more decentralized day-to-day control in the divisions comes initially as a response to the increasing vertical-information needs of the separate product groups. Decentralization of day-to-day issues is essential, although, in fact, centralization of information usually increases.
Managerial style	Difficult to generalize as we now have several different structures. But there is a noticeable increase in concern for people, and people or human-relations oriented styles are encouraged.
Integration	Separate divisions operating as cost (or profit) centres lead to the rapid emergence of new devices for more reliable vertical information flows. This is the period of complex management by objectives, head-office task forces and central training programmes, all of which are designed to help satisfy the increasing need for both vertical and even more lateral information flows.

Figure 8.7 Divisional structure

- People have different expectations.

Given these changes, highly centralized structures are not workable. The divisional form of structure is seductive in that it reduces large size to manageable units. It was first developed in the US and subsequently spread to Europe and then the rest of the world. Yet it is not a panacea—there are many problems with this form:

- Divisionalization is inevitably divisive, thereby increasing the need for integrative mechanisms.
- Inter-divisional competition, especially over allocation of funds, is also inevitable, often leading to major political conflicts.
- Employees' identification with the overall organization is likely to decrease because of identification with a division.
- Divisions themselves grow too large and diversified, and no longer have a logical base for grouping products.
- Head office–division conflicts may run rampant in a system in which divisional general managers are told to 'run their own shows' yet are subject to a whole range of head-office guidelines, even if those guidelines are 'suggestions' rather than commands. (As head office controls the future careers of divisional managers, it is inevitable that head-office executives have considerable influence on the divisions.)

If large size within a division makes the divisional form unworkable, it is difficult to return to a purely functional authority structure. Most frequently, the structure becomes a hybrid or mixed structure, and the neat logic of the divisional structure becomes blurred. Divisions may be retained as profit centres, but head-office departments are given functional authority within divisions. Another possibility is a matrix structure whereby a second logic for grouping activities is superimposed on the divisional structure.

Task differentiation in a divisional structure

With reference to Fig. 8.8:

- The head-office functions are given the title director, general manager, or vice-president.
- The major functional differentiation is repeated in each division (see the food division, for example).
- Each division can be run and evaluated as a unit. Within a unit, strategic businesses are identified as SBUs.
- Once operating, divisional structures can divide again—for example, the food division can divisionalize into a non-frozen packaged foods division and a frozen foods division, etc.
- The most important prerequisite for a divisional structure is a standardized information system so that divisions and/or SBUs can be compared.
- Most fights between divisional managers and head office occur because of:

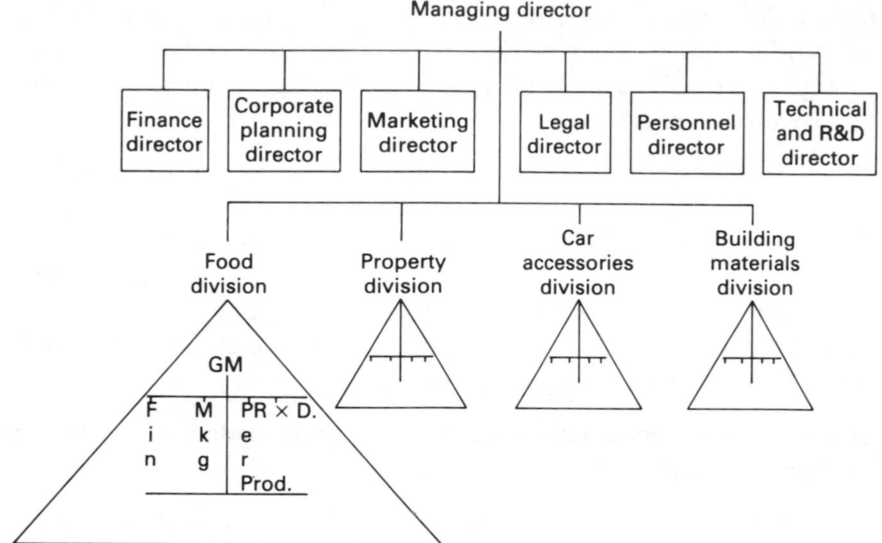

Figure 8.8 Task differentiation in a divisional structure

- The allocation of head-office overheads.
- Head-office interference in the day-to-day running of the division.
- Failure to specify clearly exactly what authority the head-office directors have compared with local functional heads.

Controversial areas must be the subject of clear definitions if conflict is to be minimized.

- Market size is a major problem. The cost of duplicating head-office functions in each division may be prohibitive. A second problem may be the spread of consumers over a vast area.
- Banks, government departments and insurance companies prefer to call geographic divisions 'regions'.

CONGLOMERATE STRUCTURE

A conglomerate is a fairly rare type. Basically it is a very large trans-national divisional structure. It is characterized by:

- Size—large and diversified.
- Multi-divisional—unrelated products.
- Involved in five or six industry categories.
- Usually grows through acquisitions or mergers.
- Sales of several hundred million dollars.
- Simple divisional integrating devices.

The conglomerate consists of many product divisions, each of which sells products to its own market rather than to the other divisions, although there will be internal sales and transfers. The consequences of the diverse activities are:

- A small, highly professional head-office group (compared with an expansive, large group in the divisional form).
- Problems in comprehending the various technologies and markets.
- Independence among the groups, which allows one group to expand operations in its area without affecting other groups.
- A loss of some overall benefits from cooperative effort, but gains in smaller, competitive, manageable units.

The lack of interdependence among major units leads to three important characteristics:

- Major sub-units tend to be self-contained to a considerable degree. The basic organizational unit in conglomerates is the divisional profit centre rather than the functional department. Thus, although the corporate office may provide certain staff services, each product division has nearly all the operating and control functions necessary to do business in its particular industry.
- The main area of interdependence is between the product divisions and the corporate headquarters. Subject to the constraints imposed by overall corporate goals and resources, most divisions in a conglomerate can operate independently of their sister divisions. Thus, comparatively little direct inter-divisional coordination is required.
- Product divisions enjoy considerable independence of the corporate headquarters. Because of the number of broad-range industries encompassed by its product divisions, the corporation is obliged to permit them considerable autonomy in both strategy and operations. Corporate control tends to be exercised through evaluation of the economic aspects of funds rather than through direct participation in formulating the division's product–market strategies, unless production occurs only at the head office or in a few locations. In this case, autonomy on products is lost and a product–location matrix is used.

There have been many critics of the conglomerate form, most claiming that it is as unworkable as it is uncontrollable. My own view is that it should be workable, provided that the vertical information system is reliable, but this does assume that divisional managers and their sub-divisional managers are honest and will provide reliable data. Often this is assuming too much, and it may be preferable to break the massive conglomerate into separate or subsidiary companies or to recentralize the controls even further, so that the person on the spot is little more than an ambassador, enforcing (usually at great cost in terms of personal rewards) the centrally determined decisions. This second choice is only sensible if product groups are similar (e.g., computers and calculators).

THE SUBSIDIARY COMPANY

If we go to the end of our structural continuum, the subsidiary company has achieved far more independence from the central office, the remaining tie being a financial reporting link through a modified management information system. Here, the objectives are multiple within subsidiaries; markets are quite different and of diverse complexities; functions are duplicated without concern for overall costs; different sorts of people work in the different subsidiaries; and any generalizations about the whole company are so general as to be useless. As the units become more autonomous, the variety and number of integrative mechanisms between units declines. There is no need to elaborate lateral information flows—the units operate best on their own, doing their own thing, unrelated to the other parts except in a consolidated balance-sheet. Heterogeneity and diversity have replaced the predictability and homogeneity of the bureaucratic form.

DUAL-AUTHORITY HIERARCHIES

In this analysis I have concentrated on the three most common forms of hierarchy—bureaucratic, centralized functional and divisional. Yet increasing market pressures are compelling even the most centralized structures (e.g., banks, insurance companies and government departments) to find alternative forms. These often violate the traditional guidelines for good design and represent the only innovation in hierarchical design this century. They are called *dual-authority structures.*

Fig. 8.3 suggested three variations of centralized structures:

- Project teams
- Product management
- Matrix structures

Most frequently, these are three variations of a centralized departmental structure. They are all 'project' or task centred and are increasingly common, sometimes being referred to as *mixed structures*. I will look briefly at the project-team structure and the matrix structure. Product-management structures (which are a sub-class of project-team structures) occur in organizations with centralized marketing, finance, personnel and production functions where a need exists to integrate product marketing laterally. The product manager is the integrator, taking a product as his or her function but integrating functional inputs to that product. Product management is usually a precursor to divisional management.

The common characteristic of mixed structures is a lateral grid which is superimposed on the vertical hierarchy. In this sense, teams, workshops and semi-autonomous work groups are also variations of the centralized departmental or functional structure. They indicate a major attempt to stay close to the market, that is, to the customer or client.

Project-team structure

A unit in this structure consists of a group of specialists drawn laterally from diverse disciplines, working under a single manager to accomplish a fixed objective. It is an organizational form which allows efficient performance of interdependent activities that cross functional and/or the firm's boundaries.

The members of the team are often part-time members, belonging to a functional department (or an external organization), accountable to both the functional head and to a project manager (who may also be called a product manager, an integrator or a coordinator).

The manager and team operate independently of the company's normal chain of command. The manager is accountable for the project's success or failure, though not always for the people assigned to the project tasks. Fig. 8.9 shows a project structure. This form of project-management structure—where the project manager has complete accountability for the task and all resources—is used only on very large projects.

A more common form is the functional-alignment structure illustrated in Fig. 8.10 on page 194. Functional-alignment project managers are usually not assigned complete accountability for resources. Instead, they share them with the rest of the organization. They may have a project organization consisting of a handful of employees on temporary assignment from the regular functional organization. The functional

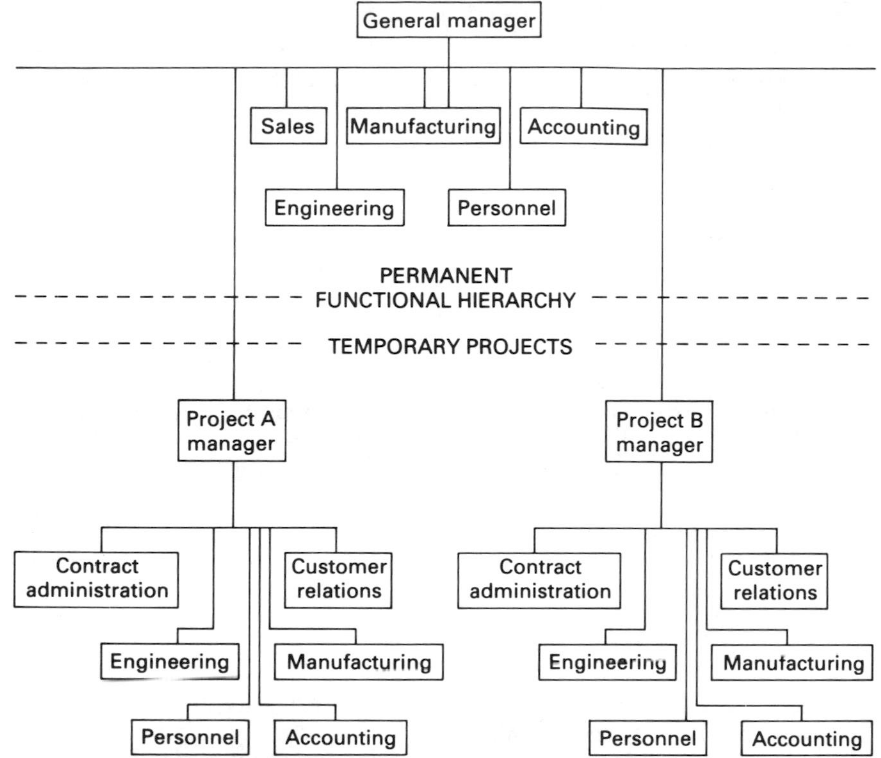

Figure 8.9 Typical project organization in the aerospace and construction industries

managers, however, retain their direct line authority, monitor their staff contributions to the project and continue to make all major personnel decisions. This 'two boss' design is not without problems, and a resource-allocation manager is usually introduced to resolve potential conflicts between project managers and functional heads.

A project-team structure is suitable in a large, centralized organization, when the structural design variables are different for a specific project. The conditions are set out in Fig. 8.11 on page 194. The project may last three months or three years, but its life-cycle is always finite. The objectives require the skills of diverse experts, and the client needs a responsive group with which to deal. Initially, the centralized system tries to cope but, after successive breakdowns in the functionally organized departments, and after considerable client pressure for results, this laterally derived task force is created. The project manager is primarily a team-builder whose expertise, I believe, should include group dynamics.

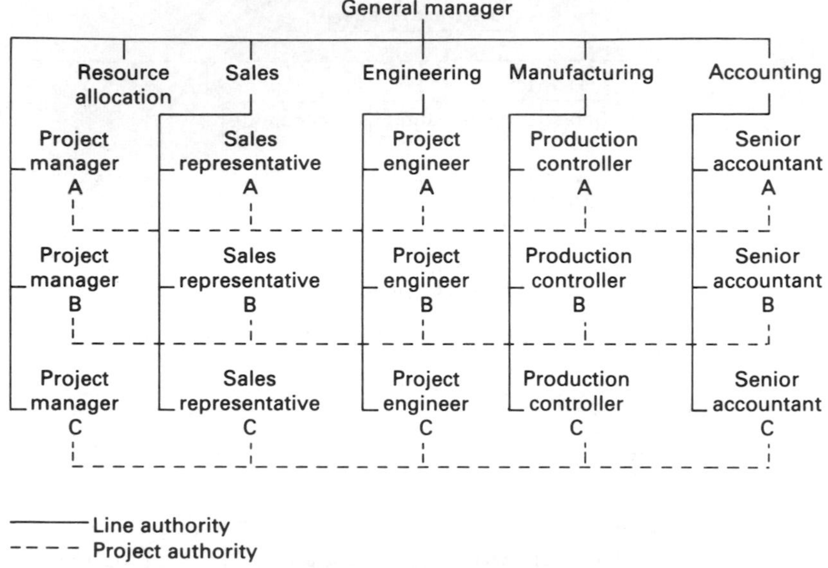

Figure 8.10 Project organization in general industry

Objectives	Clear, specified as ends, quantifiable in cost.
Time orientation	Short and finite.
Task differentiation	Very high, often reinforced by differentiation by skill—e.g., architects, engineers, quantity surveyors, accountants.
People	Self-starters and experts in their own fields; strong self-esteem goals. Numbers involved usually fewer than 20.
Technical system	May have considerable influence, but does not restrict the *ad hoc* movements of the team.
External pressures	Unusually high.
Managerial style	Team-builder: task-oriented.
Integration	Lateral links vital. Task-force operation. Project leader is integrator function.

Figure 8.11 Project-team structure

Matrix structure

Structures of this type were first developed in research and development organizations as a way of exploiting the advantages and minimizing the disadvantages of the functional structure and the project structure. The functional form has the advantage of centralizing disciplines and developing expertise. The project form has the advantage of focusing on the client's needs. Both functional and project forms have disadvantages: the functional form keeps like functions together but tends to ignore the customer; the project form concentrates on the customer, but divorces specialists from their disciplines.

The matrix structure attempts to overcome the disadvantages of these two structure types by asking an individual to be responsible jointly to both customer and to function; that is, this is a dual-authority structure, thereby violating one of the traditional sacred rules—unity of command (i.e., one person one boss). Function and customer (or territory and product, or service and patient) have joint responsibility for integrating the quality of the service, product or project the organization is delivering. In this sense, it is a highly volatile, unbalanced structure in which conflict is inevitable. For example, project managers whose primary function is to get the product or project to the customer are matched against functional managers who are concerned with design, quality, safety, etc. When these two opposing forces are well balanced, the organization can achieve technical excellence and product delivery (e.g., multinational consumer goods—electronics, computing, toiletries, food).

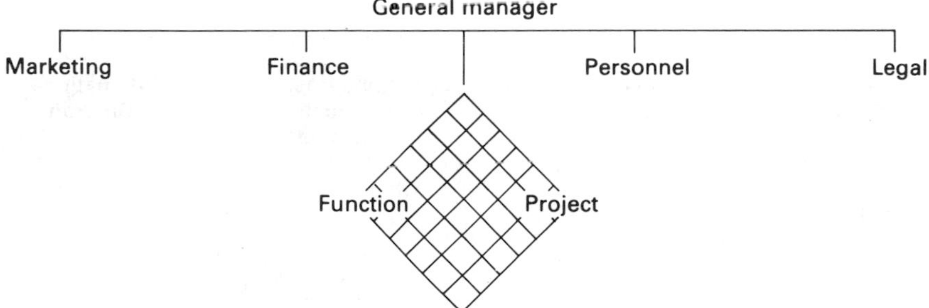

Figure 8.12 An example of a matrix structure

The matrix in Fig. 8.12 is shown in a state of balance. The angle of incidence of the two axes (function and project) to general management is equal. If the functional axis gets more power (i.e., has more support or resources from the top manager) then the matrix will swing. The angle of incidence between the function axis and the top will be smaller. Conversely, with less power the project axis will increase its distance from the top, reflecting its reduced power and influence. If this continues the structure will return in *practice* to the functional form. To make this finely balanced hierarchy work requires trust, a willingness to compromise, and enormous market pressures to provide common external enemies. Without the 'enemy' either the level of conflict swings the matrix back to a functional or project form *or* top management spends most of its time resolving the conflicts to preserve the matrix.

Matrices come in a variety of forms. Some allow the domination by one of the two lines of authority on certain issues and dominance by the other line on different issues. Some are permanently biased one way or the other. In multinational matrix structures, it is often the reputation of the local managers which determines the distribution of power in their locations; for example, in the structure in Fig. 8.13, the managing director of the French company reports through two axes: the product–marketing line (with *product* profitability responsibility); and the international division (with *international*—including French—profitability responsibilities). The country manager has accountability for the total profit from the French company *and* for the profitability in France of every product line. (Often these dual accountabilities are contradictory.)

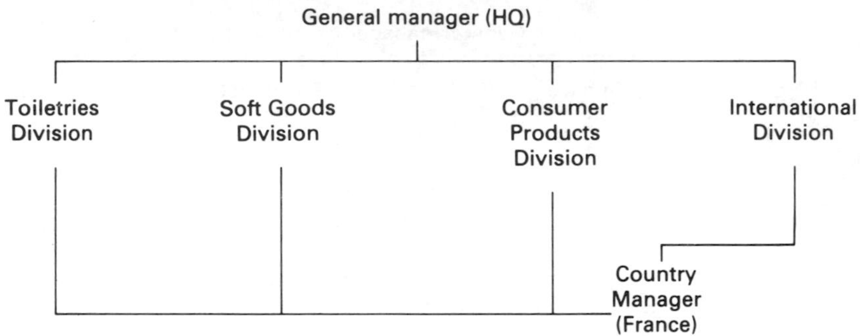

Figure 8.13 Multinational matrix structure

In this hypothetical case, it is possible that the French manager has every other product manager in the other divisions demanding action on their products as well. Resolving conflicts becomes a major part of the general-management function. It also requires the general manager (at headquarters) to force conflict down the structure so that the two axes (or those positioned on the two axes) will mutually resolve their problems.

Most frequently the research and/or marketing functions are in matrix forms and the rest of the organization is not. Hence the *extent* of the matrix is a key factor; for example, in the London Business School nearly 200 people operate within a matrix but the number regularly affected by it is a quarter of the total.

In other organizations, much larger numbers of, say, salespeople are in matrices (e.g., the computer-manufacturing companies), but the traditional functions of production, finance and personnel are not organized as matrices. The greater the number of people involved in a matrix the more complex it becomes.

The conditions indicating suitability for a matrix structure are:

- A clear dual focus.
- Scarcity of resources across products or projects.
- Excessive market pressures demanding faster information processing.
- A group of members who can tolerate ambiguity, will trust others and will focus on the market, *not* on political activity.
- A general management capable of pushing decisions down to the matrix *and* willing to communicate the essential values, beliefs which become the 'glue' for balancing the system.

The configuration of design variables would indicate a matrix structure as shown in Fig. 8.14.

Matrix-structure projects are most frequently seen in task-force exercises—the US Polaris and Apollo projects are two of the best-documented uses of this structure. Medical or surgical teams, new-product groups, research and development teams, and creative buzz groups in advertising agencies are frequent users of the matrix form.

Schull and others have identified several forms of matrix on a continuum. At one end is the routine matrix, at the other end the heuristic matrix.

- *The routine matrix* This is closest to the project team. It is contained within an overall hierarchy, is specific in choosing personnel, devises integrative mechanisms, stipulates methods of solution, etc. It is different from the project team in that it occurs for indefinite time spans (e.g., multi product, transnational).
- *The heuristic matrix* This has more autonomy. The problem has first to be defined, personnel are chosen as needed, controls are problem-related, and *ad hocracy* allows problems of extreme complexity to be solved by people with creative, professional skills. It is usually seen in research work, where the integrator is the major

Objectives	Clear, quantifiable.
Time orientation	Very short to medium-term.
Task differentiation	Dominated by *two* clear central factors (product/category, customer/service, project/function, programme/discipline).
People	Low structure goals; high concern for autonomy, professional independence. High tolerance of uncertainty, ambiguity; capacity to trust (to the other axis), capacity for intermittent relationships.
Technical system	Highly variable, often transportable to problem—e.g., in hospital, transported to patient in emergency. In manufacturing too inflexible to include matrix.
External pressures	Very high or highly uncertain, complex, often hostile. Essential ingredients for matrix as external pressures make structure workable. Without this the two axes will conflict destructively.
Integration	Lateral links under pressure are immediate; skills work on problems together under less pressure (e.g., in multinationals). Integration is the key managerial function through face-to-face discussion. Vertical integration—matrix feeds into a traditional structure. Communication problems and 'feeding up' conflicts appear inevitable. Senior officers resolve conflicts unilaterally or refuse to resolve, thereby forcing those involved to trust and co-operate. If unresolved, matrix 'swings' to one-function dominance.

Figure 8.14 Matrix structure

researcher. Concern for positional power is secondary. Power is given to those who have the expertise to solve the problem.

There are many writers who believe that the heuristic matrix is not a structure at all. Certainly, it is little more than an informal group. Yet it can be effective in solving highly uncertain, complex problems *if* the necessary professional skills are available. The major difficulty with this structure is finding people who can endure the endless change, from one group to another, the uncertainty and the unpredictability of their working day. Placing individuals with strong certainty or stability goals in such a structure can cause major psychological problems.

Further out on the uncertainty continuum is the self-designing organization. Here uncertainty, irrationality and 'muddling through' are dominant characteristics; other features are ambiguous authority structures, unclear objectives, contradictory assignments of accountability, unclear statuses, overlapping jobs, volatile rules, unstable behaviour patterns, vague official communication channels and trial-and-error methods of analysis. Under conditions of great uncertainty, this sort of organization produces conflicts, collisions and cohesions which generate answers. Yet to those obsessed with neatness and so-called rationality, this 'mess' is unendurable. Nevertheless, muddling through in messes is, under certain conditions, an entirely viable organizational form.

Systems

Linking hierarchies together are a host of information, accounting, control and personnel systems. We do not have the space here to develop all of these in detail; yet they are part of the structuring process, and it is often the relationship between these systems and the rest of the structure that poses a major source of conflict. For example, we design autonomous units and retain central personnel systems which do not allow the local managers to select their own staff; or we subdivide the hierarchy into divisions and then, for portfolio investment decisions, impose a strategic-business-unit analysis (e.g., PIMS) across those divisions as though the divisions did not exist; or we conduct outdated management-training programmes which have little to offer managers trying to manage a new matrix hierarchy. Coordinating the parts of a structure so that they contribute to the same overall purposes is difficult, even in those organizations seen to be successful. One reason for this is that the formulation and implementation of the strategic choices (e.g., choices of mission and hierarchy) and the design and implementation of systems occur at different rates, for different time horizons and at different times. And just when the managers believe they have got the structure integrated, the market-place changes unexpectedly and, within days, the integration is gone. One system now works against another; one part of the hierarchy works against another; a control system violates the best information we have about how to operate effectively in new conditions. It is these dilemmas which make the managerial task both exhilarating and infuriating. We never seem to get it right, simply because structure is static and the organization is dynamic. We learn to live with less-than-perfect combinations.

CONTROL SYSTEMS

These systems are concerned with collecting data, feeding that data back for comparisons with standards or targets, and providing the means for corrective action if and when deviation occurs.

Deviations are inevitable in an unpredictable world. There will be deviations from budgets, targets, quality standards, delivery schedules and machine capacity, and, most often, in members' behaviour. The more deviations occur, the more we refine and redesign increasingly elaborate control systems to allow us to identify deviations earlier and correct them. To illustrate the extent of our creativity in the field of control systems, here is a list of the areas which might be subject to control systems in a manufacturing business:

- Production
  - Quality
  - Quantity time
  - Cost
  - Machine capacity/utilization
- Finance and accounting
  - Profit and profit control
  - Capital expenditure
  - Sources of funds
  - Liquidity
  - Inventories
  - Costs
  - Cash-flow
- Personnel
  - Lost time due to industrial disputes
  - Absenteeism
  - Compensation and superannuation
  - Sickness
  - Pensions
  - Wage and salary administration
  - Levels of job satisfaction/dissatisfaction
  - Safety
- Marketing
  - Sales volume
  - Sales expenditure
  - Credit
  - Advertising costs

– Performance of sales personnel
– Customer satisfaction

There are many other areas where control systems may be useful. For example, information on profit does not 'fall' out of organizations; there are 'profit-extracting' controls to provide managers with data on progress to date and to collect often unrelated information connecting costs to revenue and profit. There is also increasing demand for the evaluation of firms' contribution to society (social responsibility), and for the evaluation, in advance, of the organization's ability to adapt to a changing environment. Finally, in complex markets, there are an increasing number of attempts to predict and, if feasible, control future events.

The important considerations in any control system are:

- The feedback should be concerned with *now*—too much data is collected on an historical basis. We need to know *before* the deviation becomes excessive.
- The feedback system should not be designed as a witch hunt among employees.
- The only justification for a control is that it shows correctable deviations from what members have decided are desired ends.
- The feedback should go up to the individual(s) involved.

There is little point in telling the general manager that quality is poor in the plant. The employee in the plant influences quality. The controls should be documented for before-and-after correction comparisons.

INFORMATION SYSTEMS

The whole field of organization design may be seen as making sure the right information arrives at the right place at the right time in order to allow a number of individuals to achieve their objectives. Indeed, it is increasingly the design of information systems which is affecting the shape of structures; for example, there may no longer be the necessity for great numbers of people on one site. Decentralized, relatively autonomous units, employing sub-contracted individuals rewarded on strictly performance-related criteria are no longer a designer's fantasy—we do it already. This transformation is a product of the reliability, speed and flexibility of modern information systems. The French, Roman and British Empires might have survived had they had such systems.

In its simplest form, an information system collects, organizes, possibly transforms, stores and disseminates information. Heavy users of such systems are those functions dependent on the flow of information—accounting, production, service, market research, purchasing, etc. Less frequent developers of systems are functions relying on opportunism and spontaneity, for which gut feel rather than reliable information is the life blood (e.g. dealers, sales representatives and counsellors). Yet even these functions do have information systems, some extremely effective and yet simple. Complexity and investment in hardware and software are often confused with effectiveness. Flexibility, simplicity, dependability, security, cost effectiveness and user satisfaction are more important criteria.

It is impossible to generalize here about the design of information systems. References to that subject are given at the end of the chapter. However, several important design principles dominate the literature.

- Top-management support and user involvement are crucial to success.
- Information can confuse not clarify; the principle should be to clarify, to reduce uncertainty not increase it.
- Designers should be prepared to accept the administrative realities that exist—transforming an existing system in the name of neatness or some equally narrow objective is naïve. Compromise is inevitable.
- Finally, as more and more of these systems affect the resultant structure, designers should check to see the relevance of their system to the total organization design.

PEOPLE SYSTEMS

The number of controls and systems devised for controlling and predicting the behaviour of the members of our work organizations is mind-boggling. There are selection systems, induction systems, training systems, performance-measurement systems, reward systems, career-planning systems, promotion systems, discipline systems, human-resources-planning systems, and redundancy and retirement systems. There is not room here to do more than mention them. Further information is provided in Chapter 9. However, one of these systems does stand out as pre-eminent in the overall design—the reward system which is discussed in the next chapter.

Summary

The design of organizations is analysed here as a rational process. In fact, the development of structure is most frequently a rather unsystematic process reflecting the trial-and-error efforts of members.

The major components of structure are strategy, (including purpose and objectives), policies, goals, tactics, tasks, jobs, functions, hierarchy and systems. Together, these devices attempt to introduce rationality into organizations.

I have examined the formulation of strategy, the selection of purpose and objectives and the human problems associated with these activities. I then looked at each of the other components of structure—goals, tactics, tasks, jobs and, finally, the choice of a hierarchy.

Selecting hierarchies has probably attracted more practitioner attention than any other managerial activity. There have been a variety of 'academic' approaches to it; I concentrate on two—the so-called 'traditional' view, drawn from the observations of twentieth-century writers on recurring characteristics within hierarchies, and the sociological view (dominated by the German sociologist, Max Weber) that the form of a hierarchy arises from the distribution of authority. I conclude by suggesting that there is no one best hierarchy for any organization.

Making a design choice of hierarchy should begin with an analysis of the major variables that have been found to affect the shape of a hierarchy; these are history, the clarity of the objectives, the time orientation (short, medium, long), the task differentiation, the people involved, the size of the organization (number of people and its geographic location(s), the external pressures on the firm, the technical system it uses and the available integration devices.

To demonstrate that different combinations of these variables will lead to different hierarchical forms, I have looked at seven idealized examples—bureaucratic, central functional, divisional, conglomerate, subsidiary, project and matrix. My objectives have been, first, to show that it is the situation (the variables) which will determine the shape of the structure and, second, to provide descriptions of seven of the most common hierarchical shapes. In reality, these shapes rarely occur in a pure form; most organizations are messy hybrids of pieces of hierarchy in a range of the forms I describe.

Finally, I have examined the systems which support the hierarchy and give it life. These systems collect data, process it, store it and lead individuals to act on it. Clearly there are so many systems in organizations (ranging from how to get into the car park through to extracting the annual report) that it is difficult to generalize. However, I look briefly at three important groups of systems—control, information and people systems.

References

ON STRATEGY FORMULATION AND IMPLEMENTATION

Hrebiniak, A. G. and W. F. Joyce, *Implementing Strategy*, Macmillan, NY, 1984.

Steiner, G. A. and J. B. Miner, *Management Policy and Strategy*, 2nd edn, Macmillan, NY, 1982.

ON ALL ASPECTS OF DESIGN

Galbraith, J. R., *Organizational Design*, Addison-Wesley, Reading, Mass., 1977.

Mintzberg, H., *Structure in Fives: Designing Effective Organizations*, Prentice-Hall, Englewood Cliffs, NJ, 1983.

Nystrom, P. C. and W. H. Starbuck (eds), *Handbook of Organizational Design*, Oxford University Press, Oxford, 1981.

Schull, F. A., A. L. Delberg and L. L. Cummings, *Organizational Decision Making*, McGraw-Hill, NY, 1970.

ON DESIGNING HIERARCHIES

Traditional view

Koontz, H. and C. O'Donnell, *Readings in Management, Part 2*, McGraw-Hill, NY, 1959.

Weber's view

Weber, M., *Economy and Society*, vol. 3, Bedminster Press, NY, 1968, Chapter 11.

Modern view

Child, J., *Organization: A Guide to Problems and Practice*, 2nd edn, Harper and Row, London, 1984.

Hrebiniak, A. G. and W. F. Joyce, *Implementing Strategy*, Macmillan, NY, 1984.

ON CONTROL SYSTEMS

Dunbar, R. L. M., 'Designs for organisational control', in *Handbook of Organizational Design*, P. C. Nystrom and W. H. Starbuck (eds), Oxford University Press, Oxford, 1981.

Child, J., *Organization: A Guide to Problems and Practice*, 2nd edn, Harper and Row, London, 1984.

ON DESIGNING INFORMATION SYSTEMS

McCosh, A. M., M. Rahman and M. J. Earl, *Developing Managerial Information Systems*, Macmillan, London, 1981.

Wainwright, J. and A. Francis, *Office Automation, Organization and the Nature of Work*, Gower, Aldershot, 1984.

ON DESIGNING PEOPLE SYSTEMS

Armstrong, M., *A Handbook of Personnel Management Practice*, Kogan Page, London, 1984.

Thomason, G., *A Textbook of Personnel Management*, 4th edn, Institute of Personnel Management, London, 1981.

Sayles, L. R. and G. Strauss, *Managing Human Resources*, 2nd edn, Prentice-Hall, Englewood Cliffs, NJ, 1981.

9. Managing organizations

Introduction

While there have been many theories about leading, managing has remained the poor relation of the academic world. Perhaps this is because managing is about common sense—and common-sense managers have not needed or supported a theoretical perspective in the past.

Yet many people become managers with little or no training as to what managers do. To make this worse, most of these managers begin their careers in organizations as something else—perhaps clerks, typists, engineers, doctors or economists. As they proceed up the organization, they find the time they spend on typing or whatever progressively declines and more and more of their time is spent on managing. The lucky ones are helped in this progression by management-training programmes. They learn that managing is not about grand visions (at least for most managers), but about getting the goods and services on to the market on time, in peak condition. In public-sector organizations it is about making sure that the service is provided at the right time, at the right cost, and to the satisfaction of the government and the customer.

Early theories of managing adopted a rational view which dominated business schools for nearly two-thirds of this century. Managers, according to this perspective, were meant to act rationally and plan, organize, direct and control in an adult, logical manner. Subsequent researchers found that managers did not behave like this at all—indeed, the effective managers were hard-working, action-oriented, scatty rather than logical, concentrating on the short term rather than the long term. Moreover, there was no evidence to show that managers who were hectic and action-oriented, shooting from the hip, would be more effective if they did rationally plan, organize and control. Certainly, looking at objectives, strategy and corporate planning, was a function for the rational planner, yet the amount of time that a day-to-day manager had for such activity was very limited. A typical day for the manager was loosely planned, with a variety of activities, interruptions, short time scales and rapid assessments of (invariably incomplete) information. The function required patience, a tolerance of discontinuity and a deep interest in other people's performances. For many of the experts (planners, trainers, economists, accountants, researchers, etc.), the managerial function was not an attractive one. Managers appeared to spend so much of their time massaging, correcting, enthusing, assessing and sensing that it was, at the end of the day, difficult to find tangible evidence that the manager had done anything at all. In contrast, the experts produced reports, statistical analyses, accounting forecasts and feasibility studies in abundance, thereby perpetuating an underlying belief that organizations could be administered scientifically. So dominant was this belief in the superiority of Western rationality that it was not until the mid-eighties that the assumption was seriously questioned; for example how did Japanese and Korean managers cope *without* the science of Western rationality?

Subsequently we have seen a rise in the status of the manager and increasing interest in the manager's skills. After all, it is the managers, not the experts, who actually get the goods and services into the market-place. Unfortunately, because managing is largely an intuitive process, science has not been able to offer managers a theory—they have to discover how to do it on their own. Because of this, it is my intention in this chapter to examine what some managers do and to point to the skills that may indicate whether you should become a manager or something else.

So what does the manager do?

A typical day for a manager might begin with arrival at the office at 8.30 a.m. Then there is an hour spent reading the mail and answering letters before people start to come to see the manager. Subordinates without appointments simply walk in, or the manager goes out to see them. From these interactions information is collected and decisions are made. Formal appointments occupy a considerable chunk of the morning. Between 10 o'clock and midday our manager interviews an applicant for a job, attends a committee meeting and answers several 'phone calls. While moving from one interaction to another, the manager contemplates whether or not it might be easier to run the section with another supervisor who could look after four clerks. This concession to planning and organizing of necessity occurs on the run or in moments of day-dreaming at a meeting.

The afternoon is similarly filled with short interactions with superiors, peers or subordinates; with formal and informal meetings; with telephone calls and reports; and with an occasional memo requiring more attention. At the end of the day the manager wonders, 'What did I achieve today?' and invariably feels that time has been dissipated, that he or she must get more done tomorrow. Unlike the design engineer who looks over his or her elegant design at the end of the day, the manager may have nothing to show for all this effort and all this interaction. And to top it off, the candidate interviewed and offered a job in the morning has rung to say he doesn't want it. The interviewing process for an acceptable candidate will therefore have to resume tomorrow.

Managing is getting things done, with and through people. It is essentially a series of interpersonal relationships which often extend over many years. Communicating occupies most of the time (up to 80 per cent of it). Much of this communicating is listening, getting the facts and, on the basis of that information, making a decision or extracting a decision from another. The function has been characterized by some writers as a series of roles or parts the actor must play:

- Relating roles—to peers, superiors, subordinates.
- Informational roles—clarifying goals, informing, planning.
- Decision roles—allocating resources, resolving conflicts.

How managers cope with this disordered activity remains locked in their heads. Certainly the facts are quite different from the picture painted by the rational view of the manager. However, it is this capacity to think of many things at once, to identify which sections will produce the greatest return, to shift rapidly from one activity to another, to think laterally, to see consequences before others do, that provides the real challenge to academic researchers studying managers.

I do not want to imply that there is no logical or rational behaviour in managing. There is. All studies of managers either ask them to explain their behaviour or observe their behaviour. The supposedly changing, irrational behaviour that we can observe is driven by a logic which only the manager knows. All managers have visions of what they want to achieve; they are results-oriented; they know where they want their section or company or department to go, at least in the short term.

Skills in managing

Just as we can identify parts the manager plays, so too we can identify skills good managers use. We can categorize these into:

- Human—the interpersonal skills.

- Technical—the decision–knowledge skills.
- Conceptual—the planning, visionary skills.

No one manager will be equally competent in all skills. We have biases, interests and pet obsessions which tend to take us in one direction more than another. Hence, one manager spends large amounts of time drawing up strategic plans while another spends most of the time talking to people. Not surprisingly, when we ask the subordinates for their views of these two managers, we find the first is criticized for spending too much time on paperwork while the second is criticized for spending too little time on planning. It is virtually impossible to get the mix of time and skills right for all the people around a manager all the time. Yet running something, in the sense of increasing its performance by stimulating people to perform, is one of the great experiences of work organizations.

Skills at different levels

We can examine the managerial function further by looking at the skill mix required at different levels in the hierarchy. Unfortunately, it is too often assumed that the skills needed in a manager running a department are the same as the skills needed in running a multinational corporation; or that the manager who succeeds in situation A will also succeed in situation B; or that a person who succeeds in managing a restaurant will succeed in running a merchant bank, even though one might expect the technical skills in the restaurant and the bank to be radically different. I shall look at the skill mix at different levels:

- First-line supervisors/managers
- Middle managers
- Top managers/chief executives

At the first-line level the dominant skills are human and technical, and of these the human are usually more demanding than the technical. At the middle-manager level, the technical component reduces as managers become more removed from the productive processes; and the human skills come to dominate. However, the conceptual skills necessary to the top managers begin to appear through issues like departmental objectives, structures, etc. On a time basis, top managers' activities are dominated by human skills. The technical skills now occupy a very small amount of their time. However, on an 'impact' basis, it is the visionary or conceptual skills which become paramount.

Unfortunately, career plans rarely take account of our personal skill mix. The divisional manager who succeeds extremely well in running a division fades into incompetence when moved to head office—the skills required in the two locations are different. The young supervisor who floundered on the factory floor is dramatically successful with a team of planners.

A difference also exists in the time orientation of the different levels of managers. Those on the first-line level are preoccupied with today and tomorrow; those in the middle with the 12 month period constituting the financial year; those at the top should be thinking of 5 to 10 years ahead, not just of today.

SKILL MIX

It is impossible for me (or anyone else) to describe an optimum skill mix for you as a manager; you must do that for yourself. What I can do is describe the major activities in each of these three skill areas. I am not suggesting that each activity will be as important as the others. Again, you must decide that for yourself. What I am trying to do is bring together a lot of research and loose ends from other chapters in order to indicate what it is that successful managers do.

Human skills

What are the major human skills? All human skills involve listening and communicating. More precisely, we can expand these into skill areas used by most managers:

- Recruiting, selecting and inducting.
- Goal setting and getting commitment.
- Negotiating.
- Training and coaching.
- Motivating.
- Appraisal and performance review.
- Rewarding.
- Team-building.
- Continuity, direction and linking past to future.

RECRUITING, SELECTING AND INDUCTING

First, design your job and, second, find your people. Who would be the ideal person for the job? Let's go back to a rational view, thereby making the manager's life easier, especially in times of unemployment, when one advertisement can produce thousands of applicants.

Recruiting
Questions to be considered in recruiting are:

- Should we change the job (or fit the job to the person)?
- What sort of person do we want for what job (age, goals, qualifications, experience)?
- Where do we look?
- Do we recruit internally and/or externally?
- How wide should the net be cast? Nationally? World-wide? Or just in our city?
- How will we reach the person? Search? Advertise? Employment agencies? (One example of a poor recruiting technique is a block advertisement buried in a Saturday newspaper where those who may be interested are unlikely to see it. It is even worse if the advertisement is aimed at a specific group of people known to read one particular professional journal.)
- What are we prepared to pay to find the person?

Like all personnel procedures, recruiting can be described quite simply. However, highly emotional issues arise when the procedures are implemented; for example, should the firm promote from within or recruit outside? My view is that it should not commit itself to either, but should choose the best path for each specific job. It is true that recruiting outsiders may upset career paths and damage egos of some employees, but the alternative—only promoting from within—can produce 'organizational incest' as exemplified by the stereotyped models of the good 'company man' or 'company woman' found in some banks and government departments. Organizations need new blood; bringing in outsiders is one way of achieving that. There are many organizations in government and business where the turn-over rate for middle and top management is below 5 per cent in a year. In these situations, a conscious policy of injecting some outsiders is very practical and regenerative. I would suggest that a healthy turn-over figure for middle management is between 15 and 20 per cent; less than that may indicate organizational incest.

Selecting
Important questions in selection are:

- What precisely is the job?
- What is the person specification?

To formulate what precisely the job is, we need a *job description*, or what in some government organizations is called a *duty statement*. The job description describes the job objectives and gives a broad sweep of the tasks to be done. It should not, in my view, give an extensive list of duties. We have become preoccupied with specializing and splitting jobs into duties to such an extent that the objectives get lost. I would prefer to see:

- A precise statement of the (multiple) objectives of the job.
- A precise statement of the criteria by which the individual will be evaluated in doing that job.
- A broad description of the major tasks.
- A statement of the authority (control over resources) the individual will be allocated.
- A statement on where the job fits into future plans and where the occupant may fit in after three to five years.

As we move closer to the base of the hierarchy, individual job descriptions are usually replaced by group descriptions, which should also concentrate on the ends not the means, on the duties not the objectives.

The person specification identifies the 'ideal' candidate for the job in terms of physical condition, education, experience, abilities, goals, social skills, etc. Invariably we overplay the 'ideal' and are disappointed when we do not find it. However, much time is wasted in selection simply because the organizational members have not stopped to identify the sort of person they want. Selectors also need to decide:

- What information do we need to gather?
- How best (cost and time) can we gather that information (e.g., by interviews, references, tests, ballots or assessment centres)?

The cost of data-collection (e.g., interviews) must be weighed against the importance of the job. If costs permit, any methods should be used which give a little more insight into the person.

The order in which the techniques are used is also important. Are applicants to write or 'phone for details? If they telephone, the first selection criteria can be handled on the telephone. If they write, then it may be preferable to ask them to complete the firm's application form, so that the forms of different applications can be compared. Extracting relevant data from a six-page letter of application is an expensive exercise.

If the applicant satisfies the criteria of the application form, then test the application by checking references and 'phoning previous (but not current) employers. Finally, see the person. Interviewing time is the most expensive cost of selection.

The appropriate methods of selection vary from job to job. Obviously, if you were selecting a new managing director you would not use the methods described above; nor would you use them for selecting the floor-sweeper. But, whatever the position, the selection process is designed to match person, job and team. The cost of mismatching is one of the largest, if hidden, costs in industry.

Inducting

Chapter 3 discussed what happens when an individual joins an organization. The behaviour change in new members may amount to little more than the fact that they are doing a job in a new situation. However, the change is likely to be more substantial than this. Attitudes, values, goals, identifications and friendship patterns are all likely to be affected by the move into a different organization.

The process of induction should be designed to make the changes (or socialization) as easy and as predictable as possible. Excellent examples of well-planned induction can be seen in religious organizations (e.g., the Jesuits) or in the armed services. In these long-established organizations, induction training superficially transforms the outsider quickly into a member of the organization. In contrast, the importance of induction is only beginning to be recognized in work organizations, although numerous studies have shown that the induction method affects both the rate of turn-over in the first six months and the rate of integration.

Probably the most important facet of induction is the transfer of loyalties (or identifications) to the new organization. Previous relationships (especially peers at church and school) claim the loyalties of the recruit. Yet to satisfy his or her wish to belong, identification must be transferred, in part, to the work organization. This is an important process, and one we need to examine here.

Many stages of establishing one's identity have been observed in children; one of these stages occurs at puberty. In traditional societies, when children reached puberty and recognized that their parents were not infallible gods, their identification was transferred from parent to religious institutions—gods or religious leaders became the parental substitutes. In an age when this transfer from identification with parents to identification with religious figures is occurring less, the need to identify, to be inducted into a new institution has become stronger. This need to identify with someone or some institution has created a multi-million-dollar market for new 'gods'—a market which pop idols and sports stars have been only too willing to serve.

Many managers assume that when teenagers begin work they have resolved their identification problems. On the contrary, most of them are still trying to find out who they are and what they want to be. Induction into the work organization is a most important occasion. And if the induction is badly handled, they are likely to leave and search for another place to work where they will feel comfortable. On average, the search for a career identity goes on into the mid to late twenties and some people never discover what they want to be.

I believe induction training should tell the recruit what the purpose of the organization is:

- How the company and/or department is structured.
- What makes the organization different from others.
- What the achievements of the organization are.
- Practices in the organization that may be different from practices elsewhere—what behaviour restrictions apply that do not apply elsewhere.

The objective should be to make the individual think and feel, 'What a great place to work!' The next stage of induction is the *situational* induction, which should be handled by the boss. Here important questions are:

- What is the job?
- What is the boss to be called?
- What restrictions are applied to behaviour (dress, hair, etc.)?
- Who are all the members of the team?
- What 'hygiene' (heating, lighting, salary, equipment) requirements have or have not been satisfied for this individual?
- How does the reward system operate (including benefits, bonuses, pension, holidays, etc.)?

Induction is easiest on the *first day* of employment. It is easiest to change behaviour (in minor ways) when the new member is anxious and insecure. By the second day, when the peer group has told the informal story of life in the organization, the best time for induction is past.

GOAL-SETTING

The chapter on organizational design (Chapter 8) explains the structuring process that begins with the major strategic choices: What business are we in? What are our objectives? What are the goals of this department, division, job?

Goal-setting, on the other hand, involves telling individual employees:

- What they have to do.
- How long they have to do it in.
- How they have to relate to others.
- How we will evaluate their performance.

If you do this their performance will improve.

Humans are goal-directed. They need clear statements about where they are going and what they have to achieve. Yet, time after time in organizations I am struck by the lack of clear objectives, goals and targets. In desperation, individuals devise their own. What makes this observation more startling is that all research on performance of individuals and groups stresses the fact that clear, unequivocal goals with frequent feedback correlate positively with superior performance.

One explanation for the absence of clear goals is that managers assume that the goals are so obvious that people will be insulted if they are told them specifically. In a survey of over 500 managers in all sorts of companies, it was found that 25 per cent or more of the subordinates did not have clear goals which had been agreed with their manager. One might conclude that the goals may be obvious to the manager, but they are not to the co-workers. Differences in goal direction and in time orientation mean that not all individuals pursue goals with the same single-mindedness, enthusiasm or concentration as some managers. This apparent lack of direction is often perceived as laziness. It is not. Many people just do not think in goal-directed ways hour after hour, day after day. Hence it is the function of the manager to ensure that goals are clear.

Even more important is commitment to those goals. There is not much point in agreeing on goals if the people involved are not committed to them. A lack of commitment occurs when the people involved have not participated in setting those goals. Commitment increases with participation. Conversely, imposing goals produces less commitment. One explanation for the success of some Japanese managers is their capacity to get commitment to goals.

NEGOTIATING

Negotiating is an 'enduring art form'. It involves getting agreement among different people about how they will 'do business'. Conflict or struggle is an essential component. The people involved place the arguments in a different order of priority. Fortunately, a common interest means that compromise, rather than war, is possible. The importance of the common interest allows those participating to manipulate the perceptions of their adversaries by relating arguments to that common interest. Each party may be motivated to misrepresent its position in an attempt to outwit the opponents and defend its own position. This process means that adversaries tend to regard their opponents' arguments with scepticism. In contrast, opponents tend to believe their own arguments are valid. Distortions are inevitable.

The negotiation process, i.e., what is actually going on between the people, is the vital learning medium for the manager. Negotiation can be seen as the manoeuvring of people through guile within broadly agreed (if unspecified) rules of the game. For example, it is rarely acceptable to tell lies or to resort to threats. Rules are established by tradition or by extrapolating evidence from previous encounters.

The more complex the issue, the more important it is to prepare in advance. Some broad guidelines in this planning may help managers:

- *Define the situation* What exactly are the situation, the issues, the information, the values and beliefs involved? What cause-effect explanations are available?
- *Identify the constraints* What options are possible within the situation? Technology, formal processes, past experiences, the capacities and behaviours of the adversaries, market conditions, etc., may all impose different limits.
- *Identify the expectations of the opponents* What will they be seeking? How will they respond? One's style of negotiating will colour the perceptions of the opponents' likely behaviour and vice versa. Tough negotiators tend to see their opponent(s) as deliberately obstructive. What they may fail to see is that values very central to the

opponent are on trial. In contrast gentler negotiators run the risk of assuming that the opponent is not willing to compromise, that concessions will be small.

- *Selecting a strategy* This step involves a decision as to whether to negotiate or not. A delay of several days may allow a shift in power or a new fact to influence the negotiation. If the negotiation must proceed a manager should decide what is the *ideal* outcome and the *worst* acceptable outcome on any item. Prescribing the *upper* and *lower* limits allows the negotiator to define his or her behaviour controls. In team negotiations (two or three members), gaining previous agreement on the range of outcomes is vital. It is the single most powerful control the team can devise.
- *Choosing tactics* Is this a one-to-one negotiation or team-to-team? Most of the negotiation in which a manager is involved is one-to-one, but in industrial relations issues it is usually team-to-team. Agreement on the roles team members will play (who negotiates? who observes? collects information? makes notes? etc.) is vital. At any time there should be only one negotiator. Tactics may be accommodative, coercive or persuasive, offensive or defensive, attitudinal or situational. They may be chosen to signal 'management' resolve or to signal expectations about the range of options. They may seek to resolve the conflict without resentment or to 'draw blood'. The list of possibilities depends on the situation. What managers should do (and most do this subconsciously) is prepare their tactics.
- *Revision of strategy and tactics* As negotiating invariably involves a shift by both parties, revisions to the strategy and to the tactics are inevitable. If this occurs then the whole process discussed above may begin again from a re-examination of the situation to the choice of alternative tactics.

Successful negotiating involves two important ingredients. First, the stages in the negotiation must be a series of smooth, structured steps which avoid becoming involved in trivial issues. The central issues are foremost and all steps are directed towards those issues. The second ingredient of successful negotiating is the negotiator. Studies of successful negotiators show:

- They avoid direct confrontation.
- They hold back counter-proposals rather than responding immediately.
- They consider a wider range of options.

- They plan in terms of the range of options rather than a fixed point or a sequence of steps.
- As issues remain central, they can shift their steps to suit the processes of the situation. They do not become upset if their sequence is broken.
- They can slow down the negotiation, reduce ambiguity, clarify by restating the issues in their terms.
- They label behaviour to reduce uncertainty, to clarify and simplify.
- They use verbal techniques to facilitate: 'Would it be helpful if we . . . ?' 'Do you think it would be helpful if . . . ?'
- They involve the opponents in clarifying: 'Could you help me to understand this?'
- They summarize on behalf of all involved.
- They advance single reasons insistently and avoid long-winded, multiple-reason explanations.

Negotiating is an important managerial skill. For those wishing to read more in this field, there are references at the end of the chapter.

TRAINING AND COACHING

There are numerous excellent publications on training, which do not need any elaboration here.

Training has five basic forms:

- *Induction and skill training* Inducting and training people to do the job they were hired to do (technical skills).
- *Interpersonal-skills training* Communicating, selling, coaching, etc.
- *Management education* Training potential and current bosses to be better managers (human, technical skills).
- *Management-development training* A continuous programme to enhance the individual's development. This is normally restricted to executives and is seen as long-term development (conceptual skills).
- *Renewal or resuscitation training* Restimulating members who are suffering from organizational fatigue.

A great deal of work has been done on skill training. Similarly, management education and development are universally accepted, and the programmes offered are comparable all over the Western world. Resuscitation training is only beginning to appear. The word 'training' is used very loosely here. Organizations do stifle people and some form of rejuvenation is essential even if it is only a social event. Organizations are unable to cope with all the creativity their members have to offer; they are basically repetitive systems. For these reasons, human potential is killed, thwarted, not wanted, and major alienation problems like 'mid-career crisis' and 'burn-out' occur.

Whatever the training, a rational view would see five steps:

- Identify the need for training.
- Define the objectives.
- Design the programme.
- Conduct the programme.
- Measure the effectiveness of the programme against the objectives.

The simplicity of this plan is deceptive. Training, especially managerial and resuscitation training, is exceedingly difficult to evaluate. But trainers can hardly continue to ask top management to support their often elaborate and costly programmes merely on the basis that they must be good for 'the system'. They probably are—even if they only make people less satisfied with the system and more determined to improve it—but this sort of gut feeling may not be enough to justify continued costs.

MOTIVATING

Inspiring individuals to perform better is probably the most important of the manager's human skills. This is the day-to-day, year-in-year-out activity of managing. It is one of the most researched skills in the managerial literature, and is possibly the one providing the greatest return to the manager.

In Chapters 1 and 2, I discussed individuals' goal profiles. Motivating individuals means creating an environment in which they can satisfy their goals. This is what individuals do during their leisure, without a supervisor to assist them. They pursue those activities which interest them or the people they are with.

This same individual goes to work and the self-motivated pattern is assumed to stop. It does not. The same relatively simple link between personal goals and motivation still holds. If people want power then the manager can motivate them by offering them the possibility of wielding power. If they want money, then the manager can motivate them by creating the opportunity for them to get money. And the converse also holds. If people want power and are offered money, their motivation patterns will change (they will become less motivated). If they want money and are offered friendly relationships, then their motivation patterns will change. So what we must aim for is getting the individual's goals as close as possible to those of the organization.

Understanding motivation means understanding three links:

- Goal profile
- Energy
- Reward

In an ideal world, we would select those individuals whose goals were the same as those of the organization. We would select those individuals with the energy to pursue these goals persistently, over long periods of time. Finally, we would design a reward system which allowed individuals to achieve their goals while at the same time contributing to the goals of the organization.

This is fine in theory. In practice, though, things are rarely so neat. Individuals are often unsure of the goals they wish to pursue—goal clarity is a high-achiever concept and is not widely distributed in the population. And even where there is clarity, time orientations vary widely, so that the goal is clear for Edith for 12 months ahead while for Roger it is clear only for 5 minutes ahead. Second, the goals of the individual are rarely the same as those of the organization, other than for short periods of time. Goals for both individuals and organizations shift. For individuals (as we saw in Chapter 2) the goals shift in a relatively predictable pattern, but for organizations the shift is less predictable as it is so closely related to the goals of the senior managers. A third problem with our neat picture is that the energy levels we detected at recruitment are certainly there, but whether individuals choose to devote most of that energy to work, or to jogging, or to family discussions or to another organization is debatable. Finally, to add to our problem, the official reward system (money, promotion, free time) is very rarely linked directly to the individual but it is linked to an 'averaged' individual and therefore has little or no direct effect on motivation at work.

So we are confronted with a managerial problem—how to get the individual's goals, energy and reward linked together for as much of the time as possible, knowing that the tentative balance is likely to disappear at any time. We all have our 'on' and 'off' days. Getting these components together is the function of the manager. First, managers need to know what the goals of the individuals are. In Chapter 1, I gave many clues about the goals of individuals. Managers need to observe, listen to and read what individuals are telling them. Thousands of pieces of information are released, day after day, about what is important to that individual. Rather than the eight categories I cited in Chapter 1, the manager will find that two or three goal categories are enough; it might be recognition and highly structured jobs which excite this person; it might be friendship and creativity which excite another.

Once managers can identify the goals that excite the individual it is their job to link the requirements of the task to those goals—i.e., to find a fit between the expectations of the individual and the requirements of the organization. And, as with all compromises, there will be periods of mismatch as well as periods of exciting match. It is bad management to pretend this is not so—this is reality and we need to help people see it as such.

The second managerial task is to link goals to energy. There are two aspects of this. First, individuals have the choice of whether or not to expend energy in the pursuit of the task they have been allocated. The second aspect is the team or group of which that individual is a part. A manager's skill is to gain positives from both—the individual is induced to release energy, as is the group of individuals collectively. It is the capacity to enthuse, to uplift, to point to possibilities, at both the individual and the group level, which is one mark of the difference between a true leader and a mere manager. Leaders can enthuse, excite and uplift both individually and collectively, so that energy is released.

Finally, the manager should design a reward system which works. Most official reward systems do almost nothing for motivation. Salaries and wages paid regardless of performance do not affect motivation—unless there is a danger that they will be withheld. Salaries and wages paid on assessed performance can have a profound effect in the short term on motivation, provided money is a primary goal of those individuals. Unfortunately, for most managers (unlike most parents), changing the official reward system (salary, wages, bonuses, benefits) is not possible. However, managers do have at their disposal a system of intrinsic rewards which motivates most of us to continue contributing energy, and that intrinsic reward system works on our goals. These include success, accomplishment, friendship, fellowship, identification, promotion, recognition, power, autonomy, creativity, growth, achievement, satisfaction and being part of the winning team. These are all interpersonal and intrapersonal outcomes of linking goals, energy and rewards. What I am proposing here is that the leader (as opposed to the manager) is a person who, through communicating and listening sensitively, points to links between what I am doing, what my goals are, what the organizational goals are and what the pay-off for me will be in the event of success. If my manager does this well, I will be motivated to release energy.

APPRAISAL AND PERFORMANCE REVIEW

Having selected, inducted, trained, set goals and motivated a person, the end of the feedback loop is to appraise performance. Appraisal schemes are one of the most controversial of the manager's procedures. There have been numerous studies illustrating how destructive/beneficial/useless they are. Yet, while it is easy to ridicule the objectives of appraisal, it is impossible to ignore the continually cited need we all have for feedback on how we are doing.

It is not my intention here to design an appraisal system; it is rather to suggest why appraisal systems are so controversial.

The objectives of appraisal are multiple:

- To provide a two-way boss–subordinate review of the subordinate's performance over the year.
- To feed back to the senior managers data on the performance of an employee or a group of employees.
- To tell individuals what their strengths and weaknesses are.
- To provide data for reviewing salary and other rewards.
- To help with identifying training needs.
- To provide an inventory of talents, skills, qualifications, etc.
- To provide input for human-resources planning, career-path planning and numerous other devices.

Given the breadth of objectives and the contradictory nature of some combinations of objectives (feedback on self and salary review), it is not surprising that performance review is still handled badly in most organizations.

There are also cultural values which militate against its success; for example, it is not regarded as good form in our society to tell other people what their weaknesses are. There is also the question of individual rights and secrecy. And who will be honest with the boss if that boss controls the individual's future—especially in a contracting or shrinking organization.

One irony of our hesitations in reviewing performance is that the very same people leave work, go home and there use a direct feedback system in which all members of the family have a fairly good idea of where they stand—feedback in families is direct and constant. Deviations are not tolerated for long. Performance on family tasks is immediately appraised and rewards are offered for good performance.

My own impression is that the size of the organization has killed appraisal. Once it is standardized, hidden in head-office files, passed surreptitiously from boss to subordinate and back again, then the most important feature of reviewing performance, i.e., that it is the opportunity for a two-way analysis of boss–subordinate relations, becomes institutionalized. Any real openness is lost, as we play out our power games under the scourge of literacy—writing and filing information until it chokes us.

Feedback can improve performance, under certain conditions:

- Open and honest feedback from manager to subordinate.
- Objectives, rather than means, are the focus of attention.
- Objectives are jointly set by manager and subordinate (not imposed from above).
- Performance review is related to future objectives, not past failures.
- Criticism is offered in a helpful, friendly way, not aggressively.
- Honesty prevails—we should tell people openly what the chances for them are in the organization, rather than perpetuate the myth that everyone will be managing director one day.
- Most importantly, reviews should occur where the people work. Most data discussed should remain confidential to the individual and his or her boss.

If you have to devise a more formal process:

- Separate the different objectives of performance reviews and use different people to collect different data. We should not attempt to appraise performance *and* work out training needs from one procedure.
- The appraisal should be restricted to the section or department in which the individual works.
- The official documentation should be restricted to one or two pages, and should be compiled only if the personnel department *really* needs such documents.
- All official documents should be destroyed after three years.
- Research on appraisal has shown that self-ratings are superior to

ratings by the boss. Better still (but costly) is a combination of ratings by the individual, the boss, peers and subordinates.

- Rather than use extensive documentation, groups should be encouraged to use the team-critique method of team-building to assess the performance of the team; in other words, attempt to make the appraisal more like that which exists in a family—not a once-a-year activity, but a continuing process related to the objectives important at the time. In small organizations, this *is* how appraisal is handled.
- It is naïve to imagine appraisals and salary reviews are separate questions. They may be separate processes.

Performance review is a very large field of study. References are given at the end of this chapter.

REWARDING

If I have done well, reward me. It I have done badly, then let me know—but let me know that I have the capacity to make it next time.

There are numerous rewards available in any organization. They are both extrinsic (salary, bonuses, cars, expense accounts, offices, furnishings, pensions, prizes, etc.) and intrinsic (flattery, praise, achievement, challenge, freedom, etc.). Some rewards (e.g., salary) attract people to the organization, others lock them in (e.g., pensions); yet others (e.g., short-term bonuses) actually affect the day-to-day performance of the individual. Most of the traditional rewards (e.g., salary) have little or no direct effect on day-to-day performance. For this reason, it is not surprising that managers do not refer to salary on a day-to-day basis. Indeed, salary may only be mentioned in the annual performance review or the annual salary review. Day to day, it is the intrinsic feedback (recognition, praise, satisfaction, etc.) that works for the manager. Telling me I have done a good job, that my design is excellent, that I have the potential to do even more, to be uplifted, to grow, are the rewards that an effective manager uses, consciously or unconsciously. Generating confidence creates the climate for growth. Generating failure creates the climate for stagnation and decay. Why is it, then, that our large work organizations concentrate on negative feedback?

Productivity increases when three factors are linked:

- Task—is attractive, exciting, challenging.
- Individual goals—can be satisfied through effort spent on the task.
- Rewards—related to task can meet some of the individual's goals.

In most organizations the reward system has little or nothing to do with the task. It may have something to do with the individual's goals but the primary purpose of an organization is the task—not the individual's goals. Getting congruence between task, the individual and the reward is the key to increased productivity.

There is not room here to go into reward systems in detail. References are given at the end of the chapter. After years of inactivity, suddenly innovative reward systems are appearing in work organizations. The topic is complex and needs careful analysis, as any organization already has a multitude of official and unofficial rewards. Changing them is potentially very exciting but also risky. What guidelines can we use here?

- Decide what behaviours and performances the rewards are designed to influence (attracting new staff, moulding desired behaviours, encouraging above-average performance, reducing staff turn-over, encouraging individual or collective activity, reducing or increasing inter-divisional competition, encouraging entrepreneurial activity, etc.). The major focus should be the task the individual is required to perform. Too often the task is ignored and conformity in behaviour patterns attracts the highest reward component.
- Recognize that there are many extrinsic (salary, pension, wages, bonuses, share options, medical insurance, health checks, cars, expense accounts) and intrinsic (challenge, power, recognition, autonomy, creativity) rewards in the firm. Some inevitably contradict others. Rewards for conforming behaviour may be in conflict with rewards for innovation. The greater diversity of different behaviours the corporation requires the more certain it is that one universal reward system will fail. Different units, sub-units, groups, divisions and countries may need quite different reward systems. There is no sanctity in a universal reward system based on equity if that system has no relationship with what people actually do day-to-day. Unfortunately this is true of many salary and wage systems.
- High achievers in a career sense may prefer performance-related rewards based on their performance of the task(s). However, lower levels in the hierarchy are likely to prefer group-based rewards. Indeed, one difficult managerial decision is the hierarchical level at which the reward system shifts from an individual to a group base.
- Clear, agreed performance criteria are essential. They need to be multiple (up to five or six).

- The performance criteria may be both quantitative (number of sales, profits, units produced, customers served, fees earned) and qualitative (customer or client satisfaction, industry reputation, perceived value to the company). Simple, clear criteria and simple, clear performance measures are far better than complex criteria or measures. As compromises are inevitable, the selection of performance criteria and measures should be guided by the principles of clarity and simplicity.
- The most effective reward systems occur when individuals satisfy *their* extrinsic and intrinsic goals by performing the tasks required by the organization. This is called goal congruence, and it is enjoyed by entrepreneurs, many professionals, and some sales personnel. The challenge for a manager is to help individuals find personal goal satisfactions in the work they do for the corporation.
- Be creative. We have shown an amazing lack of creativity in reward systems. Most of them have been designed in the interests of the accounting function. For example, in salary systems individuals are paid monthly through bank drafts and never see the money they have earned. How much more effective it would be if a manager came into my office and each week handed me, in cash, the money I had made. As we move closer to a cashless society this scenario is unlikely. But there are other tangible signs. Gifts and prizes have enormous motivational value simply because they are tangible. Recognition of a job done well is still one of the most effective ways of rewarding a person. Team effectiveness is still important to most of us. Managers often say there is nothing they can do about the reward systems. I think this is false. The effective manager uses a plethora of tangible and intangible rewards on a continuous basis. Ironically, most of these tangible and intangible rewards cost nothing or very little in actual cash.

TEAM-BUILDING

Organizations exist so that individuals can cooperate. Building cohesion, and minimizing conflict and disintegration are fundamental skills of the manager. Collectively we refer to the outcomes of using these skills as team-building.

Cohesion is affected by the frequency with which people are brought together and by the sharing of values and beliefs. Most team-building literature concentrates on meetings of the team (committees, task forces, management meetings, board meetings, etc.) and emphasize the fact that the skills needed by the team-builder are broader. They include creating a climate in which the team can critically assess its own behaviour: How are we doing? How can we do it better? Through this process effective interpersonal relationships are highlighted, group processes are analysed and the group's culture evolves. Clarification of the parts people play and positive attempts to build on their strengths follow.

Team-building is also used with reference to teams which work together all the time. These are not people from different departments, functions or firms but are the 5, 10 or 15 people who work alongside each other in the office, factory, etc. Here the process of building cohesion is helped by similarity of task and goals. Much of the cohesion is developed through informal out-of-work activity. Thus social events (births, marriages, birthdays) become the excuse to build more cohesion into the team. Cohesion develops orally through interaction; the more the team is brought together, the more they share values and beliefs and the more cohesive they become.

External threats (competitors) and an articulated corporate culture are also conducive to cohesion. As both these influences have been discussed in some detail in Chapter 6, we do not need further clarification here. Finally, the example of the manager's behaviour provides the strongest clue to greater cohesion. It is the manager's capacity to provide leadership, to give meaning to what people do, to lead by example, and to enthuse, energize, talk, repeat, and repeat and repeat, the basic messages, that differentiates the stronger from the weaker team. There are, inexplicably, managers who imagine that putting a group of people together generates a team. No football manager would make that mistake—an enormous amount of time and expense is invested in moulding the team members into a cohesive whole.

The positive outcomes of team-building are the resolution of pointless conflict, the potential for greater productivity, an increased sense of identification with the firm, and a consequent reduction in the tendency to withdraw temporarily or permanently.

CONTINUITY AND DIRECTION

Team members need continuity, tradition, ritual and ceremony to give them that security and confidence in which individual and team growth are possible. Managers are the only links able to provide that continuity. They have at their disposal three directions for linking, which draw yet again on their human skills:

- *Linking over time* Past to present, to future. Transmitting policies, practices, beliefs and values. How did we get here? What will we do now? Where will we be next year?
- *Linking laterally* Linking the manager's function to other functions, the manager's group to other groups, insiders to outsiders. Finding a place in the whole for the team.
- *Linking vertically* Linking the manager's team to his or her superiors. Linking (delegation) his or her part to those of immediate subordinates. Linking the team to the functions below them in the hierarchy.

Some writers refer to the manager as a decision centre in the middle of many information networks. It is a useful description. By maintaining these links the manager provides the sense of continuity members need. Very few individuals can operate in totally unpredictable, fly-by-night operations; most of us need a sense of continuity, permanence, even destiny.

The list of human skills that managers might use extends far beyond those I have cited here. Indeed the list is infinite. Political skills, disciplining skills, skills for defusing conflict, protecting their teams, going in to bat for their team members, confronting, correcting, uplifting—these are but a few of the human skills in the manager's portfolio. I have tried to highlight what I see as the recurring skills, but there are many more.

Technical skills

By 'technical skills' I refer to those skills which can be learnt. It is more difficult to learn the interpersonal skills discussed above. Many of the technical skills required of a manager have been discussed in other chapters (e.g., planning, organizing, controlling—see Chapter 8), so let us briefly bring them together here. These are the skills most books on management review, probably because they appear to be so sensible, rational and teachable. Reality is less predictable.

The major technical skills of managers are:

- Planning
- Organizing

- Delegating
- Problem-solving
- Deciding
- Controlling

Add to these those specific to the situation. For example, the banker has lending skills; the creative director has particular creative expertise; the surgeon has operating skills. As it is impossible to generalize about these functions or skills, I will not attempt to do so. Suffice it here to say that managers who do not share the technical skills of their teams (be they accounting, production, marketing or mechanical) have more difficulty in controlling that team than do managers who have comparable professional or craft skills.

PLANNING

Much of the management literature claims that planning is the weakest managerial skill. Lateral thinking in rapidly changing situations does not fit well with the vertical, cognitive rationality of the planning sciences.

In Chapter 8, I looked at structuring in detail, beginning with the important strategic choices and developing tactical plans from those choices. It is sufficient here to note that there is nothing as time-wasting as plans without commitment to action, yet organizations are full of plans that went nowhere.

ORGANIZING

This skill relates to developing the linkage between goals, tasks and people. In Chapter 8, I looked at this skill in detail. The essential components were:

- Establishing the strategies, including the objectives.
- Identifying the tasks necessary to meet the objectives.
- Collecting like tasks into jobs, jobs into functions, and functions into units, divisions and corporations (choosing a hierarchy).
- Allocating tasks to the relevant individuals or groups.
- Integrating the tasks through lateral and vertical systems (production, financial, personnel, marketing).

Central to the skill of organizing is the question of manager's authority. I use the term 'authority' to refer to the right (a formal approval by superiors) of the manager to control resources (people, finance, information, plant, equipment, ideas, energy). Whatever the structure the manager designs, it is the authority overlay that gives it the potential to affect behaviour. Authority gives a power base to managers. Whether they are able to use that authority (i.e., whether they have power) is in the hands of their subordinates.

Responsibility or accountability is a second important concept in organizing. The term 'responsibility' is used very loosely in practice to mean that a person will be accountable for the performance of specific tasks. Accountability is a much better word to use—responsibility has ethical overtones which are not important to organizing work—we all hope that managers are responsible people (in a moral sense).

DELEGATING

The skill that links authority to accountability is delegation. It is both a technical skill, used in designing a structure, and a human skill. And it is the human skill which causes problems. Throughout childhood, delegation is discouraged. If I am not very good at languages I am not permitted, in our school system, to delegate my language assignments to someone who excels. Indeed, with the exception of within one's family, or if one holds an office (prefect, house captain, etc.), there are almost no opportunities to learn to delegate during our formative years. Even at college, we are not permitted to delegate—we must do all the work ourselves. It is, therefore, not surprising to find that when we are asked to become managers, say in our mid-twenties, we show poor delegation skills. The sheer weight of accountability eventually forces most of us to learn (through bitter experience) to delegate to others, yet some very senior managers never learn and continue throughout their careers to do everything themselves.

It is ironic that many of the poorest delegators will admit quite openly that this is one of their worst skills, yet they continue to hold on to tasks they know they should delegate. I do not believe that training courses change this behaviour in people. What may have an effect is increasing the workload to the point where more must be pushed down the hierarchy. If this fails, then the only other option is to explain that progression depends on getting rid of what you are doing now. The most pressing human problem for a chief executive in a slow or no-growth situation is what to do with the people waiting to move up the hierarchy. Individuals who fail to delegate and continue to do what they have been doing for some time are not the chief's problem. The people who present the problem are those who do delegate what they are doing and then come back to ask for more. Delegation is a vital variable in who gets promoted.

PROBLEM-SOLVING AND DECISION-MAKING

For a manager, problem-solving involves:

- Finding potential problems.
- Identifying, articulating and diagnosing problems.
- Searching for and generating alternative solutions.
- Evaluating the alternatives } *decision-making*.
- Choosing from the alternatives }
- Implementing the chosen solution.

Most of the time managers do not segment their work into these rational steps. They see, collect information, search their experience (or lack of it) for alternatives, make a decision and go into action. The whole process is over within minutes, even seconds.

There is a vast literature on this topic. I wish to highlight just a very small part of it.

First, a useful classification of problems is whether they are recurring or new. *Programmed decisions* are those that relate to problems that recur—because they have occurred before, we devise ways of dealing with them. Hence procedures, rules and methods are devised in order to reduce the necessity to 'invent the wheel' every time a problem recurs. Solutions are absorbed into the structure of the organization.

Non-programmed decisions occur when the situation has *never* occurred before. We have no past to draw on—we are novices. Fortunately the number of these we face in a lifetime is not great. When they do arise, we tend to talk to the people closest to us or to those who have had similar experiences. Usually gut feel, 'sixth sense' and confidence in that sense will account for the subsequent managerial decision.

Second, finding or sensing future or potential problems is one of the important technical skills. Prime sources of such problems are deviations from expectations (for example, individuals' behaviour patterns change, the number of units produced falls, there is a sudden increase in customer complaints). A second source is subordinates or superiors who bring them to the manager: 'What do we do about hiring a replacement for Bill?' 'Can we spend more than we budgeted on the sale campaign?' A third source of problems is the market-place! 'What is the government planning?' 'What have the suppliers decided to do?' 'What are the competitors' new products?'

Some managers appear to have a highly intuitive capacity to sense and articulate a potential problem and to begin tactics to reduce or solve the problem. This capacity to sense outcomes is impossible to formulate in a scientific way. Some managers just know that the industrial relations issue is explosive, so they immediately start a defusing process—chatting, raising questions and preparing individuals in advance. Yet other managers, without this capacity, appear to let the problem smack them in the face, unaware that it was ever emerging.

One way to extend one's capacity to foresee problems is to keep in touch, to relate to people all the time. Managers who are always locked in an office doing paperwork are in danger of not foreseeing, of being so out of touch that the problem does eventually smack them in the face, simply because their communication channels are too restricted. Scanning, listening and searching, by more or less continuous interaction, is the link between problem-solving skills and human or interaction skills.

We tend to think that managing is about solving problems. Merely solving problems is not the key to success—it simply allows other people to meet the organization's objectives. But, as well as being something to be solved, problems are opportunities. Creating opportunities comes from a single event or a sudden insight into a possibility. For both problems and opportunities, managers collect information until they sense they have enough. What is enough is clearly related to their willingness to take risks, to feel confident in their judgement. Once that threshold of 'I have enough' is reached, a decision will be made. Both the mental capacity to collect information and the level of information people feel they need before they can take a decision vary from person to person.

Finally, some managers, given to procrastination, persist with collecting more and more information until the opportunity has come and gone and may have become a problem. Indeed, procrastination is probably the least researched activity of managers. Making no decision at all is not necessarily procrastination; many problems resolve themselves—there is little in organizational life that has not occurred before. Issues centre on events which subside, die, re-emerge, etc. By procrastination I mean deferring action when action is needed. As a consultant, one of the most frequent questions one asks is, 'Why has no decision been made?' and often the matter is not controversial or difficult to resolve. For some reason, some managers just will not or cannot decide.

The mental processes by which humans make decisions have attracted a great deal of research. Unfortunately, the resultant decision-making models are almost useless. On the one hand, we can (as we have seen in Chapters 1 and 2) identify goals individuals have; on the other hand, we can watch outcomes of overt behaviour. The problem for models of decision-making is that the black box linking goals to behaviours remains just that, a black box. Certainly, there *are* descriptions of how people make decisions, but these descriptions simply reveal something of those people. They reveal very little about how the decision was reached. What is abundantly clear is that the rational models prescribed in so many books on management are not the way decisions are reached in practice.

CONTROLLING

Organizations are assessed by outsiders by the results they achieve. This means that the activities of the insiders are sufficiently coordinated and controlled to increase the probability that the objectives will be reached. There is certainly no evidence that chaos is effective. However, there is no way all the activities of insiders can or should be controlled all the time. Despite the remarkable number of control systems we have devised (accounting systems, personnel systems, production systems, etc.), we still seem hell-bent on devising more and more, even though some writers have suggested that the effective organization may need to be clumsy, muddling through, wandering, and loosely controlled.

Because of our traditional obsession with control, the technical skills managers are believed to need are dominated by control skills—especially those relating to numerical controls. Accounting skills (budgeting, preparing financial statements, ratio analyses, audits, break-even analyses, etc.) are all considered to be important in the manager's repertoire. Yet it is the human problems which continue to dominate the day-to-day life of managers.

Conceptual skills

The capacity to 'see the big picture', to see the whole in motion, is not widely distributed in the population. Yet it is this capacity to conceptualize that becomes more and more important the closer the manager is to the top of an organization. Clearly, the more wide-spread the organization is geographically, the more this capacity becomes paramount.

Conceptual skills are used in corporate planning; in articulating the organization's corporate values and beliefs (the creed or philosophy); in designing the total formal structure, especially the hierarchy; in integrating the different control systems so that they do not compete unnecessarily with each other; in selecting corporate strategies; in designing visual presentations; etc. Because of the apparent shortage of these skills, a multitude of models, paradigms and check-lists (including many in this book) are offered to managers to help them see the big picture. Most of these models or diagrams are developed by academics and consultants who have highly developed conceptual skills—it is one reason why they have chosen the career they have. In contrast, practising managers often have difficulties in seeing what to do with the beautiful model they are being offered, even if the model is only an organization chart.

Conceptual skills are difficult to teach. They involve the capacity to take information and process it laterally and vertically. As the processes involved are partly genetic and partly the product of environment early in life, subsequent attempts to develop conceptual skills have been disappointing. For years management-development enthusiasts believed that one way to expand a manager's conceptual skills was a course in strategic planning. Recent research shows that it is doubtful whether the skills are expanded through such courses at all. The models and check-lists issued on the course are what the managers gain; they force them to investigate all parts of the problem, but they do little to help them see the big picture.

Some of the most interesting research in this field has shown that the brain may be dominated by the left or the right hemisphere. Our society has traditionally encouraged the left-hand side to develop—for speaking, reading, writing, counting, time management, etc. This is in sharp contrast to the role of the right-hand side of the brain, which is more influential in understanding complex patterns and ill-defined relationships—it is used in gut feel, creativity, insight, etc. Our preoccupation with the left has been worsened by our mania for rationality. Further, people have assumed that males were dominated by the left-hand side and women by the right. Subsequent research has not supported this sex bias. It *has* supported, however, the proposition that in Western education systems we stress the left-hand side, while in Eastern cultures stress is also given to the right. There is even evidence to show that occupations are related to hemisphere dominance—artists show a right-side dominance, accountants a left-side dominance. However, this is still a very controversial field.

The development of conceptual skills relies on sensing the messages from the non-verbal, intuitive and spatial thought processes. It also requires the unrestricted collection of data in a non-organized, free-flowing way. What happens to that data inside the head of the right-side-dominant person is not clear, but new products, innovations, even brilliance, are possible. But it is certainly ironic that we seem to try to extend managers' conceptual skills (right side) by providing them with vertical, verbal, sequential and logical models. Not surprisingly, this has had little effect on those conceptual skills. We should first rid ourselves of the view of management as a Western rational process. Management is also about gut feel, insight, following hunches, dreaming and magic. In our obsession to reduce the world of management to vertical (as opposed to lateral) verbal lists, we are in danger of killing the very process which produces conceptualizations of what is possible.

Summary: so who should manage?

In Chapter 1 we identified one important dimension of managers:

- A desire to have power over others.

In Chapter 4, we identified the skills associated with power:

- Well-developed human and political skills in order to influence those above, alongside and below the manager in the hierarchy.

In this chapter we have added three sets of skills:

- Human skills for what is primarily interpersonal activity.
- Technical skills for providing operating structures.
- The conceptual skills for seeing the picture now and in the future.

Finally, let me add one more criterion:

- The want, the goal or desire to manage—to run something, to be in charge, to be accountable for the performance of others.

References

ON WHAT MANAGERS DO

Fayol, H., *General and Industrial Administration*, Pitman, London, 1949.

Mintzberg, D., *The Nature of Managerial Work*, Harper and Row, New York, 1973.

Stewart, R., *Choices for the Manager*, McGraw-Hill, London, 1982.

ON HUMAN SKILLS

Buchanan, D. A. and A. A. Huczynski, *Organisational Behaviour: An Introductory Text*, Prentice-Hall, London, 1985.

Schermerhorn, J. R., J. G. Hunt and R. Osborn, *Managing Organizational Behaviour*, 2nd edn, John Wiley & Sons, 1985.

ON NEGOTIATING

Margenau, J. M. and D. G. Pruitt, 'The Social Psychology of Bargaining', in G. M. Stephenson and C. J. Brotherton (eds), *Industrial Relations: A Social Psychological Approach*, John Wiley & Sons, London, 1979.

Morely, I., 'Negotiating and Bargaining', in M. Argyle (ed.), *Social Skills and Work*, Methuen, London, 1981.

ON REWARD SYSTEMS

Beer, M., B. Spector, P. Lawrence, D. Quinn Mills and R. Walton, *Human Resource Management*, Free Press, NY, 1985.

Child, J., *Organization: A Guide to Problems and Practice*, 2nd edn, Harper and Row, London, 1984.

Galbraith, J. R., *Organization Design*, Addison-Wesley, Reading, Mass., 1977.

ON TECHNICAL SKILLS

Adair, J., *Management Decision Making*, Gower, Aldershot, 1985.

Cooke, S. and N. Slack, *Making Management Decisions*, Prentice-Hall, London, 1984.

ON CONCEPTUAL SKILLS

de Bono, E., *Lateral Thinking*, Ward Lock Educational, London, 1970.

Springer, S. P. and G. Deutsch, *Left Brain, Right Brain*, Freeman, San Francisco, 1981.

GENERAL BOOKS ON MANAGING

Drucker, P., *The Practice of Management*, Heinemann, London, 1954.

Green, C. N., E. A. Everett and R. J. Ebert, *Management for Effective Performance*, Prentice-Hall, Englewood Cliffs, NJ, 1985.

10. Leading organizations

Introduction

For centuries, people have been analysing leadership. Why is it that in certain situations an individual emerges who stimulates others to a higher level of achievement? The obvious starting-point in attempting to understand this phenomenon is to look at the individual and identify in him or her some personality traits which are unusual. This approach (*trait theory*) has so far failed to produce a common set of characteristics from which we might choose a leader. Yet it is this tendency in all of us to label potential leaders as 'ambitious', 'decisive', 'charismatic', etc., which invariably brings a discussion of leadership back to a trait approach. So let us dismiss this approach first. There is no set of personality characteristics that has been found to recur in leaders. Indeed, the reverse is more likely to be true—leaders are noted for being different from each other in personality traits.

A second approach to understanding leadership expands trait theory to include the tasks to be completed, the factors affecting the situation both leader and followers are in, and the personality traits of the followers. While it is irrefutable that leaders emerge in specific situations and that some great leaders are not effective in their first attempts at leading (presumably because the situation is not right for them), it is also blatantly obvious that leadership is a process involving leader, led, task and situation. To say leadership is a relationship may be helpful but this *situational theory* does little to explain the leader.

Style theory largely superseded both trait and situational theories in the seventies, for a whole range of reasons but particularly because it provided a structured way to get people talking about managers and leaders at work. For this reason, the importance of style theory was probably overstated. Yet it did highlight the relevance of the task–maintenance mix within the top group of an organization. It also drew attention away from personality traits to the actual behaviour of the leader, even if it restricted the analysis of a leader's behaviour to two dimensions. Attempts to measure a person's inclination to either of these 'styles' were more problematic. Indeed, it is possible to give the same person any two of the recognized commercial questionnaires about task and maintenance preferences and to produce radically different results (see Blake and Mouton, Reddin, Hershey and Blanchard).

More recently, researchers have concentrated on what a leader does on a day-to-day basis. Some researchers have shown that successful leaders play a variety of parts or roles in a single day, from counsellor to magician, from visionary to disciplinarian. Others have claimed that it is the leader's capacity to link the followers' actions to goal achievement and rewards that distinguishes the effective from the ineffective. Others still, called *contingency theorists*, believe that it is the leader's capacity to perceive the 'vitals' of the situation, and to provide the behaviours and paths through and out of that situation, which separates the good from the less good.

Confusion among researchers persists. The test of leadership theories is whether they are useful for those who are in situations requiring leadership. Certainly trait theory, style theory, situational theory and contingency theory have all contributed in sensitizing practitioners to differences among styles, tasks, goals of followers, etc. It is undeniable that those individuals who are perceived to be good leaders are highly sensitive to the needs of the situation; and, on a day-to-day level of interaction, this is important. But much of the discussion of leadership is not about repetitive day-to-day activity. It is about the flash of brilliance, the one piece of behaviour that changes history. Unique flashes of insight of any sort are difficult subjects for general theories.

As this book is aimed at managers, I will adopt a slightly different, and I hope more useful, approach. I will concentrate on the visionary side of leadership, and pose a number of questions:

- What is leadership?
- Who makes it to the top?
- Is managing synonymous with leading?
- What do leaders do and how do they lead a team in balance?

Finally, I propose that leaders are examples for followers.

What is leadership?

Leadership is the capacity to mobilize in competition or conflict a potential need in a follower. In this sense, leadership is a relationship or process of mutual stimulation and elevation that converts arousal into engagement and results. As such, the process is interdependent; leaders give meaning to possibilities in followers.

Who makes it to the top?

Many thousands of managers make it to the top of organizations but few are leaders in the way I have defined leadership. Those who do make it to the top of large organizations do have some common characteristics (but not personality traits). What these common characteristics tell us is that moving to senior management in private and public organizations is not an equitable process. Much of the conditioning essential to expending energy in the pursuit of a career is programmed in by parents and schools. Those who make it tend to be:

- *First child or first son* That is, *special*—proportionally more first children reach the top than do second or third.
- *High achiever* Those who are highly motivated to succeed, who are competitive and who take their careers seriously.
- *High energy levels* The energy required to persist, to be disappointed and to fight back in the hierarchy-climbing stakes.
- *Longer time-span* Those at the top think longer term (three to five years) than those lower in the organization.
- *Goal-directed* An endless pursuit of goals, even to the point of creating goals when none are necessary.
- *Politically active* This may relate to the success of first children, who possibly learn their politics in the family with the arrival of the second child.
- *Loners* Content with and confident with their own company.
- *Field-independent* Psychologically capable of differentiating the important from the unimportant, the central from the peripheral.

None of these characteristics is necessarily related to socio-economic background. Some of the highest achievers are the children of process workers. However, it is true that the managerial and professional classes do inculcate the achievement goals in their children more often than do parents lower down the socio-economic scale. Most children model their behaviour on their parents' level of achievement, and stretch slightly beyond it. If we look at careers in hierarchical terms the child of managerial or professional parents has less distance to stretch to the top. Fortunately, there are those exceptional children from groups lower down the scale with enormous energy to stretch, but they are rare.

WHAT OF THE GREATS?

If we study the great leaders of history, do we find that they share the same characteristics as those who get to the top of work organizations?

For example, were all history's famous leaders first children? Most of them were, but there were exceptions—Napoleon and Nelson were fourth children. In these two cases, and indeed in most of the exceptions to the first-child rule, there was an explanation of why the child was treated as special. For example, Stalin and Hitler were fourth children but the three older children died at birth. Gandhi was fourth, but he was the first child of his father's fourth marriage. In contrast, taking a random sample of great leaders, William the Conqueror, George Washington, Alexander the Great, Joan of Arc, Winston Churchill, Benjamin Disraeli and F. D. Roosevelt were all first children. What is significant about being first is that it makes you special. For those great figures who were not first children, the 'special' effect still held. On all other characteristics—being goal-directed, being a high achiever, high energy levels, longer time-span, vision, etc.—the leaders of history appear (as it is impossible to test them) to have rated highly but were not necessarily exceptional.

WHAT DO THOSE AT THE TOP BELIEVE?

Let us put the question another way: What do the people at the top think? Studies of chief executives indicate that those at the top believe in indicators of potential. The terms vary from one study to another, but the patterns are the same. The most prized factors are:

- Ability to work with a wide variety of people.
- Early overall responsibility for important tasks.
- Strong achievement goals.
- Experience of leading a group early in career.
- Wide experience of several business functions before mid-career.

If pressed, the chief executives are likely to add to this list some gentler and moral characteristics like 'concerned for people', 'integrity' and 'trust'. Unfortunately, the perceptions of those at the top may bear little resemblance to the facts. But that is not the issue. The important issue is that these people describe an idealized model and it is this 'star' model which influences not only the choice of potential leaders but the characteristics that the would-be manager, or leader, presents to the world of work. Yet, time after time, those who reach the top do *not* fit the ideal model, suggesting that either the selection process, or the model, or both, are wrong. We find so-called managers but few leaders running our public and private organizations.

Managers and leaders

In Chapter 9, we looked at the role of a manager. Many managers are not leaders in the sense that I am using the term here. Managers are concerned with a variety of activities which sustain the task(s) for which the organization exists. These activities are subject to frequent interruptions and involve a large number of mostly oral interactions, extending far beyond the immediate work group.

Leaders are also involved in these day-to-day activities, but the leaders are distinguished from day-to-day managers by their capacity to rise above the usual, to elevate to another level. Leaders have moments of inspiration, even glory. Managers need not be inspirational or glorious at all. Hence, some managers are leaders and some leaders are managers, but the two words are not synonymous.

What do leaders do?

The first task of a leader is to bring into consciousness the followers' sense of their own goals, values and purposes. In this sense, the leader elicits meaning for what the followers want to do. By this process, the leader makes the followers more conscious of aspects of their identity (function, profession, background, nationality, grade, etc.) and gives that identity relevance. By sharpening awareness and providing purpose, the leader strengthens the values which are the source of vital change: values like victory, justice, cooperation, achievement and salvation can focus attention on the essential tasks. They expose to followers the narrowness of petty rivalries, competitions and conflicts which limit achievement through unproductive behaviour.

Astute leaders do not try to impose values on followers; they elicit the goals of the followers. The leader elevates performance by bringing those goals into consciousness, by giving the followers the chance to satisfy their wants, desires or hopes. Values exist only when there is consciousness. Hence, when the team wants to win, if the leader articulates that goal and provides the values surrounding the means for achieving that goal, then the aspirations of the followers become focused, and enormous amounts of energy are released in cooperative effort.

This is not a rational process. It is largely an emotional, inspirational process. The leader's fundamental act is to induce in people an awareness, a consciousness of what they feel; to articulate their goals so strongly, and to define their values so clearly, that they can be moved to purposeful action.

John Gardner describes the process for political leaders, but the same sentiments are relevant to leaders in work organizations as well: 'Leaders must offer moral leadership. They can express the values that hold the society together. Most important they can conceive and articulate goals that lift people out of their petty preoccupations, carry them above the conflicts that tear society apart and unite them in the pursuit of objectives worthy of their best efforts.' The major difference, then, between managing and leading is the leader's capacity to lift people up, to articulate purpose, to give reality to higher values, to resolve conflicting aims as a means to the fulfilment of the followers. Conflict, in leadership as in all interpersonal relationships, is essential. Conflict is the democratizer of leadership; it causes the leader to walk about, to expand the field of combat, to reach out for more followers, to search for allies, to inspire more people with a feeling of purpose. It organizes and strengthens the articulation of values.

Only recently has the 'magic' and 'religion' of organizations been studied seriously. Various books, such as *In Search of Excellence* and *The Winning Streak*, point to the culture of organizations as the glue which cements disparate elements together. Both these studies (one American, the other British) of successful companies reflect the importance of articulated uplifting values. They also illustrate that the easiest way to inculcate a set of values is through a leader. If we need further illustrations of this phenomenon we need only study any religion to find that the leader gave vision, articulated values and elevated followers to believe in a collective superordinate goal.

Leadership and balance

So far I have largely ignored the followers. Leaders who uplift do so through a political process. Style theory is very useful for understanding this process. Style theory proposes that there are two dominant behaviours in interpersonal relationships: task-oriented behaviour and maintenance-oriented (or people-oriented) behaviour. They are the foci of social power. Between these two extremes lies a great deal of academic controversy and limitless combinations of the two idealized 'styles'. A task-oriented style of managing is present when managers are likely to define and structure their and their co-workers' jobs towards achieving a goal. Hence, direction, structuring and defining ways and means are characteristics of this style. (The same factor was found in Chapter 5 on groups and again in Chapter 6 on organizations as cultures.)

Maintenance-oriented behaviour occurs when an individual relies on trust, mutual support, avoidance of conflict and concern for the ideas and feelings of others to achieve the goals. In Western society, the traditional sex-role allocation gave the male the task-behaviour model and the female the maintenance-behaviour model. The allocation of behaviours based on sex totally ignored the fact that only about half of adult males prefer task-oriented behaviours, the other half preferring maintenance-oriented behaviour! The same is true of women. Preference appears to be determined not by sex but by such factors as birth order, role model (i.e., father or mother) and the parts played by other members in the family.

Both these behaviours or processes can occur in us all, but most of us have a bias one way or the other. In contrast, leaders appear to be capable of advanced behaviours in both styles in much the same way as religious deities are an unusual combination of task and maintenance behaviour. Indeed, most images of gods exhibit some confusion about the sex of the god, reflecting both the tougher and the gentler natures of the traditional sex-role allocations. If we study the lives of the great male leaders of history, then we find that the equal influence of *both* parents, or the absence of the father, caused the potential leader to be brought up to be sensitive to both maintenance and task behaviours. If we talk to the followers of tough, autocratic leaders, we will find the same paradox—the image of the tough, insensitive leader is softened by myths about his or her gentleness.

The most significant contribution of style theory is not the idea that managers or leaders prefer task or maintenance behaviours but that they are sensitive to both these processes at work. Describing the behaviour of a leader as 'task-oriented' or 'maintenance-oriented' has very limited explanatory value on its own. Indeed, it takes a social scientist to differentiate which is which. It is not surprising that these are not terms used by leaders. Yet leaders do, consciously or not, appear to recognize that their success depends on the balance within their team. Their own behaviour is merely the stimulant to that team's interactions.

For this reason, the choice of a team is vital. And for the same reasons leaders will tell us, 'Susan had to go. I just could not see how we could work together', or 'I just like having Jasim around—he seems to add a calming dimension to the team', or 'We get on well together—but you should ask them yourself, don't take my word for it.' If a balance of social power is achieved within the team of followers, then the elevating function of the leader can operate. If it is not, then the team will descend into trivia and interpersonal sniping, and the leader's elevating function will not be able to operate. Instead a preoccupation with the ordinary rather than the extraordinary will prevail. And it is just this situation which I find in so many organizations.

The importance of the top team may also help explain why the numerous attempts to identify personality characteristics of leaders have failed. As leadership is an interpersonal relationship, the behaviour of the followers must be as significant as the behaviour of the leader. And regarding the behaviour of the followers, I am proposing that a balance of social power between the followers and the leader holds the second clue to success.

FOLLOWERS' BALANCE

How does balance arise? What do we mean by it? Is it stable or can it be disturbed? I will look here at the processes which underlie the development of a balanced group of followers. It is clear to me that leaders appear to do this intuitively. They sense imbalance and move to deflect or correct it, most frequently through verbal exchanges and by drawing attention to the superordinate goals within or the enemy without. They reinforce it when it occurs by promoting the team and its achievements rather than their own. They see themselves as pivotal to the balancing of relationships, in exactly the same way a parent may see his or her function as maintaining balance or equilibrium in a family. In fact, let me first explore the process of balance in a family, as it is an experience all of us have had.

Most families will have one adult who prefers to adopt the task-specialist role most of the time, and another adult who prefers to adopt the maintenance or human-relator role most of the time, depending on the situation. (For a comparable analysis see the Fred and Myrtle case study in Chapter 6.) If one of these adults withdraws, even for a little while, the members of the family will redress the imbalance in power, and the missing role will be adopted by another person or divided between two or more people. For example, if one parent usually adopts the maintenance-oriented role and withdraws, then either the other parent (who may usually play the task-oriented role), or one of the children, will adopt the missing role. When the children are very young, the imbalance occurs often if one parent is away frequently on business. When the traveller returns, the spouse may comment, 'Thank goodness you are home. I have had a dreadful time with the children.' In other words, an imbalance of social power and influence occurred during the parent's absence—one of the apparently essential roles was missing. Most frequently, as the children get older, one of them will take over the human-relations or maintenance role when one parent is away. Less frequently, the remaining parent plays both roles. The only problem with children adopting roles is that, when the missing parent returns, he or she usually presumes that the child will be willing to relinquish the adopted role. Conflict is often the result, especially where a task-oriented parent withdraws and then returns and tries to re-establish a dominant role. How many families have heard the lament, 'Why is it the children start fighting as soon as you come home?'

In Western society, cultural norms have tended to decree that boys should be socialized to adopt a task-oriented role and girls to adopt a maintenance role, but the realization that half of adult men do not want to play task-oriented roles at work or at home has been extremely beneficial for male-dominated work organizations—in very general terms, half the males will be task-oriented most of the time and the other half will prefer maintenance-oriented roles, so balance is quite possible. It is not so possible in female-dominated organizations in which career-seeking task-oriented women may be deserted by their maintenance-oriented colleagues, who withdraw temporarily or permanently to have a family. Balancc is not as easy to achieve among a population whose bias is task-centred. Conflict is inevitable.

Sex category is not the major determinant of the role a child learns to play. Birth order, other children, age differences between children, and adult role models are more influential in role preferences than the sex of the child. First-born children and first-born sons have a much higher propensity to seek and adopt task-oriented roles in organizational life. Third- and fourth-born children have a higher propensity to play the maintenance role in organizational life. However, before we divide the world too simply, there are many deviations from these findings. For example, a female, fourth child, after three sons, is likely to be task-oriented and highly motivated to achieve, especially if the mother dominates family interactions.

CHANGES OF BALANCE

So far, I have assumed that family roles are fixed. But the requirements of the situation (especially the task) are just as important in determining role adoption in a family as in organizations. We may see an individual who habitually adopts a warm, nurturing, supportive role in the family adopting a task-oriented, dominant role in a crisis. Conversely, task-oriented managers can learn to be sensitive and to use a human-relations-oriented style when appropriate.

The arrival of relatives on a visit totally changes the distribution of power in a family and forces compromises and accommodations if the unit is to remain relatively conflict-free. In our cell-society of two parents and two children, we may be in danger of losing the flexibility of the extended family and be unable to merge temporarily with other people into a single unit. Having people to stay becomes too much trouble!

Similarly, when a person leaves home to enter an organization, he or she is likely to adopt a different pattern of behaviour. The situation will be different, the task different, the rewards different and the expectations of peers different. Sometimes the shift in behaviour is dramatic, suggesting that the situation, rather than the individuals' experiences to date, is the dominant variable in understanding the shift. However, people will usually revert to a preferred style which they modify slightly as they move from one situation to another.

As we move from situation to situation, adjustments have to be made; for example, many people who successfully play a leadership role at work find it impossible to move back to their family without a transition zone, such as a drink at the pub. Those who do not use the pub as a diversion may find it takes them 20 minutes or more to move back into their family and adopt their family role. If another child comes to stay, we make allowances for the child to settle in and adjust to a new situation; yet how many families have conflicts simply because no provision is made for the re-entry and change in role of an employee, especially the newly employed eldest child ('what's wrong with him/her/Dad/Mum tonight?'). In a society which permits an individual many roles in widely different and often geographically dispersed situations, it is inevitable that stresses arise from role confusion.

In summary, I believe that an individual's preferred way of behaving is largely a personal behaviour pattern developed over long periods and influenced by many childhood, familial and organizational experiences. However, the appropriateness or relevance of the behaviour is a function of the perceptiveness or sensitivity of the individual to the demands, tasks, expectations, etc., of the situation.

What is clear about leaders is their capacity to sense what the situation needs in order to allow balance to exist. If the situation needs a new balance of power (e.g., less structuring, more coaching and counselling), the leader will modify his or her own behaviour, or the task, or the behaviour of the other actors. By such sensitivity he or she continues to lead, to embody purpose for the common welfare. We will find leaders actually search for equilibrium and power balance.

EQUILIBRIUM IN ORGANIZATIONS

Whatever the preferred behaviours (task or maintenance) of the leader, there will be accommodating behaviours among those supporting him or her. The dictator, supported by acquiescing maintenance-oriented subordinates, has been well documented in history.

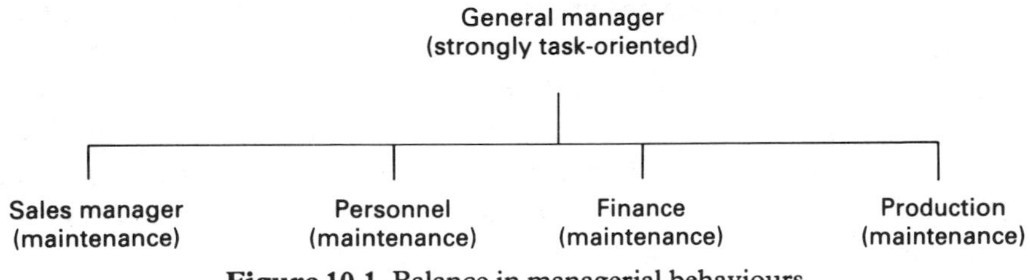

Figure 10.1 Balance in managerial behaviours

Fig. 10.1 shows an example of balance from a study of managerial behaviour among the top group of a chemical company. This group was dominated by one man, yet was in balance most of the time—and this sort of combination is often very effective. However, if a new chief executive were appointed who preferred to play a maintenance or human-relator role, then we would find that a task-oriented person (sometimes seen as wielding a hatchet, or at least sweeping with a new broom) would emerge fairly quickly to restore the balance.

Combinations which are effective in work organizations vary considerably because of the variety of behaviours each person may adopt in response to the situational demands. Strongly task-oriented people can adopt conciliatory human-relator styles when confronted with conflict between two other task-oriented members of the group. In this way, the group balance (rather than disintegration) prevails—shock waves are absorbed as individuals adapt their expectations about power.

So much, then, for the followers. Let me conclude with the leader's function as the exemplar—the model for others.

The exemplar

Achieving a balance of social power and elevating the activities and values of followers are interpersonal achievements. Successful leaders are visible examples, walking about, parading, talking, having fun, generating stories, creating rites and 'religious' festivals. Success produces myths. Stories are transmitted, mostly about the leader's personal life, habits, relationships, beliefs, interests, hobbies, etc., and not about the logical operation of the business. One enormous disadvantage of the rational view of management was the assumption that the best leaders operate like machines—scientific, analytical and unemotional. Yet the reverse is true. Leaders are lovable, irrational, irritable, often disorganized. It is difficult for followers to love a machine. What followers search for is humanity, frailty, mastery, for stories with which they identify. Clever leaders provide all this by example, by developing jargon, by endless conversation, by isolating the essential values and promoting them, perhaps by the use of video recordings to extend their wave-lengths. Through this process, the leader makes an impact upon a culture and begins to change it. It is the values and beliefs of that culture which stimulate balance, cooperation, commitment, loyalty and the release of energy.

To reinforce his or her oral activity the leader generates rituals and ceremonies, drawing up a calendar of events—festivals, ceremonies, dinners, training programmes and conferences through which the elevating messages can be transmitted. It is no accident that religions have events every three months of the year, with mini-festivals in between. If we examine the activities of an organization, we can ask whether there is a well-planned series of events through which the values can be expressed and articulated, or is the so-called leader sitting alone in his or her office, unseen and unheard by the rest? Being a leader is an interpersonal activity. Conceptualizing the vision, repeating the values, the beliefs and the stories is exhausting. If that is not your idea of fun, then avoid the top job. There are already enough managers who think that leading an organization is done by remote control. People need to see, hear and feel for their leaders. If the leader is the same as me, why should I follow him or her? My leader must have a vision, must be different from me in significant ways and create opportunities for the difference to be sensed. That is an interpersonal not a mechanical process.

Summary

Few fields of human activity have received as much attention as leadership. Yet the results are disappointing. Two dominant theories are trait theory and style theory. Trait theory proposed that there was an identifiable set of personality traits from which we could select a leader. This has not been supported by the research. Style theory related the leader to his or her situation, to the task, the structure and the followers' expectations, and proposed that two behaviour patterns or styles were common, a task-oriented and a maintenance-oriented style. Like trait theory, style theory also had limited explanatory power. However, it has proved extremely useful as a basis for analysing the social-power relationships of the leader and followers.

Task-oriented behaviours (structuring, verbalizing, directing and deciding) and maintenance-oriented behaviours (team-building, conflict-resolving, helping, coaching and reconciling) bind social systems into collective efforts. The mix of both styles is critical to the leader's success. In this way, sensitivity, particularly to the selection of the top team, is crucial.

We see leadership as primarily an inspirational process whereby the leader creates a power balance and articulates and gives meaning to the activities of the followers. This is done by identifying the goals of the followers and providing the means for their satisfaction. Through this process the followers are stretched and uplifted.

People who get to the top of organizations do tend to have some common characteristics (first born, achievers, etc.) but when they get there there is no inherent quality which will turn them into leaders. Most will remain managers concerned with the day-to-day activity of the firm, unable or unwilling to elevate and give vision to the followers.

The inspirational act of leaders demands a medium for expression. Through ritual, rites, ceremonies and other oral activities, leaders transmit their articulated values in order to transcend the ordinary and give meaning and relevance to much that is repetitive in work organizations.

References

ON TRAIT THEORY AND STYLE THEORY

Hunt, J. W., *The Restless Organization*, John Wiley & Sons, Sydney, 1972, pages 166–83.

ON GOAL THEORY

Hackman, J. R., E. E. Lawler and L. W. Porter, *Behaviour in Organizations*, McGraw-Hill, NY, 1983, Chapter 6.

ON WHO MAKES IT TO THE TOP

Ghiselli, E. E., *Explorations in Managerial Talent*, Goodyear, Pacific Palisades, 1971.

Margerison, C., 'Chief Executive Perceptions of Managerial Success Factors', *Journal of Management Development*, **3**, 4, 47–60, 1984.

Margerison, C. and A. Kakabadse, 'How American chief executives succeed', *AMA Survey Report*, NY, 1984.

ON WHETHER LEADERSHIP MAKES ANY DIFFERENCE TO PERFORMANCE

Smith, J. E., K. P. Carson and R. A. Alexander, 'Leadership: it can make a difference', *Academy of Management Review*, **27**, 4, 765–76, Dec. 1984.

ON INSPIRATION

Burns, J. M., *Leadership*, Harper and Row, NY, 1978.

Gardner, J. W., 'The Anti-leadership Vaccine', *Annual Report of the Carnegie Corporation of New York*, NY, 1965, pages 3–12.

Goldsmith, W. and D. Clutterbuck, *The Winning Streak*, Weidenfeld & Nicolson, London, 1984.

Handy, L., *Understanding Organizations*, Penguin, Harmondsworth, Middlesex, 1985.

Peters, T. J. and R. H. Waterman, *In Search of Excellence*, Harper and Row, NY, 1978.

11. Changing organizations

Introduction

Change is one of the most debated topics in the behavioural sciences. The tentative literature of the sixties has developed into a tidal wave of books, papers and monographs on the subject. Why?

There are several explanations for this explosive interest in change. First, the market-place has changed dramatically. Second, people are no longer prepared to allow the gap to widen further between what we get in our organizations and what we want. Alienation is as common now as it was in 1960. Third, improved communication provides instant feedback on the failure rate of organizations. Almost overnight, major institutions disappear without a trace. Organizations are swallowed by others after years of independence. Whole industries have disappeared. Of the largest 100 firms in America in 1900, only 2 remain now.

Finally, the life and death of organizations in a socially, politically and technologically changing market gives support to the controversial theory that all organizations have life-cycles. Death is inevitable. Learning how to adapt and change is the only path to survival. Managers must see themselves as agents of change.

Whatever the reason for an obsession with the management of change, changes in technology, employment, international markets, the regulation of financial markets and the concentration of wealth around the world have put enormous pressures on organizations to be effective. This is not the first time this has happened. The thirties saw immense pressures on organizations, as did the forties, fifties and sixties. The difference in the last two decades of the century is that the feedback on success and failure is instant. Hiding one's flaws becomes less possible; knock-on effects become more immediate.

Levels of change

Organizations are changing all the time. They are dynamic, and the structures, systems, hierarchies and people involved are evolving all the time through behavioural integration. The endless search by individuals for new experiences, more efficient methods and more exciting lives means that different functions evolve while others die. This day-to-day level of change is not what concerns me in this chapter. Here we are concerned not with incremental change but with induced change; that is, a conscious decision is made to change the organization, its systems, processes, people, structures, products or whatever.

Induced change can occur at different levels of significance. It can be:

- Routine
- To meet crises
- Innovative
- To transform the organization into a very different social system (this occurs rarely).

Another way of regarding these changes is to rank them by magnitude, from *first-order* to *fourth-order*. The disadvantage of such a classification is that a routine change may be first-order for the firm but fourth-order for those involved; for example, the building of a new plant to a standard model may be routine for the planners, but for the local community in a green-field site it may be a mega or fourth-order change.

ROUTINE CHANGE

These changes solve problems. They aim to maintain the steady state by restoring equilibrium. They may be major and expensive but they are not designed to transform the firm or change it radically. Examples are improving the product or service (in terms of quantity or quality), lifting the sales volume back to a previous level, increasing profitability through faster processing, improving cooperation and reducing conflict.

These are the sort of changes that preoccupy managers day to day. There is nothing startling or mysterious about them and, indeed, this is true of most of the change managers handle—it is routine, problem-solving, designed to shift the deviation back to normal conditions.

CRISIS CHANGE

This, as its name suggests, relates to a crisis—a deviation has occurred unexpectedly. This form of change allows very little time for consultation and is most commonly indicated by a unilateral, central decision. Examples are unexpected changes in the price of resources, an unexpected industrial dispute, an accident, the death of an indispensable member of the top management team, an unexpected take-over bid, a power black-out, etc.

The great advantage the manager has in these instances is that individuals will be prepared to allow their behaviour to be changed quite radically to meet the crisis. Conversely, as the changes are not predictable, the amount of preparation possible is very small. Manuals may exist for an accident, say, and procedures are followed, but the crisis arises from the fact that this is non-programmed or heuristic problem-solving.

INNOVATIVE CHANGE

Like routine changes, innovations are occurring all the time in organizations, simply because people use trial-and-error methods to find easier, better and faster ways to achieve results. This creativity produces innovative change. The decision to seek new ways of working, new products, new structures or new systems may be indicated by a task force or by an expert who is assigned the function of innovating.

Innovation is encouraged under certain situations:

- Flat structures with few reward differentials or other divisive differences.
- External pressures that are high, or perceived to be high.
- Top managers who are professionally trained and confident in their capacity to manage.
- Decentralized power.
- Carefully constrained and minimized formalization.
- A bias towards quality, rather than volume, of output.
- A de-emphasis on efficiency in terms of cost. Costs are added to price.
- People who are highly satisfied with their jobs.
- Personnel policies which allow individual discretion.
- Guaranteed resources (a powerful élite can innovate more readily than a powerless senior team).
- A government interested in sponsoring innovation through co-ordinated tax, trade and tariff policies (e.g., Japan, Korea).

TRANSFORMING CHANGE

The process of transforming an organization has only recently attracted attention. Two aspects of the subject have been of interest in academic circles in relation to turn-around strategies:

- Radical changes as a method of managing a crisis and thereby turning failure into success.
- The shift in fortunes of many national and international organizations in the fluctuating markets of the seventies and eighties; this is especially the case in Europe, where unemployment and dramatic market upheavals have led to the collapse of major corporations.

Transformation change occurs under certain conditions:

- External pressures are extremely high.
- A life-cycle points to death unless drastic action is taken.
- A new team is introduced to manage the transformation from the top.
- Massive shifts in personnel are possible (e.g., by early retirement and redundancy).
- The chief executive is a visionary and has the capacity to enthuse, articulate and communicate his or her vision of the future.
- Feedback on the turn-around is widely disseminated, such that failure is shifted to success.
- The confidence of the top team includes making the strategic decision (to cut products, close markets, shut plants) without becoming emotionally involved in the process. For this reason, the top team may see two stages: the turn-around phase ends with the departure of the chief executive; phase 2 sees the arrival of a less visionary, more stable manager (e.g., at British Leyland) who consolidates the turn-around.

The eighties saw an unprecedented level of transformational change in North America (e.g., Chrysler, Hewlett Packard, ITT, AT & T), the UK (Leyland, ICI, BP, ICL, British Steel, Telecom) and the rest of Europe (Peugeot, Fiat, Olivetti, Volvo). These changes reflected an increasing recognition by senior managers that neither government nor the current corporate team was capable of propping up a sick business. Drastic transformations were seen to be the only solution for turn-around. And drastic means just that—massive shifts in labour, world-wide structural surgery, multi-million-pound investments in new technology, huge sales of non-productive assets and a much tougher attitude towards the selection, assessment and rewarding of employees, especially the team at the top.

The risk of the experience of the eighties is that people will begin to see this change as the norm. Organizations responding sensitively to their markets should not need this sort of induced change. Those that did need it were over-staffed, inflexible and struggling to survive. Their excuse for this situation was that the market had moved too fast for them to see it. When they did see it, transformation was begun, invariably by a new top team. What this has shown us is that the organization life-cycle theory (of birth, growth, maturity and death) may be false; provided the transformations are made at the appropriate time, survival is possible.

Whatever the level of change (whether routine, crisis, innovative or transforming), we can identify a general pattern for the process. First, there is a problem—something is perceived to be not right. Second, there is a period of political activity, stimulated by a powerful coalition which leads to a change in strategy, people, tactics, or all three. Third, the people adapt and the changed unit survives.

If we analyse this process after the event, we tend to turn it into a superbly rational one. In fact, most induced changes are only loosely rational, are politically haphazard, often faltering, sometimes advancing with remarkable speed, often stagnating, thereby reflecting the idiosyncratic nature of the people involved. For change to occur at all it must do so first in the heads of those people—drawing new organization charts does not change behaviour. Hence, the process is characterized by stop–start, unexpected outcomes, major differences in the rate of learning, resistances, crises, reinforcements, etc., rather than by rationality. Managers who have been through an induced and planned change know the energy it takes, in massaging, manipulating, prodding and coaching individuals to move with the change. Contrary to what is suggested by most of the stories about change, it is usually a long, slow, drawn-out process requiring enormous amounts of energy and a powerful commitment from the manager.

Steps in the process of change

Change is triggered by a problem or a vision of a problem—a deviation from what was wanted—or by an opportunity. Most descriptions of the process from here on make it look rational, but this is rarely the case. Let us first look at the rational case, then at the realistic one. The rational case has seven sequential steps.

- *Data-collection* What is the evidence of the problem? What are the symptoms?
- *Definition of the problem* What precisely *is* the problem?

- *Diagnosis and identification of the cause(s)* What is causing the problem?
- *The plan* What shall we do?
- *The action* Implementation of the plan of action to correct the deviation (intervention).
- *Consolidation* Stabilization.
- *Evaluation.*

Data-collection

The first formal clue to a problem usually appears in the end-result variables—the figures for profit, sales, market share, absenteeism, etc., are above or below standard. This information is the most powerful trigger for change; it has a validity which is difficult to reject, especially if the information is documented and has been reliable in the past.

The information pointing to a problem or opportunity launches a data-collection phase. To be effective it requires two conditions:

- Top management must support the data-collection.
- The data must be reliable and irrefutable.

Methods of finding data vary from situation to situation. Some of the common sources are:

- Surveys
- Documents, reports and accounts
- Data files
- Interview reports
- Workshops and seminars
- Observations

First let us look at a few common-sense guides to data-collection. As change is a learning process in which individuals learn new attitudes, behaviours, values, etc., it is important that the symptoms of the problem and the data surrounding them are presented unequivocally to those with power. Many innovative ideas fail simply because the data were weak, non-existent or unreliable. Second, in presenting the symptoms of the problem we should avoid data overload. Most people can only absorb half a dozen points at a time. The tendency of consultants using attitude-survey data to overload clients with the distributions for 200 employees on 60 questions has been the subject of much criticism. Third, most change comes from top managers. Bottom-up change is very rare. Therefore, initiating change is a selling process for anyone except the chief executive. It is exactly the same process as selling any other idea, product or service. If you consistently find your ideas are rejected you should look at the way you sell your information on the problem—do not assume it is the information or data which let you down.

The most frequently used data-collection technique is the interview. For example, if I were looking at an organization for an overview of its management I would begin with those at the top. I would always interview the top two levels of any unit, i.e., the managing director and his or her functional heads. Thereafter I would interview by sampling functions and geographic units, depending on the nature of the contract and the problem presented. Interviews would last one to two hours and would cover most of the variables I used in Chapter 7. But my prime interest would be to learn how the firm got to where it is and how the current problem arose.

Documents provide the second most common source of data. Apart from the obvious sources, like balance-sheets, annual reports, profit-and-loss statements, monthly accounts, sales reports, personnel records, production records, etc., there are usually a number of important secondary sources. For example, studies of specific industries (check libraries, stock exchanges, business schools, brokers, consultants, newsletters, government agencies, etc.), trade magazines and professional institutes may have important information. Finally, any industry has a series of highly developed grapevines. Depending on the problem presented, it may be important to tune into those grapevines. Executive-search consultants, for example, live off the willingness of people to gossip about each other.

If attitude-survey data are available (or can be obtained), they can provide an immediate snapshot of the state of the organization. Surveys have the great advantage of allowing comparisons with other organizations. This means that standardized questions must be included in the survey, whether it is based on a questionnaire or on an interview schedule. The disadvantages of questionnaire surveys are that they take time and provide no insights into why the results arc as they are.

Probably the least utilized data-collection method is observation. Yet any manager knows that watching, especially watching interactions between individuals and the technical system, can reveal far more than any interview or survey. Similarly, observation reveals information about the culture of the organization, its values, beliefs, etc.

Physical layout, entrances, exits, canteens, etc., are all valuable sources of information. Observing a board or senior management team can reveal more about the power play than any number of interviews.

One final comment on data-collection. Our strength is also our weakness. Accountants may be blinded by their accounting information and ignore data with which they feel less comfortable. Conversely, I have seen behavioural-science colleagues totally ignore the accounting information, the market-share results or the sales figures, and concentrate on the interactions of the top team, working on the thesis that if the top team sorts out its relationships then all will be well. That is an extremely naïve view, especially when we consider that most change is triggered by the market-place, and good accounting data and/or market-research data reflect the state of the market and can provide irrefutable triggers for change. 'We are going broke! Look at the figures', does focus the mind.

Definition of the problem

Having gathered the symptoms and the surrounding data (often in one's head), we need to ask what exactly the problem is. So much of our time in organizations is consumed with treating symptoms that the problem is often lost. For example, sales decrease so we train the salespeople; yet the problem could be that the product is obsolete or incorrectly priced.

Questions you might ask are:

- What is the scope of the problem?
- Is the problem recurring? Has it recurred over time?
- Is it being recognized for the first time?
- Is it being re-recognized, having been ignored before?
- Is it now or expected in the future?
- Is it a refashioned problem, an old problem newly defined?
- Is it unrecognized? Has it low visibility, low awareness?
- What number of people are involved?
- What sort of people are they? Have we data on how they learn?
- How extensive is the spread of the problem?
- What is the location of the problem? Geographically? Socially? Organizationally? Technically? Strategically?
- What remedies have been tried? By whom? When? With what results? What rumours followed?

- Why have these failed? Why have they been partially successful? What do we learn from these experiences? Are the stories true?

If we regard change as a selling (or political) process, then a clear identification of the problem (or opportunity) provides a simple message to sell. A confused, poorly articulated definition provides the foundations for major resistance to change.

Diagnosis and identification of causes

Linking symptoms or evidence to a statement of the problem and then to causes is probably the weakest area of change management. It is almost impossible without some model of an organization, not because the model is right but because a comprehensive model will force the sort of consistency checks that the doctor makes in relating symptoms to illnesses through the model of the human body. Most managers have common-sense models; they do not call them models or even checklists, but they do have them. Rarely will all the variables of a model be necessary, but by including them in the diagnosis the danger of overlooking an important influence is reduced.

The diagnostic model developed in Chapter 7 reappears here. You will recall that I proposed three sets of variables (organizational, intervening and end-result) to cover the important influences on organizations.

Diagnostic conclusions will have emerged during the data-collection phase. For example, the absenteeism problem will be seen to be caused by the way jobs are designed; the company's failure to penetrate the European market will be seen to be caused by the inexperience of the people in the marketing function. Employees make diagnostic assumptions all the time as a way of explaining and rationalizing the problems

Organizational	Intervening (process)	End result
Formal structure (strategies, hierarchy, systems, etc.)	Leadership style, power (philosophies, decisions, communications, etc.)	Profitability
		Share of target market
		Growth
Informal structure	Satisfaction	Productivity
Technical system	Dissatisfaction	Customer satisfaction
Individual variable	Cooperation	Employee turn-over
External pressures		Absenteeism and sickness
		Image

Figure 11.1 Variables for analysing an organization

or opportunities they see around them. A shortage of theories about cause and effect is usually not the manager's dilemma. The dilemma is that the theories are extremely simplistic. For example, the absenteeism problem may be partly caused by the job design, but it may also be related to the recruiting policy, the reward system, the managerial behaviour of the boss and the feedback loop from other parts of the organization.

The most persistent error in diagnosis is *either/or* theorizing—either it is the job *or* it is the manager. In reality, there is rarely a single cause. Organizations are not so simple. For this reason, effective diagnosticians are good conceptualizers—individuals who can conceptually deal with a multi-variable, dynamic total picture and who are not given to simple either/or, linear linkages. Unfortunately, the capacity to conceptualize at a higher level of abstraction is not common. Nor is this capacity directly related to intelligence or any other ability. Some managers at very senior levels have superb capacities to conceptualize. Many others do not have a capacity for conceptualizing and diagnosing and this is reflected in a succession of temporary solutions to symptoms instead of a direct attack on causes. It is also a reason for the importance given to the whole field of strategic management at business schools—it is one way to provide managers with models and check-lists designed to cover the total system rather than a small part of it.

The data-collection step should have provided us with process data ('How did we get here?') and variance data ('How does this compare with our experience?). Both sorts of information are important in the diagnosis. The problem we are examining is always explained by past data. However, we can expand our insights from a single case. Comparisons for variance can be made with other organizations, with other people's expectations, with industry data, with scientific and theoretical predictions. This is an automatic process for consultants or experienced general managers; from their wide experience, they draw diagnostic conclusions in the same way as the medical practitioner, partly on experience, partly on fact, partly on gut feel, mostly on a rather unfocused lateral-thinking process. Whatever the check-list the manager proposes to use, that is all it is—a check-list to ensure that nothing has been forgotten. Those who are good at diagnosis invariably have great difficulty in explaining how they do it. When compelled to explain, they fall back on to their models and turn a lateral-thinking, intuitive process into a logical, rational one. In desperation, the right-hand side of the brain asks the left-hand side for an explanation.

A rational diagnostic procedure is to relate the information collected at the data-collection stage to each variable of the model and to assess whether there is a link. Begin with the external pressures, because that is where the trigger for change is most frequently found. Thereafter, work through the other variables in the model. What do we know of that variable? What influence might it have on the problem as defined? Would that variable (e.g., formal structure, strategy, style, etc.) produce the symptoms of the problem we have defined?

The final step in diagnosis is to link variables together into a whole and attempt to conceptualize the whole system in action. If this is not your strength, it may be worth while asking for help. Linking markets to structures and then to end-result variables is not easy.

This rational explanation of data-collection and diagnosis is not what happens in reality. The pseudo-scientific approach adopted by most external consultants is rather more like a sponge—absorbing, informing, mixing collected data with a model, rejecting data that doesn't fit, testing and re-testing, and by a process of elimination coming to a conclusion about cause and effect. This is the same sort of heuristic problem-solving technique that creative people use. Where consultants may have a slight advantage over others is that, by moving from organization to organization, they gain wide experience and retain some objectivity—examining from a variance perspective is possible. Moreover, good consultants know when they are being seduced by the people in the client organization and can distance themselves from it (often simply by going away). Thus by employing a highly developed capacity to absorb and conceptualize, and by ensuring distance, the consultant arrives at a conclusion: the symptoms are these; the problem is X and it is caused by Y and Z. The difficulty for clients occurs when they ask the consultant how he or she got there. In some cases it is the reputation of the consultant which carries the conclusion—past experiences have shown him or her to have a way of being right. Conversely, if the consultant gets it wrong too often, the consulting practice dies. Consulting in this field is a highly exposed activity, but, even more, it exposes the internal change-manager who must live with the outcomes of a diagnosis.

The plan

Involving other people in the diagnosis introduces the beginning of the change-planning process. Diagnosis attracts attention to issues which may have been ignored, such as: Where is the team going? What are the real problems? Many is the case where the problem presented initially is dropped because a more significant problem emerges during the diagnostic phase.

Plans for routine or innovative change will be radically different in intention and content from a transformation plan.

STEPS IN THE PLAN

Having conceded that the plan will depend on the situation, can we generalize? The answer is yes—the plan for induced change is like any other plan, with the same logic.

- What are the objectives of the induced change?
- What measures, standards or end-result variables will tell us when we get there?
- How will we get there?
- How long will it take?
- What resources will we need?
- What will it cost?
- Who will introduce and manage the change?

How will we get there?

Change does not occur in a vacuum. It occurs, as I have emphasized, in the heads of members. Hence the question, 'How do we get there?', means, 'How do we get people to learn?' Asking people to learn involves power. The more power managers have, the greater the chance they have of getting people to learn new ideas, new techniques or new systems. The greater the threat to the survival of those people, the greater the chance that they will learn quickly. The less threatening they perceive the problems to be, the more resistance there will be and the longer learning will take. The less threatening the problem, the more the people affected may have to be involved in the design of the learning programme. Routine changes will produce more resistance than transformational change if members perceive the changes as routine and not survival-based.

Learning also involves re-learning—not merely learning something new but trying to unlearn what is already known. This requires a common language and may mean that some form of initial training is necessary before the real changes can begin. The disadvantage of developing the language is that it is time-consuming. The advantage is that once learnt, the changes can be explained more easily.

It is difficult to discuss the learning process in other than very general terms. Individuals learn, groups learn, even collections of individuals in organizations learn. Obviously, whatever level of learning we analyse, some individuals are far better prepared for the learning than are others. For example, as I have said before, there are many members (including senior managers) who cannot conceptualize at an organizational or departmental level; that is, they cannot 'see' what the organization might be like if it were changed—it is like driving a car blindfolded. This conceptual incapacity produces enormous uncertainty and resistance. The macro-picture is just not possible for them. In contrast, the consultant or the academic specializes in conceptualizing and pushing models of the world on to others. One outcome of people's limited capacity to see the big picture has been a preoccupation with techniques (the means) for learning rather than the ends of learning. To overcome this, it is vital to produce pictures, diagrams, scale models, charts, etc., so that the learning objectives can be 'seen', so that people can get a picture of their future state and what it will look like. And as with all visual learning (as opposed to aural), forgetting can be minimized.

Three phases have been identified in successful learning (see Fig. 11.2)—the *unfreeze* phase, the *change* in values/attitudes phase and the *re-freeze* phase. Most failures occur in the unfreeze—the selling phase. This is when managers try to convince others that they need to change their attitudes, behaviour, structures or systems.

Since the sixties, there has been an explosion in creative techniques for taking people through the unfreeze phase and on to the learning curve. Manuals, games, groups and video exercises have developed just to deal with this important stage. What is worrying is that the medium often becomes more important than the message; playing games becomes the objective rather than a means to an end. And the end is to change the organization by inducing people to learn to behave differently.

If we relate stages in learning and the preparation of members for learning, then we can explain why some organizations use certain techniques and others use different ones. There is clearly no one 'package' suitable for everyone. For example, where conceptual skills are well developed and where learning from experience is understood, then problem-solving discussions, which cut across functions, as well as

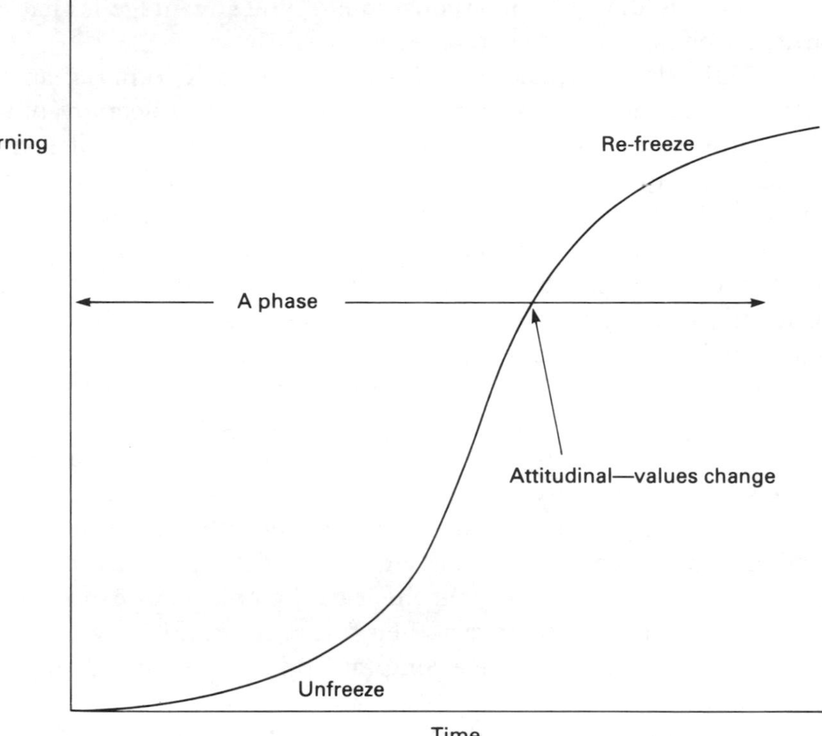

Figure 11.2 The learning curve

encouraging highly personal and open exchanges of feelings, are possible. In highly centralized, economically protected organizations, where conceptual skills and the understanding of organizations as social systems have not been encouraged, the unfreeze phase may require highly structured, safe 'management development' programmes, which approach but do not reach experiential learning techniques. After participating in such a 'safe' programme, a second programme may move the same participants further towards dealing with complex but uncertain issues. Two or three different training situations may be necessary before sufficient learning has taken place so that real issues are tackled openly. Failure to prepare people for learning is the major source of failure in inducing change. Only in a crisis, such as the death of an organization, can the manager reduce the unfreeze phases.

Individuals learn in different ways. Some (e.g., accountants and engineers) prefer neat, vertically structured learning exercises; others (e.g., creative and caring functions) prefer highly emotive, affective

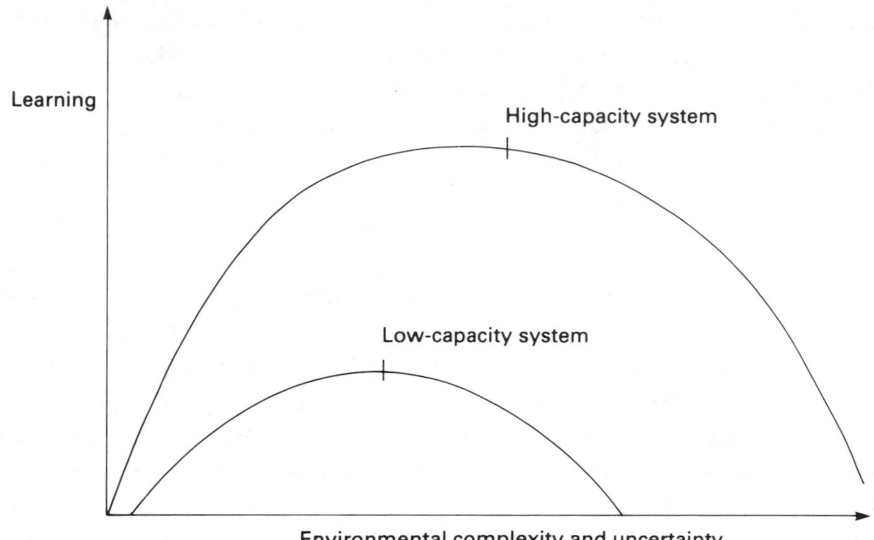

Figure 11.3 Learning in organizations related to environment. Capacity for learning is affected by conceptual skills and previous learning. If complexity and uncertainty are too great, learning declines.

learning techniques; others (e.g., academics and consultants) prefer conceptualizations of reality; yet others (salespeople, line-supervisors and craftspeople) learn most readily by doing something rather than talking or thinking about it. Some generalized assessment of the people involved makes good sense, so that the wrong methods are not used on the wrong people. Change is about selling—choose your unfreeze technique carefully.

A perceived threat (to survival) can stimulate the rate of learning. Readiness can be increased by environmental uncertainty and complexity; that is, if the market-place is unpredictable, then the members' learning increases to cope with that lack of predictability. However, if the uncertainty is too great, learning decreases, as Fig. 11.3 shows. There appears to be a U-shaped relationship between learning, and environmental complexity and uncertainty. Similarly, as learning increases among members, a more complex and uncertain environment is necessary in order to optimize learning and thus to raise members' capacity further. Where there is a high level of environmental certainty, behavioural techniques may have to be used among members in order to initiate the desired learning. Most of these techniques (e.g., T-groups and confrontation groups) fabricate high levels of internal uncertainty and are most frequently found in organization-development exercises in protected organizations for which market pressures are not sufficiently threatening to induce people to change (e.g., public utilities and private oligopolies such as banking and oil).

Learning is not continuous. Individuals need periods of consolidation in order to rethink, examine, absorb and digest. Over-stretching the process can lead to breakdown. Too much information too quickly may lead to random behaviour. Learning is a stop–go process depending on the whole range of personality and ability characteristics that the members represent. If catastrophe or organizational death is the objective, then it may not matter if people behave randomly when subjected to intense ambiguity and uncertainty. However, this is rarely the objective of induced change—it is more common in the early stage of crisis. Disturbed, random behaviour patterns, once developed, can take years to repair.

If you are planning the change, then your plan should take the complexities of learning into account. It is easy to facilitate the learning by ensuring that those involved:

- Understand the threat to their positions.
- Perceive the problem as a real one.
- Understand the diagnosis and believe it to be correct.
- See the plan of action as sensible.
- See rewards in the change for themselves.
- Have a common language to discuss the problem.
- Have the learning capacity required.
- Have the resources to implement the plan.
- Are capable of managing the transition.

There are a number of techniques for increasing the capacity to learn. Workshops, search meetings, survey feedback seminars, encounter groups, problem-solving task forces, team-building exercises and group-therapy sessions are all familiar techniques to an increasing number of managers, as well as to specialists working in the field. The choice of technique will be determined by *timing* (How long have we got?), *content* (What is it we need to learn?) and the *people* (How best do they learn?).

Broad choices about technique and content can be influenced by the two major learning strategies available. They can be seen as opposite ends of a continuum, running from '*Involve* those affected' to '*Tell* those affected'.

- Change attitudes → Change behaviour → Change structure (*Involve*)
- Change structure → Change behaviour → Change attitudes (*Tell*)

Most frequently change involves both strategies.

Of the two broad approaches, the second (that is, change the structure, which will change behaviour, which will lead to a change in attitude) has more empirical support behind it, even though the change literature stresses the first as it is more participative. During periods of recession, unemployment, falling sales, etc., the second is easier to invoke. In periods of abundance, growth and harmony, the first strategy becomes popular.

How long will it take to get there?

The time it will take to achieve change depends on the sources of energy. The market-place energizes most change. Indeed, if the market is not 'working for' a change that the manager wants to introduce, then the latter has artificially to generate the energy inside the organization. War (external threat) produces extraordinary cohesion and solidarity within a society; inordinate changes are tolerated, and people learn to cope with amazing speed. This is so because the threat to survival is clear. Changes in technology, falling market share, falling profits or high turn-over of staff are all environmental or externally generated pressures which induce change. Threats to survival—i.e., the possibility that the organization will cease to exist *at all*—will stimulate rapid change. External forces energize most internal change.

Energy sources within the firm are the members and information; some managers just have more energy, can engender more enthusiastic activity, and can persuade people more successfully that their vision or their solution is worth while. A second trigger for releasing energy is information—sufficiently bad feedback can release energy to change the situation, but exciting good feedback can also stimulate more action.

Whatever the internal or external energy source, we must first ask, 'Is there enough energy here to make "getting there" feasible?' Energizing others requires power. All change involves power. Much of the literature on change comes from a North American view of consensus power, despite the inescapable evidence that Western work organizations represent one of the last bastions of centralized authoritarian power. The people who initiate most changes are at the top. It is true that some changes are initiated from below, but the vast majority of significant changes in the life of an organization originate from the top—hence our preoccupation with concepts like leadership.

Power strategies for inducing change usually do something *to* people rather than *with* them. The greater the manager's control over resources (authority or positional power), the greater his or her facility to energize change.

The more sensible the change, the less resistance there will be to that change. The more the change relies on positional power to push it through, the greater the amount of surveillance needed to ensure that the change is actually followed through. The greater the use of positional power, the greater the probability that 'drag' will occur—that is, that people will attempt to hold the past situation or return to it. For this reason, it may be necessary for the power-broker to 'take the structure' (for example) beyond the position he or she hopes it will settle at, simply to counter structural drag. (There have been some interesting European examples of matrix structures being used in this way.)

The lower the perceived need for change, the more positional power will be necessary to energize the change. The greater the magnitude of the change (say, a change from a functional structure to a divisional structure—i.e., transformation), the more use will be made of positional power and market pressures. The smaller the change, the less energy (from inside or outside) will be necessary.

The major cause of failure of unilateral power strategies is the lower commitment of those affected; hence the vast literature on how to persuade people to accept a change (whether the method of persuasion is money, promises of other rewards, consultation, friendship, participation, love, involvement, etc.).

Although there are numerous classifications of power strategies (from dictatorship to participation), they are not very helpful for the manager. More important to the manager is ensuring that the energy source is adequate to get the change introduced. The effectiveness of chosen power strategies will depend on:

- The recipient(s)—an individual, a group, a division.
- The level of the expected change—conceptual, behavioural, technical, procedural, structural, etc.
- The magnitude of the change—routine, crisis, innovative, transforming.
- The relationships involved—interpersonal, intrapersonal, intergroup, intra-group, organizational, inter-organizational.

In assessing your power to introduce change, check both your power base *and* the power of your function.

- The individual's power base—authority, expertise, access, contacts information, experience, charisma, articulacy, etc.
- The power of the individual's function—its centrality to the major tasks, the ease with which it can be substituted, its capacity to cope with uncertainty, its relationship with completion of the primary task of the firm.

Power does not only reside in individuals. Organizations can be studied as a complex structure of coalitions. Some groups or specialists have advantages (e.g., communication skills) which allow them to exercise more power to energize more change. Leading functions, new specialisms, new skills and new people all ensure shifts in the distribution of power. Further, external organizations (suppliers, governments, etc.) or other parts of the same firm (e.g., head office) represent energy sources in an institutional form.

Who will introduce and manage the change?

Having collected our data, diagnosed the problem and developed a plan, we now need action. Implementing a plan is the most difficult part of the change programme. Anyone can design a change; very few of us are competent at introducing change, simply because so many of the problems that arise are unpredictable. Think of the relatively simple change of moving a family of four from one house to another. Is it ever plain sailing?

The shorter the time-frame, the less feasible is a sequential process (step by step) for implementing our plan; and the more intense the pressure for change, the shorter the time-frame. On the other hand, though, the shorter the time-frame and the more pressure for change, the more acceptable will short-term, dictatorial, drastic action be. Indeed, experienced managers learn that many changes they would like to introduce have to wait for a crisis simply to allow a highly centralized authoritarian decision to be accepted.

Most routine and innovative changes do not occur under crisis conditions. For this sort of induced change, people prefer a sequential phasing rather than a concurrent implementation. Similarly, the more significant the problem and the longer the time-frame, the more a phased introduction will be essential; there is neither the conceptual capacity nor the pressure of time necessary to induce a rapid change.

Once action begins, the firm does not immediately shift to a new configuration of components. There are three stages in the implementation process:

- The organization as it existed prior to the change.
- The organization as it will exist following implementation.
- The transition state that exists as the firm moves from one to the other.

The implementation phase begins with informing those who will be directly affected by the change. This is preferably done face to face. Usually the face-to-face meeting will be private, between the boss and his or her team. The implementation plan will be used to explain the change, its rationale and how it will improve the organization. Participation in the details of the plan may or may not be encouraged, depending on the time-frame, the number of options, the strength of conviction of the top managers that they have it right. Studies of change show that participation does assist large-scale change. It is most important in these first meetings that visuals (charts, models, diagrams etc.) are used to increase the learning. Second, it is vital that those attending participate in a discussion of the design. People must be encouraged to express their reservations and their support for the changes. It should not be a one-way lecture, even when there *is* only one option. The manager needs to know, in advance, where he or she has room to manoeuvre and where he or she does not.

If face-to-face communication is deemed the best medium for 'selling' the plan to the rest of the employees, then the managers attending the first meeting will conduct similar meetings with their teams and the information cascades down the organization. It is important, if the face-to-face method is chosen, that the time between beginning the process and ending it must be short, otherwise the grapevine will run ahead of the meetings at the different levels, and the managers will have to correct all the rumours before they can get an open discussion about the planned change.

Face-to-face meetings (backed up with visuals) are the most reliable way of transmitting important messages, simply because the manager can get instant feedback and has the advantage of both verbal and non-verbal signals from subordinates. However, it is also costly. Therefore, individuals who are only indirectly involved may be informed by video cassettes, by memoranda, by mass meetings, by staff letters or newspapers, or by noticeboards. However, these one-way communications must be monitored via the grapevine in order to assess people's reactions.

MANAGING THE TRANSITION

Informing people that a change is to occur does not mean the change *will* occur. Changing organizations, other than those in crisis, requires enormous amounts of energy, repetition and vigilance. For this reason, many routine changes are never implemented—they never become part of the learning experience of the members. To avoid a 'dying' learning curve, i.e., failure, we have to massage the transition from the current state to the transition state, and then to the desired state. But how?

Basically, there are four transition-management options. All are structurally based.

Manager manages change

First, the manager accepts total accountability for introducing the changes. Positional power, energy and repetition are used to ensure that the change (the learning) becomes internalized by a critical mass of people. Learning is promoted through face-to-face meetings with those involved.

Manager and task force (subordinates)

In slightly more complex cases, the manager may create an internal task force of some of his or her senior colleagues who collectively preside over the transition. Traditionally, this might have been a management committee, but it is now likely to be an *ad hoc* task force designed to terminate with the end of the change programme. The team might include all or some of the immediate subordinate managers. Together this task force manages the transition. Sometimes resources like clerical, research or secretarial assistants are added to the team. To ensure that the change does focus attention away from the normal, day-to-day work of these people, meeting times are fixed to discuss the change and its progress. Often meetings are off-site, to signal to the task-force members and to others that the team is concentrating on the change. This has the advantage of avoiding interruptions, telephone calls, etc., although there is also the disadvantage that it might suggest that the change is 'off-site', whereas it is not.

Manager and task force mixed membership

In more complex cases, the manager has to use a different transition-management structure by attaching a task force or change team to him- or herself; that is, he or she adds to the normal hierarchy a group of specialists (sometimes including external consultants) who watch and preside over the transition phase. The task force does not have the manager's authority to implement, but it does have the authority to persuade, to answer questions, to deflate opposition, to push for performance indicators of success, etc.

Specialist change manager

Finally, where the change is complex and long-term, a change manager is added to the hierarchy, reporting directly to the top manager. This is an additional resource whose full-time work is to manage the change transition. Usually this person is supported by a task force of other managers but he or she can also draw on external and internal consultants. In this case, the transition-management function has authority in its own right and can authorize resources to be employed in the transition phase.

The transition-management techniques appropriate to one situation will not necessarily suit another. The important function of the transition manager is to be concerned with *now*. He or she walks about, answers questions and defuses problems. With the long-term end kept firmly in view, this is not a situation for sitting in an office doing more planning. Transition is about massaging, guiding, persuading and rewarding those learning how to use new structures, systems or processes, in a way not unlike a teacher in a school. It involves encouraging, enthusing the sceptics, pushing the conservatives, providing an example and convincing the rational resisters, until the momentum for the successful implementation of the change begins to show. Successes are broadcast, failures are played down. Learning thus leads to attitudinal and structural change without the unnecessary blood, sweat and tears that the conservatives said would occur. The exchange involved in change has begun to occur.

Multi-variable change

Unfortunately, none of this change is a simple, linear process. Change cannot occur only in one variable (strategy, structure, task, market, people, technology), and, even with the best preparation in the world, the manager cannot predict all the outcomes. Variables which should not be affected do become involved; structures which were not planned to conflict with, say, the marketing strategies do in fact do so; reward systems that were not seen to affect cooperation levels begin to do so; divisional structures which were not perceived to be divisive turn out to be so. Transition management involves the consequences of these interdependencies—what I have called in earlier chapters the inter-variable relationships. And it requires a highly sensitive capacity to see linkages, preferably in advance.

One advantage of a diagnostic model or check-list is that it reminds us of some inescapable truths about the variables. For example, the variables change at different rates. Hence, policies change at a much slower rate than, say, external pressures. The sort of people employed changes much more slowly than do their informal relationships. Second, we should remember that a change in one variable (say, formal structure) will lead to changes in other variables. Third, both positive and negative outcomes result from planned change—there will be gains and losses. And finally, as change occurs in the heads and in the perceptions of the members, there are variations in their capacity to absorb change, to learn, to tolerate ambiguity, etc.

As most changes involve several variables and several strategies at once, the transition phase is difficult to describe. It is just this reality of managing that makes change so difficult to explain. It also makes it well-nigh impossible to give specific advice without a specific case before us. However, there are two research findings which help in the implementation stage.

Change involves structures and people. The sort of structures that are relevant during the search for alternatives are different from those relevant for implementation and managing the transition.

- Search stage—a loosely structured, decentralized authority stimulates creativity by stimulating individuality.
- Implementation stage—implementation is facilitated by centralized authority, a high degree of formalization, and simplicity. One simple, central message is preferable to a multitude of local messages. Individuality, of necessity, gives way to collective conformity.

The greater the need for change, the more the structure will differentiate analysis, diagnosis and search from implementation. The greater the uncertainty, the more the innovative and implementation phases should be differentiated. The more radical the change, the more the diagnosis/search stage should be decentralized (perhaps even with the establishment of a task force). However, the more complex the change and the more radical the change, the more centralized structures will be essential to push the change through.

Stabilizing change

Change (whether transformation, routine, crisis or innovative change) by definition means that the transition phase has shifted the configuration of the firm and its market into a new stage of its evolution. That is, the change has stuck. The organization's members have not succeeded in pushing the firm back to its previous position. Variables have been altered; the firm is no longer what it was. Consolidation is essential.

Consolidation is primarily about structure and systems. Hence, hierarchical changes are documented, reward systems are altered, information systems are modified, performance criteria are confirmed, job descriptions are edited, locations are closed, plant is sold, etc. This period of consolidation is usually a much shorter one than the period of transition. And the process has one enormous advantage—some of the changes, because they are now documented, are visible. There is a new manual on reward systems, on induction programmes, on authority charts, etc. Like the action plans which finish off so many management-development programmes, this documentation of the consolidation or stabilization stage simply makes public the results of the political process. As the process is lost to history, the needs of members for rationality and order demand evidence of the change. Without it, people feel insecure; rationality has to be shown to be successful, effort has to be shown not to have been wasted. An interval in our lives has ended.

Consolidation is also important as a bench-mark in the life-span of the organization. In fact, change does not end—it becomes blurred and merges into the dynamic whole. Consolidation exercises overcome this lack of finality by suggesting a definite interval—an end and a beginning.

People will react to the period of consolidation in a variety of ways. For the conservatives (those who resisted the changes most volubly), it is back to normal—restoration of the steady state. After all, the threatened change was not as bad as they had imagined. But they are certainly not looking for any more changes.

For the radicals, whose energy was important in launching the change, a return to a steady state is not attractive. They will desperately try to invent new changes, to continue the heady rate of activity that they have come to expect. As most of us cannot absorb major change on a continuous basis, the radicals will meet resistance and will become isolated. Indeed, they may be best advised to leave, to find another organization where major change is imminent. Unfortunately, locked in by pensions and commitments, they hang on, depressed that the potential has not been exploited far enough. Managers should counter these sceptics with undeniable evidence of success.

As for the majority, we adjust to major changes and continue our tasks, tidying up loose ends, convincing ourselves that it was worth while, searching for confirmatory information (accounting, sales or personnel data, etc.). Managers should counter our hesitation with frequent statements of, 'We are winning'. Most of us will not search immediately for new ventures. We need time to absorb what has happened before we launch new initiatives.

For those who initiated and managed a major transition, the end of the era may signal relief. Transformation is draining—the endless repetition of the plan, the endless political activity, the endless energizing of others' activity. Early retirement or a less demanding job (in head office?) may become attractive. Yet for other top managers the reaction is the reverse—they become intoxicated by the rate of change. Instead of consolidating, they search for more and more change. Inevitably, most of this fails—people cannot absorb it unless it is routine or, at most, innovative on a small scale. Time and a new senior group will eventually put an end to this self-indulgent exercise. Even entrepreneurs, whose radical changes become myths and legends in the cultures of our organizations, proceed with a very stable set of values and beliefs; their major changes conform to a pattern, even if the details were, at the time, unpredictable.

It is becoming clear that those managers who are first-class at initiating change may be less competent at managing the transition and even less competent at consolidation. The daily business press dubs manager A a 'fix-it person', while manager B is a 'new ventures person'. An analysis of the life-cycles of organizations reflects this distinction. What was necessary to launch the business is not what is needed when there are 300 employees. What this means is that in attempting to predict outcomes, we should remember that those who begin the change process may not be the best people to consolidate it.

Evaluation of change

In a rational world, the evaluation of a change should be based on the performance criteria it was designed to affect. In just the same way as managers evaluate an investment decision, so they should evaluate a change programme. Yet this is rarely the case. Most important change in organizations remains unassessed and undocumented. Case studies are beginning to provide the sort of longitudinal research data that allow an assessment to be made, but these are still fairly rare.

One of the problems with assessment is in deciding whether the results were the product of the change or not. Was it a change in attitudes, stimulated by the market, that led to the improved result, or was it the new technology that was introduced in parallel? Isolating cause and effect in an on-going dynamic system is fraught with problems, yet that is no reason for avoiding it.

A more fruitful approach may be to ask, 'What can be learn from successful changes?' Most successful changes are those that members believed were successful rather than those that were proved to be successful on specific performance criteria. Nevertheless, when members of organizations or change consultants are asked about success, they do report very similar findings. These are listed at the end of this chapter.

Resistance to change

Resistance is any conduct which attempts to preserve the status quo in the face of pressures to alter it. It is the most frequently cited reason for failure—'They (the people) didn't like it!'

The greater the use of compulsion in achieving change, the lower the degree of commitment of those involved. Nevertheless, even this research finding can be modified during a recession (a crisis) simply because tolerances of 'tough' policies will be greater.

There is a spectrum of possible reactions to the objectives of a change programme:

- Acceptance
  - Enthusiastic cooperation and support
  - Cooperation
  - Cooperation under pressure from management
  - Acceptance
  - Passive resignation
- Indifference
  - Indifference

  - Apathy
  - Loss of interest
  - Minimal contribution

- Passive resistance
  - Regressive behaviour
  - Non-learning behaviour
  - Protests
  - Working to rule

- Active resistance
  - Minimal work
  - Slowing down
  - Personal withdrawal
  - Committing errors intentionally
  - Sabotage

We tend to see resistance as unhealthy. However, it should be expected and seen as healthy—it tells us something about the people involved.

There are numerous sources of resistance, including cultural or belief barriers, group solidarity, rejection of outsiders, conformity to past norms, conflict, 'group think', the distribution of authority, structural divisions, technology, managerial philosophy and managerial style. However, contrary to popular theories, most people do *not* resist change *per se*. Many wait, and may have to wait all their careers, to see it. The most frequent cause of resistance is the *way* the proposed change is introduced. It is true that some personality characteristics do not correlate well with change (e.g., age, strong security goals, depression), but most people do want some change and many have been waiting for many years for changes to occur. Ask employees what they would like to see changed and you will find that they are full of ideas.

Managers need to recognize the different forms of resistance:

- Ignorance—'I don't have enough data to decide.'
- Delayed judgement—'I will wait and see how it goes before I decide.'
- Comparisons—'Other solutions are better.'
- Defensive stances—'I don't think this will work', 'There is no way this will work', 'It cannot be allowed to proceed.'
- Deprivation—'It will be far too costly for the firm.'

- Anxiety—'I know I won't be able to operate the new system.'
- Guilt—'I realize things need to change but I like the current way we work.'
- Alienation—'This will mean separating me from my people and my division.'
- Experienced rejection—'Here we go again. We tried this once before and it failed.'
- Loss of power—'It means giving up control over our budgets.'
- Default—'I am just not interested in computers.'
- Erroneous logic—'There are sound reasons for rejecting this proposal. It didn't work in London so it won't work in Geneva.'

The list of *political games* people can play in resisting change is endless—undermining, circulating malicious rumours, ridiculing the change agents, questioning the motives of managers and blaming the initiators for any small organizational hiccup are all familiar tactics.

Resistance is best met with face-to-face confrontation. Usually it indicates that the objectives or the sources of pressure for change have not been explained. Rumours begin to circulate and, unless the resistance is seen as constructive and confronted in an open way, the pain and hurt may continue for years. As in all situations of conflict, it is best to hear out the complaints, let the anger surface and then try to build on calmer behaviour. Also, be realistic; in radical change some resistance is inevitable and healthy—it reminds change managers that they have to sell the idea to the people.

If, 'How do we get there?' is about learning, energy (power) and resistance, then, 'Who will introduce and manage the change?' is a question about two plans—implementation and communication:

- *The implementation plan* Formal, written down, outlining the objectives of the change, the performance criteria, the techniques, the methods. This is the rationale for changing anything at all.
- *The communication plan* This is the plan to inform those affected by the proposed implementation. This plan concerns itself with how, when and where information will be transmitted, and by whom.

If participation by others is sought, and generally it is, then this should be stated in both plans.

Change is a political process

I have proceeded most of the time in this chapter on the basis of a rational or planned view of change. In fact change is *not* the rational linear process we are describing, so why do we pretend it is? Because having a plan gives us confidence—we believe it will work and it is the confidence to proceed that is the major outcome of planning, not the plan *per se*. The plan is rarely ever implemented as it was intended. It is difficult to predict the consequences of any choice. So what happens most often is not, in fact, a logical process but a slow political process in which relationships are changed, and new relationships formed; through this interaction, individuals with political skills opportunistically build up an idea of what is possible. Rather than logical, it is an intuitive gut feel, a lateral-thinking process, in which there is no beginning or end, just a shift of perceptions over time.

However, the rationality of the plan is important for another reason as well—the manager who wants to introduce change should know that rationality 'sells'. By presenting a rational programme, with both an implementation and a communication plan, managers have a far greater chance of beginning to influence the process of preparing the climate for the changes they envisage. However, the view of many managers (and academics) that the rational process is how it really occurs is mistaken.

The situation, particularly the external pressures, largely determines change processes. The manager's capacity to react to that context is a political skill. The tension necessary to energize can come from outside or inside the organization. The inside force is the manager who pushes, persists, argues and knows when to withdraw, and when to fight. He or she must champion the change if it is to succeed. If the external pressures are low, managers must ask whether, individually, they have enough energy to convince a potentially reluctant membership through argument, discussion and selling skills that they are right. Most change depends on a few people, and for this reason it can easily fade and disappear. To avoid this, politically astute managers build on the context as it is; they do not attempt radical change but build on the processes of change that exist at any time in any organization. They know with what they are dealing; they know the power figures; they build their coalitions of support; they know how the people learn; they persuade the early adopters to 'buy'; and they use their sensing of external pressures to focus attention. Through these political skills they appear to have a rational model not unlike the one we have described already. But whether or not they believe in that rationality is not important—what is important is that they have an end in view.

The politically astute manager:

- Focuses on the problem and stimulates concern.
- Obtains commitment from a powerful few to solving the problem.
- Plans the rational case; sells the rational argument.
- Builds confidence and certainty; reduces fear and uncertainty.
- Stabilizes the change, consolidates, structures.

Sensing the problems begins this process. Thereafter problem-solving activities spread the concern about the problem, not the solution. Through this interactive process, the problem becomes defined and refined. By then the small group or coalition begins to link up with others—with peers, with subordinates—and thereby spreads the word of a problem–market link. Thus sensing becomes an educational process which can be legitimized by inviting a consultant or an expert just to 'talk about these issues' in a management seminar. People outside the net are invited to the educational event. Often the timing of this is wrong or the consultant might be the 'wrong' consultant. The politically astute manager then bides his or her time and tries again, sometimes a month, often a year, later, with a slightly different definition of the problem. But the awareness-lifting, sensitizing process continues until those with the power to act are compelled to acknowledge the problem. It is now impossible to pretend that the issue is something else or that the manager who first perceived the problem is a radical. These later processes I have already described.

Tenacity, energy, patience and political astuteness are the characteristics the manager needs here. For the impulsive, the naïve and the radical, the process is too long and so much of what they would like to see changed falls immediately into a void. But for the manager with vision, power, energy, tenacity and patience, major change is possible. Once the rational case (the evidence and the diagnosis) is requested by those with power, a concession has been won. Change is possible.

So what leads to success?

- Change is initiated from the top of the hierarchy.
- A clear set of objectives; a vision of the new organization.
- The change appears sensible to members.
- A set of external conditions which creates tension for change.
- Good timing.
- An intense period of selling the vision.

- Evidence of a high proportion of likely converts.
- An expectation that change will take years, not months.
- An open, experimenting culture rather than a closed, secretive one.
- Managers competent in managing the transition and the political processes.
- Good sensing systems.
- Energy, often centred in one person (but reflecting external market pressure) to push the change through.
- The participation of those affected in the design of the change.
- The use of competent experts (external or internal consultants).
- The use of tangible rewards for those involved.
- The availability of adequate resources—financial, human and material—to ensure the change goes smoothly.
- The recognition that resistance is a healthy sign, and a capacity to work with it and confront it, not avoid it.
- The suppression of inflated expectations (don't expect too much).
- The use of simple plans, not grandiose or complex attempts to plan the change process.
- The consolidation of the change by structural devices.

Summary

Change occurs in organizations all the time. In this chapter, we have not been concerned with the day-to-day, on-going evolutionary processes of change. Rather we have been concerned with managers who induce change at a faster rate. In fact, we are concerned with four types of induced or planned change—routine, crisis, innovative and transforming change.

Most studies of change present it as a rational process: the collection of data on the problem, followed by the definition of the problem, diagnosis, intervention, transition, consolidation and finally evaluation.

All change involves learning to behave in different ways. This means we need to understand how individuals and groups learn. Three stages on a learning curve are used to explain individual learning—the unfreeze, change of attitude and refreeze phases. In situations of uncertainty the capacity of individuals to learn can be increased.

After the data-collection and diagnosis stages come the plans. Plans should answer such questions as: 'What are the objectives of the change?', 'What will the end result look like?', 'How will we get there?', 'How long will it take?', 'What resources will we need?' and 'Who will introduce and manage the change?'

Introducing change needs energy. Sources of energy are the marketplace, powerful individuals and information. Without strong market pressures it is more difficult to induce change. With strong market pressures and an internal champion with the power to push the change through, success is not merely possible but realizable. Despite all the critics, resistance to change is largely a product of the methods used to introduce that change rather than the conservatism of the people involved.

Four structural arrangements are suggested for managing the transition phase. These range from the manager being his or her own change agent to appointing a specialist just to manage the motivation and politics of the change processes.

The rational model is compared with the political view. In reality, change is less about rationality than about politics—sensing the mood of the people, attracting a critical mass to one's ideas and selling the vision one has of the future. Sensing, communicating, motivating and political skills plus energy are vital for the manager of change.

The chapter ended with a list of the conditions which academics, consultants and managers have proposed to explain successful change programmes.

References

ON CHANGE GENERALLY

Hrebiniak, L. G. and W. F. Joyce, *Implementing Strategy*, Macmillan, NY, 1984.

Kanter, R. M., *The Change Masters: Innovation for Productivity in American Industry*, Simon and Schuster, NY, 1983.

Stewart, V., *Change: The Challenge for Management*, McGraw-Hill, London, 1983.

Tichy, N. M., *Managing Strategic Change: Technical, Political and Cultural Dynamics*, Wiley Interscience, NY, 1983.

ON CASE STUDIES OF CHANGE

Goodman, S., *Assessing Organizational Change: The Rushton Quality of Work Experiment*, Wiley Interscience, NY, 1979.

Pettigrew, A., *The Awakening Giant: Continuity and Change in ICI*, Basil Blackwell, Oxford, 1985.

Toffler, A., *The Adaptive Corporation*, Pan, London, 1985.

Index